SOME FRIENDLY PERSUASION . . .

Cobb and Macklin were both shaken by the sight of the big knife, and didn't want to see it again. "Ask me anything," Cobb said. "I'll tell the truth."

Macklin spread a thin nervous smile. "They're pulling our legs, Cobb. They're not going to kill us. They're lawmen. Just running a bluff."

"A bluff?" Sullivan Hart jerked the knife from his bootwell once again, grabbed Macklin by his lapel and yanked him forward, throwing the blade of the knife up against his throat. "That was my father *Los Pistoleros* killed, you rotten—"

"Easy, Sully!" Twojack Roth shouted, seeing that the blood had left Hart's face, and that his eyes had turned killing cold. Roth moved in quick, grabbed Hart by his wrist and held tight, the blade across Macklin's throat drawing a thin red line in the frightened man's skin. "He's right. We're lawmen. Don't kill him, not like this. . . ."

HANGMAN'S CHOICE

Ralph Cotton

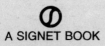

A SIGNET BOOK

SIGNET
Published by New American Library, a division of
Penguin Putnam Inc., 375 Hudson Street,
New York, New York 10014, U.S.A.
Penguin Books Ltd, 27 Wrights Lane,
London W8 5TZ, England
Penguin Books Australia Ltd, Ringwood,
Victoria, Australia
Penguin Books Canada Ltd, 10 Alcorn Avenue,
Toronto, Ontario, Canada M4V 3B2
Penguin Books (N.Z.) Ltd, 182–190 Wairau Road,
Auckland 10, New Zealand

Penguin Books Ltd, Registered Offices:
Harmondsworth, Middlesex, England

First published by Signet, an imprint of New American Library,
a division of Penguin Putnam Inc.

First Printing, October 2000
10 9 8 7 6 5 4 3 2 1

For Mary Lynn . . . *of course*

PART 1

Chapter 1

Federal Deputy Sullivan Hart lay on his side in the dirt, feeling the hot bite of the sun even through his riding duster, his gloves, and his bat-wing brush chaps. He raised his high-crowned Stetson enough to run a hand back across his damp hair. Then he leveled the hat brim down and looked over at the prisoner, Quick Charlie Sims, who lay three feet away with the telescope raised to his eye.

Bringing Quick Charlie Sims along with him was a mistake. But it wasn't Sullivan Hart's mistake. Releasing a prisoner into Hart's custody had been Judge Charles Isaac Parker's idea. All Hart could do was live with it for the time being. Quick Charlie was too slick, too unpredictable, and to tell the truth, a little too smart for comfort, Hart thought, watching Quick Charlie gaze out and down into the draw below them.

"You've seen enough, Sims. Give it to me." Sullivan Hart reached a hand out for the telescope.

"One second," Quick Charlie said, barely making an effort to respond. That's how everything went with Sims—contrary, Sullivan Hart thought. Sims had a way of turning the slightest request into some sort of contest of will. He made everything into a mental game. Hart didn't like it one bit. By the nature of his job, Sullivan Hart liked to keep things straightforward and at face value. A lawman gave an order . . . and a prisoner did as he was told. It kept

life simple. But Sims was hardheaded, tricky, and
always scheming. Hart stared at him. He felt like
rapping him in the teeth.

"Right now, Sims." Hart's tone of voice turned to
iron. He had no time to waste on foolishness. Riding
with a man like Quick Charlie Sims was like carrying
a rattlesnake in his saddlebags. It took all of his attention; and right now Sullivan Hart had no attention
to spare. There was trouble down in the draw—big
trouble from the looks of it. When Quick Charlie still
didn't make a move, Sullivan reached over his rifle
barrel. "I said *now*!" He poked Quick Charlie in the
ribs, sharp enough to make his point.

"Okay, okay." Quick Charlie Sims lowered the
telescope from his eye and handed it over to Sullivan
Hart. "Looks like your buddy, Twojack Roth, is
doing some kind of Indian death chant down there,
rocking back and forth. Maybe you better take another look."

"I've already seen him." But before he collapsed
the telescope, Sullivan Hart hesitated for a second.
He wiped a gloved hand across the rear lens, raised
it, and looked down once more into the sandy draw.
More than seven hundred yards away he saw the
Cherokee deputy, Twojack Roth, sitting in the dirt,
his big hands bound behind his back by a strip of
rawhide. "You don't know Roth," Hart added, murmuring almost to himself.

"Oh, I know him all right." Quick Charlie smiled.
"And I've seen him in much better shape."

Hart peered closer through the lens, seeing blood
run down one side of the Cherokee's face as he
rocked back and forth in the dust. Twojack Roth's
dark eyes turned upward in Hart's direction, as if he
knew someone was watching him from a long way
off. For a second it seemed as if Roth was staring
into Sullivan Hart's eyes. But he couldn't of course,
not from this distance.

"He's trying to get his hands loose," Hart offered.

"He's just biding his time, getting ready to make a move." Yet, as Hart spoke, he winced at the new sight before his eyes. Near Twojack Roth, Joe Marr, the cattle rustler they'd been searching for, stood with a rifle in his hand and a worried look on his face.

"I'd say he better make his move in a hurry," Quick Charlie Sims replied, "before this sun boils his brains out."

Sullivan Hart lowered the lens, clapped it shut, and shoved it inside his bib-front shirt. "Sit tight, Roth . . ." Hart whispered to himself, and shifted back a few inches from the edge of the cliff overhang. Holding his rifle low to the ground to block any glare of the sun off the barrel, he levered a round up into the chamber.

"What about me?" Quick Charlie watched Sullivan Hart take out his pistol from his slim-jim holster, check the rounds, then put it away.

"What about you?" Hart stared at him hard. "If I'd had any say in it, you'd still be sweating it out in a jail cell."

"But since I'm not . . ." Quick Charlie shook his cuffed wrists. "Shouldn't you give me a pistol or something? At least take these cuffs off me. What kind of fix am I going to be in if something goes wrong for you down there? You can't leave me here this way, for crying out loud!"

A trace of a flat smile moved across Sullivan Hart's lips. "Who said I'm going to leave you here?" He rose into a crouch, taking Quick Charlie Sims by the handcuffs and pulling him back from the edge of the cliff. "You're going down there with me."

Quick Charlie resisted. "Uh-uh! No way, Sully! That's even worse. Not with these cuffs on. Not without a gun!"

Sullivan Hart yanked harder on the cuffs, forcing Sims back with him. "I've had all I'm going to take from you, Sims. Now get yourself moving." Hart slung him forward, and Quick Charlie rolled in the dirt, catching his bowler hat before it got away. He dusted it against his thigh.

"Okay! Take it easy! I'm coming!" Sims rose into a clumsy crouch himself, stumbling along in front of Sullivan Hart as Hart pushed him toward the horses hidden by a stand of dried brush. "But Judge Parker is going to hear about this. You can count on it!" Even as Quick Charlie spoke, he grinned to himself. He'd been testing and needling Sullivan Hart for the past three days just to keep him on edge. Hart was wound tighter than an eight-day clock having him around. Quick Charlie knew it, and he liked it that way.

"Tell the judge whatever you want to," Sullivan Hart replied without looking back at him. "But I'd be careful if I were you. You're awaiting extradition to Colorado. Once I tell him how you've acted out here, he might decide to go on and hang you himself. Save Colorado the trouble."

Quick Charlie Sims's smile faded. His expression took a troubled turn. "What report? Nobody said anything about you giving him a report on me. Deal was I'd show you where Joe Marr was hiding out. I showed you Marr's place two days ago. Tracking him out here wasn't a part of it. You had no right dragging me along." He paused, then added as they stopped beside the horses, "You're not serious about that report, are you? It's bad enough I'm facing charges up in Creed for a bank I didn't even rob."

"I've already heard your sad story, Sims. Now get that horse between your knees and get a move on. Twojack Roth needs help down there."

Quick Charlie Sims grumbled, but swung up atop the big bay. He looked over at Hart as he stepped up onto the big black morgan cross. "Say, didn't I hear the judge mention that your pa headed out with Twojack Roth over toward Robber's Roost?"

"Yep, you did." Hart swung the rifle across his lap. "They went scouting for stolen cattle, same as us."

Sims considered it for a second, reaching up with both hands and adjusting his brown bowler hat on his head. "But I didn't see no sign of your pa down there. Did you?"

"No, I didn't. And that's got me worried."

"Oh . . ." Quick Charlie considered the gravity of it. "Sorry, Sully. I shouldn't have been giving you a hard time. If there's any way I can help."

"Shut up, Sims. Let's go." Hart stepped his horse back and slapped Quick Charlie's bay on its rump, sending it on ahead of him. "Pull up on this end of the draw. I won't put you between them and me when the shooting starts."

"Thanks," Sims called back over his shoulder. "I won't make a run for it when the shooting starts. You've got my word."

"Your word, huh?" Sullivan Hart sounded skeptical.

"That's right, my *word*," Quick Charlie called out to him. "Once I give my word on something, I never break it. I'll stick here until things are settled."

"That's real comforting, Sims." They stepped the horses down along the steep trail toward the low rolling brush country below.

On the ground in the belly of the draw, Twojack Roth sat rocking back and forth, chanting under his breath. He'd ventured a gaze all around the draw, getting a layout of the place in his mind, his wrists at work, keeping pressure on the damp rawhide, stretching it. Someone had just looked down at him from up atop the cliffs. He'd felt it. There'd been no visible sign of anyone or anything out along the line of shadowed ridges. But he knew eyes were there. Whoever was up there would soon be coming this way. And when they did, Twojack Roth had to be ready. He chanted and rocked, and slid a guarded glance past the knees of Joe Marr standing beside him toward the entrance of the cave at the end of the draw, where two more men stood with their rifles cradled in their arms. These two were well dressed but had the rough look of barroom brawlers about them. Twojack listened for any sound from within the cave. Things didn't look good for his partner, Deputy Coleman Hart. Earlier, five men had dragged Coleman Hart into the cave. Twojack had heard three pistol shots, but nothing since.

To the right of the cave entrance stood a rickety line of makeshift corral fencing that stretched along the belly of the draw, upward and out across the rocky land. Inside the corral over a hundred head of cattle milled and bawled, standing obscured in a cloud of churning dust. Outside the corral, seven horses stood hitched to the railing. These were big, well-kept horses, wearing expensive tack and saddles. Their tails were short-cropped. Their trimmed manes stood less than an inch high, like show horses. Too fancy for this part of the country, thought Twojack.

From the cave entrance forty feet away, one of the suited riflemen called out to Joe Marr, "Hey, cowboy, can't you shut that Injun up? Bad enough we've got to listen to cattle all day." He turned to the other well-dressed rifleman who leaned against the rock front of the cave and added, "What's Priest doing in there anyway? We could all be sipping bourbon in his Pullman car."

"Beats me," the other man replied. "JT Priest doesn't tell me any more than he does you." He raised a hand and swatted at a fly.

Joe Marr's ragged boot toe reached out and tapped Twojack Roth's side. "You heard them, Injun. Shut that singing up. These boys take a notion, they'll walk over and put a bullet in your head. Mine too."

Twojack looked up at him. "Do they scare you, Marr?" he asked in low voice. "Because they should. Do you think these men are going to take a chance on you? Leave a live witness here? You're in no better spot than I am."

"Shut up, Roth!" Joe Marr sliced the words under his breath, shot a nervous glance over at the two riflemen, then kicked Twojack Roth in his ribs. But it wasn't a hard kick. It was more for show. He leaned closer to Twojack's face. "I see where I stand in this, Injun. They showed up last night, met the Englishman this morning, and been here all day. What the hell can I do about it? I'm just an honest cattle rustler."

"First of all, you can stop calling me *Injun*. It might keep me from bending that rifle barrel across your back once this is all over." Twojack Roth gave him an icy stare, then began rocking again, chanting in a lower tone.

"All over? You just said yourself neither one of us is going to come out of this alive."

"Don't soil yourself, Marr. I've had a vision. In that vision I saw you going to jail for about two to five years for cattle rustling. But you seemed happy about it, because you knew that Judge Parker could have hanged you for rustling, and for shooting Dub French last year. Instead, he went easy on you for helping me and Coleman Hart get out of this mess."

Joe Marr rubbed a shaky hand across his forehead beneath his hat brim. "That's some vision, Inj—I mean, Roth. But for my money, Coleman Hart's already dead in there. How can me and you do anything to save ourselves? There's too many of them."

"We can start by you getting us over near the corral. Tell them I have to relieve myself."

"What are you going to do?"

"You'll see when the time comes. Stick close to me. Come on, act like you're helping me up. Loosen this rawhide some as you do it."

"Lord, I hope you know what you're doing here."

"You want my vision to come true or not?" Roth fixed his cold stare back into Joe Marr's eyes.

"All right, here goes." Marr raised Twojack to his feet and shoved him toward the corral.

"Hey, where do you think you're going, cowboy?" one of the riflemen called out from the cave entrance.

"He's got to pizzle," Joe Marr answered.

"Let him pizzle in his moccasin." The rifleman stepped forward from against the stone wall, but the other man stopped him.

"Let them go. It's too hot for all this aggravation."

Joe Marr reached a hand down to Twojack's bound hands as if checking them, gripping the rawhide and stretching it back and forth as he did. "Roth, you nearly got this thing loose enough already," he whispered.

"I know." Twojack Roth walked on, his calf-length moccasins stirring a low swirl of dust with each step. "I would have jumped you from behind and broke your neck if you hadn't sided with me."

"Dang . . ." Joe Marr's voice trailed off. He looked at the Cherokee's wide back, his thick neck, the long black braid of hair swinging between his broad shoulders, his faded blue denim shirtsleeves wet with sweat and drawn tight across the back of his powerful upper arms. "Well, I'm on your side now, Twojack," Joe Marr whispered. "Just let me know what to do."

"I'd give a hundred dollars to see Porter Lindsy and that big Injun go ten rounds, bare-knuckle," one of the riflemen said to the other, nodding toward Twojack Roth.

"Yeah?" The other man grinned and adjusted the rifle in the crook of his arm. "My money would have to be on Lindsy."

"Mine, too. I just like to watch two big suckers fight."

"I used to. But with all these new rules nowadays, fighting's gone to hell. You heard what Lindsy did in New York, didn't you?"

"What's that?"

"They say he showed up for a fight, and the official told him he'd have to wear gloves. Lindsy asked him why, said he didn't mind getting his hands dirty. Official said because gloves kept a man from getting hurt as bad. Lindsy said he wasn't so sure about that. Official said, still and all he'd have to wear them if he wanted to fight in New York. So Lindsy put a glove on his left hand, turned around, and smacked him twice, *bam, bam*. Once with the glove and once bare-knuckled. Turned to another official, said, 'If he ever comes to, ask him which one hurt the worse.'"

The rifleman laughed. "Porter Lindsy did that?"

"Sure did. They say that official stuttered ever since—and he was a big ole boy hisself. They say he can't read a newspaper now unless he holds it sidewise."

"No kidding?"

"That's what they say." The rifleman spat, shoved his black bowler hat up on his forehead, and looked toward the dark entrance to the cave. "How long is Priest gonna stay at this? Smelling all these cattle makes me about half sick."

"I told ya, I don't know what Priest has in mind." The rifleman leaned forward and looked toward the corral, where Joe Marr and Twojack had gone only a moment earlier. "Where were they? You see them anywhere?" All they saw were the milling horns of the cattle, and the looming dust surrounding them.

Flat on their bellies inside the corral, Joe Marr said in a choking whisper, "I can't breathe . . . can't see a thing."

"Follow me," Twojack Roth whispered back to him, inching along the inside of the fence line, Joe Marr's Spencer rifle now in his hands. "Don't get in there—they'll spook and trample you."

Joe Marr coughed against the back of his hand. "Don't tell me about cattle." He crawled forward on his stomach, raising his bandanna up across his nose.

"Hey, cowboy!" one of the riflemen called aloud

above the din of the restless herd. "Come on out where we can see you."

"Aw hell, Roth. It ain't working!" Marr drew the range pistol from his holster.

"Stay down!" Roth hissed, moving on through the dust. "Don't do anything until I get in position. When they come for you, I'll slip in and get Coleman out of there."

"Hey in there! Cowboy!" The rifleman called out again. "Don't make me come after you."

"They've got us, Roth! Run for it!" Joe Marr panicked, and stood up in the dust with his pistol blazing away at the cave as he skirted around the edge of the herd. The cattle bellowed and bolted at the sound of his pistol fire. Blue fire streaked within the dust. The riflemen crouched and fired back.

Twojack Roth rolled out from under the corral rails just in time to feel the herd begin its move, their hooves rumbling low on the earth beneath him. Joe Marr yelled long and loud. Still firing, he scrambled over the wire and rail fencing before the press of the cattle could overtake him. There was nothing Twojack Roth could do now but turn on his stomach in the dirt and fire too. His first shot went wide by two feet, but the second shot lifted one of the riflemen a foot off the ground and sent him backward, his bowler hat spinning off his head. The bullet slammed him against the stone face of the cavern.

Within the roiling dust, Roth couldn't get sight of the other rifleman as the man moved quickly across the ground and in among the horses. The man hurried to gather the reins before the nervous horses could rear against the corral rail and pull it loose. Inside the corral, the spooked herd began circling from the outside in, collapsing the rails and spilling out like water through a broken dam. They thundered up out of the draw, the earth trembling beneath their hooves.

Roth's next shot was aimed at the men who now

came running out of the cave entrance, pistols and rifles at the ready in their hands. As soon as Roth fired he rolled away, getting out from under the flash of his rifle and farther from the bolting herd.

"There goes one!" At the cave entrance, a man in a dress suit and a riding duster aimed and fired at Roth. "Get him!" But Roth was up in a crouch now, racing across the dirt and diving headlong at the last second into the cover of short rock. Bullets whined and spun off the rocks as the other men turned and fired at his position.

Above the edge of the draw, Sullivan Hart and Quick Charlie Sims had reined their horses back hard at the first sound of gunfire. Now they struggled to sidestep their horses out of the herd's path. A widening torrent of horns streaked past them until they managed to get atop a rise. Yet once there, in full view above the edge of the draw, gunfire whistled past their heads, coming from the front of the cave.

"Get down!" Sullivan Hart shouted at Quick Charlie Sims, but it was too late. Sims's horse caught a bullet in its chest and crumbled forward. Sims rolled in the dirt, helpless, his cuffed hands flailing in the air.

Hart acted fast. He threw himself forward, wrapped his hand in the morgan's reins near the bit and yanked hard, twisting the horse's head as he nailed his right boot to its side. The morgan cross let out a long whinny and went down on its haunches and rolled over onto its side. Sullivan slipped from the saddle at the last second as the horse flattened. He threw his rifle over the morgan's side and returned fire. But the big morgan cross was too unsteady under his arm, and the shot went wild. By the time he levered another round into his rifle chamber, the men below were mounting, their horses spinning beneath them as they fired and made their getaway.

"Hart! Get these off me!" Quick Charlie Sims yelled beside him, shaking his cuffed hands. Hart shoved him back, leveled the rifle, and fired again. This time one of the men pitched backward and rolled off his horse's rump, his boot still caught in the stirrup. The horse dragged him away in a spray of blood, the tails of the man's riding duster flapping in the dusty air.

Sullivan Hart levered another round. As the men raced their horses up from the draw, Hart rose onto his knees and settled himself for another shot. Through the dust he saw Twojack Roth stand up and fire. Another man toppled from his saddle. But the remaining riders disappeared over the higher edge of the draw, and in a second they were out of sight, pounding out along a low stretch of valley amid the rolling hills.

"Come on, Sims!" Hart stood the rest of the way up, pulling up on the morgan's reins. He tapped a boot to the horse's rump and swung over its back as it rose up from the ground.

"Wait a minute!" Sims missed the horse on its way up and slid down its side. Hart reached down, grabbed Sims's shoulder and hauled him up behind him.

"Coming in, Roth!" Sullivan Hart called out, putting the morgan cross forward as it shook itself out.

"Sully?" Twojack Roth spotted Hart and Sims riding forward through the dust. "I sure hoped that might be you up there." He let his pistol slump in his hand.

"Where's my dad?" Hart asked as he stepped the morgan down into the draw through the stir of cattle dust. Joe Marr came moving in from the edge of the rise, raising his arms high for safety's sake, his pistol still smoking in his right hand.

Twojack Roth nodded toward the cave entrance with a grim expression. "He's inside, Sully. Maybe I ought to go in first."

Sullivan Hart caught the meaning, but shook his head as he stepped down from the horse, pulling Quick Charlie Sims down behind him. "No, I'll go in." He looked around the draw for either Roth's or his father's horse. He saw neither. "Who were those men, Roth?" he asked as he hurried to the cave, but didn't wait for an answer.

As Hart entered the cave with his pistol drawn, Twojack Roth took up the reins to the black morgan cross and held the horse steady. He dusted himself off and turned to Quick Charlie Sims. "What are you doing out here, Sims?" he asked. "You're supposed to be in Judge Parker's jail, waiting to be shipped up to Creed."

"I never robbed that bank in Creed," Sims replied.

"That's for a jury in Creed to decide." Twojack cocked an eye at him and asked again. "Why are you out here?"

"Call it my civic duty, Twojack," Sims said. "Judge Parker sent me along to show Sully where Marr lives. Gave him my word I wouldn't cut out on him."

"Your word?" Twojack spread a wry smile in disbelief.

"Yeah, my word." Quick Charlie looked offended. "Why is it every time I say that, you people act like it's a joke? I've never broken my word in my life. What's so funny about that?"

"Nothing." Roth nodded at Quick Charlie's wrists. "Why the cuffs, if you gave your *word*?"

Sims shrugged. "Sully has an suspicious nature, I suppose. Anyway, when Joe Marr wasn't there, we followed his tracks out here."

Marr heard him as he stepped up with his hands raised, his pistol hanging on his thumb by the trigger guard. "You jackpotting rat! You brought the law down on me?"

Twojack Roth turned to Joe Marr, holding out a hand. "Give me the pistol, Joe. Right now!"

"Why? It's empty," Joe Marr said.

"Don't ask why. Just drop it off your thumb. I'm a little put out with you anyway. You didn't do like I asked you to. You nearly got us both killed."

"Sorry," Joe Marr said, letting the pistol fall. Roth caught it, checked the cylinder, and shoved it down in his waist. Joe Marr turned a harsh glare to Quick Charlie Sims. "I don't need no pistol to handle this snake. Give me a minute alone with him—I'll rip his double-crossing, gypsy head off."

Quick Charlie shook his head and clucked his tongue. "Would you really do something like that, Joe? . . . what with me standing here unable to defend myself?" He raised his hands chest high and rattled the cuffs.

Joe Marr took a step closer, past Twojack Roth, curling his hands into fists at his sides. "You better believe I would." Before Roth could stop him, Marr took another short step forward and spread his feet shoulder-width apart. "I'd do it quicker than a tomcat can scratch his—"

His words stopped in a blast of breath as Quick Charlie Sims snapped a hard boot toe straight up into Marr's crotch, lifting him up onto his tiptoes, seemingly suspended for a second. Then Sims side-stepped out of his way as Joe Marr broke forward at the waist, his knees clamped together and both hands pressed low on his belly. Quick Charlie grinned down at Marr's bowed back and raised his cuffed hands into a doubled fist above his head.

"That's enough out of you." Twojack Roth grabbed Sims by his shoulder and yanked him away before he could make his downswing. Sims stumbled and fell against Twojack's chest. The big Cherokee caught him, righted him, and shoved him toward the entrance to the cave. "Get inside, Sims." On the ground, Joe Marr rolled onto his side and let out a painful groan. "Come on, Joe." Roth lifted Joe Marr up by the back of his shirt. "You ought to know better than to fool with Quick Charlie like that."

Joe Marr struggled to his feet and walked forward, still crooked at the waist. "I'll . . . get him . . . in jail. He'll . . . wish to God . . . he was . . . never born."

"All right, now, hush up, Joe. Take a deep breath." Twojack Roth patted his bowed back as they stepped across the ground. Ahead of them, Quick Charlie chuckled and shook his head. He hated having to kick Joe Marr that way, but sometimes you had to make one move just to get to the next. He straightened his dusty brown bowler hat with his cuffed hands and walked on into the cave.

Chapter 2

Twojack Roth, Quick Charlie Sims, and Joe Marr stood back at the edge of the lantern's glow deep inside the cave. At the center of the light, Sullivan Hart sat slumped on his knees with the body of his father, Deputy Coleman Hart, raised across his lap, the dead lawman's head pressed to Sullivan's chest. "Oh, Dad . . . look at you," Sullivan whispered low. His shoulders shuddered in the circle of firelight. His high-crowned Stetson lay on the stone floor beside him.

Quick Charlie looked down from the sight of it and stood with his head bowed, his bowler hat hanging from his hand. Twojack Roth nudged Quick Charlie Sims and nodded at a spot on the stone floor where the words *Los Pistoleros* had been smeared in blood. Sims raised his face enough to read the bloody scrawl. His eyes took on a knowing glint of recognition. Then he took a step forward and said under his breath to Roth, "If you're not going over there to him, I am."

But Twojack Roth pulled him back. "No, stay here." Quick Charlie stepped back and watched the big Cherokee move in beside Sullivan Hart and lay a hand upon his shoulder. "Easy, Sully," Twojack whispered.

"Look what they did to him." Sullivan raised his bloody gloved hands, as if in some desperate plea to heaven.

Twojack stared down at Coleman Hart's gray dead face and saw where someone had sliced off the old lawman's ears, either before or after they'd shot him. His breath drew tight in his broad chest. He turned his gaze back toward Quick Charlie Sims and Joe Marr. His shoulders straightened when he saw that Joe Marr stood there alone.

"Where's Sims?" Roth asked in a harsh whisper as if not to disturb the dead.

Joe Marr looked around and shrugged, bewildered. "He was just here."

Roth started to bolt toward the front entrance, but Sims's voice came in a quiet tone from out of the darkness as he reappeared with a rolled-up canvas tarpaulin in his arms. "I'm back. Just went and got this from Sully's horse. Thought we'd need it." He untied the roll with his cuffed hands, then shook it out and spread it on the stone floor. His eyes read the blood-smeared words again. Then he stepped back beside Joe Marr, took off his dusty bowler hat, and lowered his head.

"Thanks, Sims." Twojack Roth stooped down and touched Sullivan Hart's shoulder once again. "Help me with him, Sully. Come on. Let's move him out of here . . . get him home."

Together, Sullivan Hart and Twojack Roth wrapped the body in canvas. Quick Charlie Sims stepped in again to hand Roth the ties from the canvas roll. "Here, use these," he said in a quiet, somber voice, then he walked over beside Joe Marr. The rustler still stood a bit bowed at the waist; when he shot Quick Charlie Sims a cold glare, Sims spread his cuffed hands in a show of peace and moved back a step farther from him.

When Coleman Hart's body was wrapped and tied and ready for the trail, Roth and Sullivan stood for a while looking down at it. "They shouldn't have done him that way," Sullivan Hart whispered.

"Nobody should be done that way," Twojack replied. He stooped down, picked up Sullivan's Stetson, straightened the brim, and handed it to him. He nodded at the two words written in blood on the stone floor. "Remember them, Los Pistoleros? Is that what Coleman was trying to tell us?"

"Los Pistoleros. The gunmen." Sullivan Hart translated the words and shook his head. "Yeah, I'd say so. But I haven't heard of that bunch in years."

"Me neither." Twojack Roth studied the words in the flicker of the lantern light. Without turning, he said to Joe Marr, "Who were they, Joe? Give us some names."

"Boys, I don't know. I swear I don't." He moved up into the lantern light. "Like I told you, Roth. They showed up last night, everyone of them dressed boardwalk fancy. Never asked if they could stay or nothing else. They just said they was meeting the Englishman here—and they did."

"Lord Tillford?" Roth asked. "From the Old English spread?"

"Yep, that's who they met with—except Tillford ain't no real lord, and I know it."

"He's a long way off his graze," Roth said. "The Old English spread is three hundred miles to the north . . . if they're still in business. They caught a hard freeze last winter." Beside him, Sullivan Hart stood staring down at the words scrawled in blood by his father's dying hand.

"Don't ask me," said Joe Marr. He shook his lowered head. "I'm plumb broke up over this."

Sullivan asked him in a low firm voice, "Then why were you guarding Roth? I saw it from up on the ridges."

Joe Marr hesitated, stuck for an answer. But Twojack Roth said on his behalf, "He couldn't help it, Sully. They gave him no choice. We settled up though. Joe helped me make my play on them."

Sullivan Hart nodded. "Anything else you can tell us, Marr?"

"No, not much." Joe Marr paused for a second. "Except one of them carried a golf ball and played with it all the time. I believe he's the leader."

Hart and Roth looked at each other, puzzled.

"You know, one of them gutta percha balls, like rich fellows swat back and forth with a golf stick?"

"We know what they are, Joe," Roth said. "You say this fellow played with one?"

"All the time . . . kept bouncing it up and down in his hand. Got on my nerves."

Hart and Roth stood silent, not seeming to know what to make of it. Finally, Sullivan asked Roth, "How'd they get the drop on you?"

"It was my fault. Coleman and I got caught off guard coming down into the long end of the draw. They shot our horses out from under us so fast we—"

"I'm sorry, Twojack." Sullivan Hart cut him off, seeing the painful expression on his face. "You don't need to explain yourself to me." Hart stooped back down beside his father's canvas-wrapped body and laid a hand on its chest. "He always said you're the best tracker in the Nations."

"It went wrong on us, Sully. I'm not trying to pass off the blame, but these were no ordinary rustlers or saddle tramps. It all happened so quick I didn't even get a good look at the leader's face." Roth took a deep breath. "Let's get back to Fort Smith, let the judge know about it." Without turning, he added over his shoulder, "Sims, you and Joe give us a hand here."

Joe Marr bent down beside Sullivan Hart with a grunt, his lower belly still tied in knots. But when Quick Charlie Sims didn't step forward, Twojack peered around the outer edge of thin lantern light. "Sims?" He saw no sign of him, and turned down to Joe Marr on the floor beside Sullivan Hart. "Where'd Sims get off to now?"

"He was right there beside me," Marr replied, cast-

ing a sidelong glance toward where they'd both
stood.

"Sims? Sims!" Twojack Roth ran along the narrow
stone corridor as he called out.

"He can forget it," Sullivan Hart said to Joe Marr
in a resolved voice, his gloved hand still resting on
his dead father's chest. "Sims has left us afoot here."
He shook his lowered head in the soft glow of the
lantern's light.

Joe Marr rubbed his aching belly. He spat, then
sank down on the stone floor. "That danged
gypsy . . ."

The black morgan cross was not the fastest horse
Quick Charlie Sims had ever ridden, but the horse
had power and stamina, and ate up the hill country
beneath its hooves. Sims had pushed the big horse
hard for well over an hour before he finally slid it to
a halt in a spray of fine silt and gravel at the edge
of a shallow creek. He swung down off the horse's
back before it completely settled, and dropped back
a step with the reins in his right hand, the loose
handcuffs dangling from his left wrist. He watched
the big morgan cross shake itself out and scrape a
hoof at the water's edge.

Sullivan Hart knew how to train a horse—Sims
had to give the man that much. When he'd first
swung up into the saddle it had taken him nearly a
full minute to get the big morgan to do anything he
asked of it. But that was all right—Sims admired loy-
alty in a horse. "Good boy." He smiled, stepping in
closer and looking the morgan up and down as it
scraped a hoof at the water's edge. "Kid Sully would
be proud of that run you just made."

Quick Charlie hung his bowler hat on the saddle
horn and loosened the horse's cinch. He dropped the
reins and lay himself out flat on his belly, then lowered his upper half into the thin cool stream. When
he'd raised his face and spat out a stream to wash

dust from his mouth, he lowered his face once more
to drink his fill. Then he lay there, letting the cool
stream run in braids across his arms and hands and
lap at his burning neck.

The morgan cross drew water and blew itself out,
then drew some more water until at length it raised
its dripping muzzle and slung its head and stood
with water swirling at its front hooves. Quick Charlie
raised himself up, slung his wet hair back, and took
up the reins from the ground. He moved over close
to the morgan's wet muzzle and rubbed it, then
pulled its damp head to his chest. "Let's see what I
have for you, huh?"

He held a closed hand to the horse's lips. When it
had nuzzled at his hand for a moment, he opened
his empty palm. But then, as if to lessen the morgan's
disappointment, Sims rubbed its wet muzzle and slid
his hand upward, scratching the horse behind its ear.

"Just remember . . . the hand is not always full."
He held his empty hand out before the morgan's eye
and moved it in a slow circle as if polishing the air.
"But remember also, the hand is not always empty."
He closed his hand tight, and when he opened it
again, a piece of hard sugar candy lay in his palm.
The morgan bobbed its head and spread its lips for-
ward until the candy disappeared between its teeth.
Sims patted the morgan's crunching jaw. "Compli-
ments of Judge Parker's office."

Sims took his hat from the saddle horn and put it
back on his wet head. He slipped Sullivan Hart's
rifle from the saddle scabbard and led the morgan
upstream a few yards, then hitched it amid some
pale sweetgrass in the flickering shade of a willow's
break. While the morgan grazed, Sims backed a few
feet into the willows and sank down with the rifle
across his lap.

For a moment Sims thought about taking the handcuffs the rest of the way off, but then he thought
better of it. Maybe he better wait on that, see what

wearing handcuffs might be worth to him. Twojack's
key was safely tucked behind his belt. He could get
rid of the cuffs any time. He was free now. That was
the main thing, he thought. He smiled and laid back
and looked up through the swaying willow whips
into the wide blue sky. Quick Charlie Sims, on the
run again. Some things never seemed to change.

Quick Charlie had been lying low outside of Fort
Smith for nearly four months when the three-man
posse had shown up in the front yard of the young
widow Della Stillwell's house. They'd shouldered
their way past poor naked Della—one of them having at least the decency to throw her a blanket to
cover herself—and they'd dragged him out kicking
and clawing.

In the flash of a second he'd gone from Della's
warm feather bed, naked as a jaybird himself—into
the back of a jail wagon, where two lowlife cons sat
staring blankly at him. Then, as he turned to say
something wise to one of the posse on his own behalf, a rifle butt seemed to drop down out of a fiery
heaven and smacked him down like the wrath of
God. He hadn't even told Della good-bye.

Della, Della . . . He shook his head thinking about
her, about the wine, about her dead husband's
money, and about her warm feather bed. For a moment he wondered if it hadn't been the warm, sweet
headiness of that big feather bed rather than the four
bottles of strawberry wine that had dulled his senses
and allowed him to get caught off-guard that way.
That wasn't like him at all, he thought.

But there was no point wondering about it now.
He'd been stuck in Judge Charles Isaac Parker's jail
for the past six months, awaiting shipment back to
Colorado. Della was too young and warm-blooded
to wait around for him. By now somebody had
moved right in behind him and laid claim to her. He
could just imagine it being some sort of slick-talking

hustler out to get not only what he could of sweet Della, but her late husband's money as well.

Thinking about that disturbed him, because, to be honest about it, he'd counted on getting his hands on some of the money himself, say thirty, forty thousand. Not a lot. Just enough that he could take it down to New Orleans during the winter months and turn it into a fortune on the faro tables. Quick Charlie had been on a manhunt of his own, and he needed traveling money. It would have only been a loan, of course. He would have paid her back in time. Quick Charlie always paid back his debts, one way or another.

He sighed to himself. *Well . . . when one door closes, another always opens.* As soon as he'd seen the words smeared in blood on the floor of the cave, he knew what his next move would be. Quick Charlie felt a little bad about taking off with the only horse in the place, leaving Kid Sully with no way to haul his father's body back to Fort Smith. He also felt a little bad about picking Twojack Roth's pocket for the key to the handcuffs. But neither of those two would have listened to reason if he had tried talking to them about *Los Pistoleros.* There'd been no point in wasting time.

Sims had given Sullivan Hart his word that he wouldn't run out on him in the midst of things, and he hadn't. He'd stuck around until the shooting was over. But an opportunity presented itself, and Quick Charlie wasn't about to let it get away. Sullivan Hart and Judge Parker's jail would just have to wait. Quick Charlie had things to do.

A half hour passed, and when he saw that the sweat on the morgan's sides and around its girth strap had dried into white streaks, he rose up and stretched, then stepped out of the willows. He looked all around as he tightened the horse's cinch, and swung up on the saddle. "Now that we've properly *communed*, let's get some ground behind us," he said.

Sims reined around at the water's edge, collected the
horse up, and touched his heels to its sides. The morgan cross bolted forward, back up onto the trail.

Sims only followed the tracks of the four horsemen
a few miles farther, long enough to see that they
were sticking to the winding valley trails, headed to
the northeast. He stopped the morgan on the trail
and considered the long ride ahead of him. "That's
the long way, boys," he spoke to the hoofprints in
the dirt, then looked off to his right along the high
hillside, where bare-washed stone ridging hung as if
suspended from the sky.

Sims considered the high rugged trail for a second
while the morgan cross high-stepped in place, blowing and stamping a hoof. Then Quick Charlie patted
the horse's withers as if hearing its answer, and
turned it off the trail with a touch of the reins urging
it upward, leaning forward as it climbed. The game
horse strove upward through brush and over rock,
black gravel, red clay dirt, and sand.

Evening shadows stretched long across the winding
valley trail and stood in black pools beneath deep
cliff overhangs. One of the riders kicked his horse
forward a few steps and settled it alongside their
leader, JT Priest. "Up there, Mister Priest." He
pointed along the high ridgeline to their left. "I saw
a rider through the trees . . . I'm sure I did."

JT Priest drew his horse to a halt and adjusted his
chewed-up black cigar to one side of his mouth as
he looked up. On the other side of Priest, another
man said, "Stanley's right—I see him too."

JT Priest's eyes scanned back and forth in the gray-
ing evening light, seeing the rider, but searching for
any others up there. The three horsemen bunched up
around him. He watched as the black morgan cross
stepped into view and stopped, both horse and rider
backlit now in the failing sunlight, their shadows
standing as one, cascading down the rocky hillside.

"Brazen as all get out," one of Priest's men said. "Want me to lift him out of his saddle, Mister Priest?"

"No, don't shoot," JT said over his shoulder. "Stanley, you and Norris get up there. Flank him, then bring him down here."

The big morgan began a slow walk down toward them. "Looks like he's coming on his own, Mister Priest," Ned Norris replied.

"Are you going to make me say it again, Norris?" JT Priest said harshly.

"No, sir! Let's go, Stanley." Norris gigged his horse up off the trail and onto the steep hillside, Stanley Lane following right behind him. They spread out as they climbed until they had the morgan and its rider between them, twenty yards apart. Then they turned and moved back down, keeping their eyes on the lone rider, seeing the cuffs on his wrists.

"I recognize that sucker," JT Priest said under his breath, watching the three horsemen descend in a line.

"How can you see his face in this light?" The new man, Kenny Kerns, asked, then spat and ran a hand across his parched lips.

"Kerns, if you can only recognize a man by seeing his face, you'll be blind all your life."

JT Priest sat still, watching until Quick Charlie Sims moved down and halted the morgan cross less than fifteen feet away. Priest took note of the handcuffs, chuckling low. "Is there something we can do for you?" As Priest spoke, he bounced a golf ball up and down in the palm of his black riding glove.

Quick Charlie Sims took a deep breath, playing it close and careful, and said, "Yeah . . . I could use a drink of water." He looked warily at the men on either side of him who'd moved in closer now and sat watching him, their rifles propped up on their thighs, their gloved thumbs across the rifle hammers.

JT Priest looked bemused, and tilted his chin to Stanley Lane. Stanley lifted his canteen by its strap, stepped his horse closer, and handed it to Sims. When Sims had uncapped it, turned back a long drink, and handed it back with cuffed hands, JT Priest sat gazing at him with detached interest. He finally nodded and said, "Anything else?"

Quick Charlie looked back and forth. "Any way you can get these cuffs off me?"

The men stifled a laugh, looking to Priest. "Now why would we want to do that?" Priest cocked his head to one side, rolling the golf ball around in his gloved palm. "We didn't put them on you."

"No, but his son did." Quick Charlie nodded toward the two blackened ears hanging on a strip of rawhide from JT Priest's saddle horn.

"Do say . . ." JT Priest offered a humorless smile. "So you were back there?"

"Yep, I was there. You made a mistake leaving those two boys alive. Kid Sully and Twojack Roth will be after you from now on."

"Oh? Which one is his son?" As Priest spoke, he motioned to one of his men, who sidled up close to Sims and took the rifle from his saddle scabbard. He passed the rifle over to Priest, who took it, looked it over, then laid it across his lap.

"You might as well say they both are. They'll both be gunning for you once Judge Parker hears what happened. He'll give them wide berth on this."

"And now you're going to convince me there's some way you can help me? There's something you, and *only* you can do for me?"

Quick Charlie shrugged. "No. I just came to throw in with you. I'm on the run, needing work, and figured I'd take a chance. You lost three men back there. *Los Pistoleros* is no secret now. They know you're back in business. The old man wrote the name in his own blood before he died."

JT Priest gave him a smug grin. "As I recall, the last time we spoke I asked you about working for

me, and you said you weren't going to be anybody's flunky."

"I know." Quick Charlie's eyes dropped. "But
things change. I made a mistake, a bad one. Now
I've got to swallow a big bite of pride. Let me join
you, Tuck. I'll do whatever you ask."

"I see . . ." A long silence passed while JT Priest
considered the request, rolling the golf ball in his
palm. Finally, he let out a breath and said to the
others, "Boys, meet Mister Quick Charlie Sims, also
known by some as Charlie Roma, Charlie Magic, and
The Gypsy Prince—also known in French Lick as the
man who outshot Diamond Sammy Grubbs so bad,
Grubbs swore off billiards forever." Priest looked
over at Sims with a trace of a smile. "Am I leaving
anything out, Sims?"

Sims returned the grin. "Please, Tuck, you're em-
barrassing me."

Ned Norris looked at Kenny Kerns, then the others. *Tuck . . . ?* He'd never heard anybody call JT
Priest *Tuck.*

"Watch your money around Quick Charlie,
boys . . . especially you, Stanley. I know how you
love to play checkers." Priest shot a glance at Stanley
Lane, then looked back at Quick Charlie Sims. "So
tell me, Sims. How's your golf game these days?"

Sims slid a glance over at Stanley Lane and looked
him up and down, sizing him up. *Checkers, huh . . . ?*
That was good to know. Sims looked back at Priest.
"My golf game's still good, I'm sure. Haven't played
any in a while. But I trust it. How's yours?"

"Oh, it's tolerable. Of course I only play for the
enjoyment of the game." His gaze leveled on Sims.

Sims shrugged. "Me too . . . I never take the game
too serious." He raised his cuffed hands and added,
"What do you say, Tuck? Can we get these things
off me?"

There it was again, JT Priest thought. None of his
underlings called him Tuck, and he wasn't going to

let Quick Charlie get in the habit of it. But for now
he wouldn't mention it. He backed his horse up a
step and turned it on the trail. "We'll have to leave
those cuffs on you for a while. We'll see what we've
got to cut them off back at the rails. I have my Pullman car waiting there."

"Oh, you travel in your own private car now?"
Quick Charlie stepped the morgan cross over beside
him and touched it up into a steady walk. "Sounds
like you're doing pretty well for yourself."

JT Priest smiled without answering. "It's not just
a private car, it's a private *Pullman* car. I might as
well tell you now, Sims . . . Kate McCorkle joined
my party a few weeks back. She's traveling with me
now." He paused for a second, and when Quick
Charlie made no response, he added, "You do remember dear Kate, don't you?"

"Sure, I remember Kate McCorkle," Quick Charlie
answered with a shrug, not wanting to appear as
caught off guard as he suddenly felt. "Then you certainly are traveling first-class these days."

JT Priest turned and looked him up and down. "I
arranged a pardon for her through some people I
know in Denver." His gaze narrowed as he peered
into Sims's eyes. "She owes me, Sims. She'll be be-
holden to me for a long time to come. What do you
think of that?"

Quick Charlie Sims weighed his words, not wanting to reveal any emotion. JT Priest was not the
smartest man alive, but he was no fool either. "Kate's
her own woman, Tuck. She always was."

"Oh?" JT Priest raised a brow.

Sims returned the searching gaze. "I'm not denying anything, Tuck. We had our times up close, her
and I. But we both always knew that what we had
was strictly business."

"I see . . ." JT Priest gazed forward, and after a
silence had passed between them he turned back to
Sims as the two of them moved their horses a few

yards forward of the others. "I'm sure you realize, Kate knows nothing about what I'm doing out here. If you should happen to mention anything to her about that unfortunate incident back at the cave, I'll have to have you shot, of course."

"My lips are sealed." Quick Charlie smiled, liking what he heard. He looked Priest up and down, noting the expensive suit beneath a riding duster, the thick cigar, a diamond ring glinting in the evening sunlight, and the pair of severed human ears hanging from his saddle horn. "If you don't mind me asking, Tuck, what are you doing out here? This all looks a little beneath you."

"I can't help it, Sims." Priest chuckled. "I simply have to put my hand in it now and then. Call it returning to my roots, I suppose."

Sims nodded. "I understand."

"So, tell me, Sims. Do you have any idea what Coleman Hart was doing back there?"

"I don't know. I was with Kid Sully looking for Joe Marr, the ole boy who was back there with the cattle. Why do you ask?"

"Nothing. Just curious." JT Priest rolled the golf ball in his gloved palm. "Cattle . . . I get in trouble every time I get around them."

Quick Charlie nodded as they rode along. He was in now, and that's exactly what he'd wanted. Now he had to settle back, get as far into *Los Pistoleros* as he could. JT Priest wasn't the only leader of the gang. There was another man who also used to keep a collection of ears on a string. Sims wanted him too.

"Let me ask you something important," JT Priest said. "Let's say every time you hit a ball, it goes good and straight for about seventy five yards or so, then all of a sudden cuts straight up and sharp to the right? What are you doing wrong?"

"Straight up? To the right?" Sims smiled to himself. "You know somebody who's having that kind of problem?"

"Yes, I surely do," JT Priest replied.

"That's a rough one, the straight up part." Quick Charlie shook his head. "Let me think about that. Maybe if you'll get these cuffs off me, we can hit a few balls for practice, and see what we can come up with, huh?"

"What's your hurry, Quick Charlie? I like you in handcuffs. It gives me a real sense of security."

"No kidding?" Quick Charlie grinned to himself. "I never knew I made you nervous."

"You don't." JT Priest shrugged, staring straight ahead. Yet Quick Charlie noticed how Priest's neck seemed to redden a bit at the suggestion.

Oh, yes . . . Things were moving right along for him, Quick Charlie thought, touching the morgan forward with the slightest tap of his knees.

Chapter 3

Judge Charles Isaac Parker, the Hanging Judge, stroked his fingertips down his smooth goatee and looked out through his office window. He had three good deputies missing out there somewhere. Nearly two full weeks had passed since he'd had any word from either Coleman Hart, or his partner, Twojack Roth. To make matters worse, it had been over a week since he'd heard from Coleman's son. What made this such a predicament was the fact that he'd released a prisoner into Sullivan's custody. Parker's critics would love hearing that.

While it wasn't uncommon for any of his deputies to be gone like this for long periods of time, given the demands of their job, it was unheard of to release a man like Quick Charlie Sims under any circumstances—a man suspected of both robbery and murder? What in the world had possessed him to do something like this? He chastised himself. There were those who questioned his sanity to begin with. This would only convince them that the Hanging Judge had truly lost his mind.

Charles Isaac Parker had never liked that title, but it was a mantle he had reconciled within himself. He'd accepted that from now on, wherever he went, whatever he did, he would be the Hanging Judge for the rest of his life. Although it was not a title commonly spoken in his presence, he heard it whispered too often as he walked the streets of Fort Smith. He saw it clearly in the eyes of those who would never be so coarse as to say it, as they shook his hand and told him what an honor it was to meet him.

An honor indeed . . . He gazed out through the dust-scalloped window of his office, a converted brick barracks inside the old military post, and searched the distant sky as if his deputies whereabouts might be revealed to him. After a moment he sighed and brought his gaze closer in, and looked out at the broad flag batting back and forth in the hot evening wind. Beyond the door behind him the crowded court still waited. It was 6:30 P.M., but the time of day didn't matter in this court. Federal court in the Western District of Arkansas started early and finished late, six days a week.

He would hear each case on today's docket in turn, and not adjourn until the last prisoner before him either walked out a free man, or—as most often was the case—left here in chains, dragged off to the long corridor leading down to the dark jail cells in the stone-walled basement below him. It would be easy, he often thought, for a man in his position to consider himself godlike, perched here above the squalor, the suffering, the inhumanity of that steel and stone world beneath him. But he was not God, and he knew it.

Unlike God, Judge Parker lived on a budget, and it was that budget committee far away in Washington who dictated his benevolence—they were the ones who really created the stark rancid world below him. He seldom visited the cells, yet on warm days there was no escaping the rising odor of rodent, sweat, urine, and sour unwholesome air. But this was the world he ruled, and he ruled as best he could. *So be it . . .*

Judge Parker sighed. He lifted the watch from his vest pocket, checked it, then closed it and put it away. He turned toward the door to the courtroom and prepared himself mentally to resume work. But then he stopped when he heard a quiet knock at the door and the voice of one of his deputies, old Dan Slater, say in a lowered tone, "Judge, sir? Your honor?"

"Yes, come in, Dan'l."

The door opened only wide enough for the man to slip inside the room, then he closed it behind himself. "Begging your pardon, Your Honor, but I thought you'd want to know about this right away." Deputy Dan Slater stood with his dust-streaked Stetson in his hand at his chest, a shotgun cradled in his left arm.

"What is it? News about the Harts?" Judge Parker saw the concerned expression on his weathered bearded face.

"Yes, sir, and I'm afraid it's all bad news, Your Honor." Dan took a breath. "Coleman's dead, sir. His son, Sullivan, and Twojack Roth just arrived with his body."

Judge Parker's shoulders slumped, but only for a second. "Where are they, Dan'l?"

"Over at the undertaker's, Your Honor. They also brought in the cattle rustler, Joe Marr, if that's worth anything to you now."

"It's always worth something, Dan'l. It's their job to bring in lawbreakers. Deputy Coleman Hart knew the risks better than anyone. He was with me here since the first day I took office."

"I know that, sir." Deputy Slater hesitated. "I ought to tell you before you go over there—whoever killed ole Coleman cut off both his ears."

"Cut off his *ears*? Good Lord, man!" Parker squeezed the bridge of his nose with his thumb and forefinger and shook his head as if to clear it of something. He settled himself and added, "All right, Dan'l. Please go out there and tell my bailiff I'll be back within the hour."

"Yes, sir, consider it done." He hesitated again. "Are you sure you don't want me to go with you?"

"No, but thank you, Dan'l."

Judge Parker left through the side door and walked the littered alleyway to avoid the afternoon wagon traffic until he reached the back door of the mortuary three blocks away. After knocking twice on the rough wooden door, Parker watched the undertaker's assistant crack open the door. The man looked out above his wire-rimmed spectacles at Judge Parker, a thick white bandanna masking his face. Then he opened the door wide enough for the judge to slip inside.

"I must warn you, Judge Parker," the small man whispered, his voice muffled through the thick bandanna, "the deceased is in a terrible condition. I'm afraid the heat has taken its toll."

Reeling a bit from the dank odor of death, Judge Parker snatched a handkerchief from inside his day coat and pressed it to his nose and mouth. He looked at the blackened face of Coleman Hart, his ears missing, his body still wrapped in canvas and laid out on a wooden work board. One end of the wrapping had been pulled open, revealing the rot like a dark budding flower from within the folds of stiff canvas. Judge Parker only looked for a second. He turned his eyes upward and away and stepped over to the other door. He asked in a strained voice through his handkerchief, "Are they waiting out there?"

"Yes, sir."

"I better get to them, then." He opened the door enough to step through, lowered the handkerchief, took a breath, and looked at the sweat-streaked faces of Sullivan Hart and Twojack Roth. Joe Marr sat in a wooden chair against the wall, his eyes lowered, one hand cuffed to the chair arm. Marr looked up at Parker, then back down at the floor.

At the end of a tight, grim silence, Sullivan Hart took a step forward and said, "We would have gone on after them, but we wanted him to have a proper burial first."

"I understand." Parker nodded. "Did Quick Charlie Sims have a hand in this?"

"No, sir, he didn't." Sullivan Hart looked haggard and spent. Twojack Roth looked no better himself.

"Where is he?" Parker's eyes swept the room once more.

"He's gone, sir."

"Gone? Are you saying gone as in, dead? Or gone as in, he's gotten away?"

Parker saw the answer in Sullivan Hart's eyes before Hart even spoke. "He stole my horse, sir. Luckily, we rounded up some of the other horses running astray."

Judge Parker seethed. "They're going to throw a fit up in Creed. I never should have let that man out of custody! For the life of me, I don't know quite how it came about. I had him brought to my office to question him about Joe Marr's whereabouts, and the next thing you know . . ." Parker looked puzzled and shook his head. Hart and Roth shot one another a glance.

"Nobody is to blame here, Your Honor, unless it's me," Sullivan Hart said. "I'm the one who lost him. Things just have a way of happening when Quick Charlie Sims is involved. He's too slick to deal with. I trained that morgan horse to stand on command . . . but Quick Charlie rode him out from under our noses."

"I see . . ." Judge Parker nodded. He raised a piece of hard sugar candy from his vest pocket with a tense hand and popped it into his mouth. "I want him back, dead or alive. The *alive* part is quite immaterial at this point."

"I understand, Your Honor." Sullivan Hart shook his head. "But let me make it clear, he had nothing to do with any of this. He just saw a way out for himself, and he took it. He even kept his word that he wouldn't make a run for it once the shooting started."

"His word? Ha!" Judge Parker tossed his head back in exasperation. "He promised me as soon as he got back, he'd show me how to put a man's king into check in three simple moves. So much for his *word*!"

Hart and Roth looked at each other, stunned. "Your Honor," Hart said, turning back to him. "You played chess with Quick Charlie Sims? Nobody plays chess with Sims."

Judge Parker looked embarrassed. "I heard that about billiards and checkers, but not about chess . . . chess is a gentleman's game."

"No, Your Honor, it's not just billiards and checkers. It's chess, poker, billiards, croquet. You can't play games of any kind with—"

"All right, so I was mistaken." Judge Parker cut him off, ending the matter with the toss of a hand. "Let's forget about Quick Charlie Sims for now. Tell me everything that happened out there."

The funeral was small and brief beneath a boiling thunderhead that drifted in from the southwest as if on cue. Looming swollen and dark above them, gathering itself in and churning, it seemed to wait for the preacher's final amen before busting loose in a hard, sidelong-blowing deluge. All others had left, some of them in a hunched trot, eager to get out of the rain. Yet Sullivan Hart and Twojack remained, one on either side of the grave, where the workmen had left their shovels standing in the mound of fill dirt before withdrawing out of the storm.

Sullivan Hart stood gripping his hat brim. When he looked up and across the grave, water spilled back from his hair and down the neck of his black suit coat. His black string tie lay plastered sideways on his white shirt. Twojack Roth's dark eyes stared back at him in question, and at the same moment their intentions became singular. They both walked to the end of the grave and picked up the mud-stuck shov-

els and began filling the grave. "He was a good lawman, my pa," Sullivan Hart said as they worked.

"I know it." Twojack Roth stopped with a shovelful of wet dirt and looked down at the flowers par-
tially covered by loose earth and beaten flat against
the pine coffin boards. "We got along good, him and
me." Rivulets of muddy water ran down the grave
walls and formed a dancing puddle at the bottom.

"I hate burying him without his ears." Sullivan
Hart tossed a heavy shovelful of dirt onto the coffin,
then stuck the shovel blade back into the wet fresh
mound and lifted. "What kind of men do something
like this?"

"I don't know, Sully." Twojack ran a wet gloved
hand across his face. "But we'll make them pay."

Sullivan Hart rested for second on the shovel handle. "Where do you want to start? The Englishman?"

"Might as well." Twojack nodded. "After this
wash, we can forget any tracks. With no federal marshal here right now, Parker will have to give us
jurisdiction."

"He'll give it," said Hart. "Either way, I'm still
going."

"Me too. I won't come back till it's over." Twojack
threw a shovelful of earth as if aiming for the flattened flowers. The heavy dirt hit the pine coffin top
with a resounding thud and covered them completely, stems and blooms alike.

The next morning the storm had passed, and they
stood dressed in their road clothes, readying their
horses and shooting gear. Judge Parker came into the
livery barn and stood striped in gray morning light
through the cracks in the front wall. "I have some
paperwork for you," he said. "You'll need this along
the way should your authority come into question.
From what you say about these men, they will use
every trick in the book to avoid capture, including
legal maneuvers, before it's over."

"They can try." Twojack Roth turned with a broken-down sawed-off shotgun in one hand, his Winchester rifle in the other. He slid the rifle into his saddle scabbard, then loaded the shotgun and snapped it shut as Sullivan Hart stepped over to the judge and took the papers from his hand. He looked them over briefly.

"Thank you, Your Honor." Sullivan Hart folded the papers and put them inside his bib-front shirt.

"Perhaps you should read them?" Judge Parker suggested.

"I will, sir. First chance I get." Sullivan Hart slipped the leather straps of a shoulder harness across his back and adjusted the holster up under his left arm. He picked up his pistol from atop a bale of straw. "The warrant does read *dead* or alive, I'm sure?" He checked the pistol, spinning the cylinder before slipping it down into the holster.

Judge Parker searched Hart's eyes. "You realize if you bring these men in, there are no witnesses to testify that they killed your father?"

"I saw them take him into the cave," Twojack Roth said. He turned from attending his horse and fixed his dark eyes on Judge Parker's. "When we catch up to them, witnesses won't be an issue, Your Honor."

"I understand." Parker looked from one to the other. "I just wanted to know we're all of the same mind. Until I hire a new federal marshal, I'll expect a weekly wire from you . . . if possible. If not, please keep me informed as often as you can. Coleman Hart was a good friend of mine, as you both know."

"We know, Judge," Sullivan Hart said. "We'll go as far as we need to, and we'll do whatever needs doing. That's all we can say right now."

Judge Parker backed up a step toward the livery barn door. "Good luck to you both." He bowed slightly, then turned and left.

Hart and Roth stood for a silent second, looking at each other in the gray morning light. Then Sullivan

Hart nodded and led his horse over to the door. He swung the doors open and pulled his mount to one side as Twojack Roth mounted his new silver-gray barb and heeled it out into the dirt street.

Hart stepped outside, closed the doors behind himself, and mounted the big chestnut gelding. "I miss that black morgan already," he said, stepping the big chestnut quarterwise onto the street. Without another word, they both turned their horses toward the westward trail, and heeled them forward. From his office window, Judge Parker watched them pass in the hazy swirl of morning, and stood watching them still as they grew smaller and faded into a drifting silver mist left over from the night's storm.

Chapter 4

A musky smell of buffalo wafted on the hot breeze blowing through the open car window. Along with the buffalo musk came the slight odor of wood smoke from the engine's stack, mingled with the aroma of hot oil and steam. The sound of the big idle engine pulsed and throbbed in the silence of the endless Kansas plains. Alone inside the car with his hands still cuffed, Quick Charlie Sims picked up the stack of dollar bills from the green felt tabletop and leaned back in his chair. He smiled to himself, riffled the money, then folded it and shoved it down in his shirt pocket.

When the door at the front end of the Pullman car opened, he looked up for a second and nodded as Kate McCorkle walked past without acknowledging him. She stopped at the ornate brass-trimmed bar with her back to him and poured herself a drink. Sims had only seen her for a moment when he'd first arrived with JT Priest three days earlier. She'd greeted him in a polite yet constrained manner, and had avoided him ever since.

But now that it was just the two of them alone in the car, she turned facing him, a snifter of brandy in her hand, and said in a lowered voice, "I won't even *try* to guess what sort of an angle you're playing, Charlie Sims. But the first chance you get, I want you out of here."

Quick Charlie sat looking into her eyes for a moment before saying, "Believe me, Kate, whatever I'm doing here, it has nothing to do with you. I had no idea you were with JT Priest until he told me. By then it was too late for me to turn back. I'm on the run Kate. I knocked on the first door I came to."

She studied his eyes from across the Pullman car. "Then I was right about one thing—you didn't come here looking for me." She paused for a second; and in that second Sims saw the faintest surge of hurt masked behind her cool demeanor. He reached out with his cuffed hands, picked up a short stack of silver dollars from atop the table, and for a quiet moment sat plinking them up and down. She watched, somehow attracted to the smooth steady motion of his hand.

"What did you want to hear, Kate?" The coins clicked with a gentle ring. "Did you want me to lie to you? Tell you I've been trying to find you all this time? I don't want to do that."

"Then don't." She kept her eyes on the silver dollars. As she raised her drink, she seemed to be considering something, and when she lowered the glass from her mouth, whatever it was had been resolved. "You always know when to lie and when not to—so if you're telling the truth, it must be for a reason. But I'm settled in here, Charlie. Don't ask anything of me." She gestured about the Pullman car, its polished wood paneling, the plush carpets on the floor, the expensive crystal. "I won't let you do anything to destroy this for me."

Before answering, he noted the way she'd said it. She'd swept her hand toward the fine trappings as if her surroundings might well have been bars to a cage, and her hand, in spite of its soft and casual presentation might as well have been a fist. Without revealing anything of his intentions, he answered her the only way he could. "If you're really happy, Kate, I won't destroy things for you. I couldn't if I tried."

Happy . . . ? She studied the coins as he continued

stacking them, knowing how Quick Charlie Sims's words could always be taken any number of ways. "Why *are* you here?"

He nodded at his cuffed wrists. "Like I said, I'm on the run. Right now I'm powerless to do anything for myself. I hoped to throw in with *Los Pistoleros* for a while, just long enough to get back on my feet."

She sighed and sipped her drink. "You're never helpless. Even if you were, *Los Pistoleros* is not what it used to be. They're strictly legitimate now."

"Oh? And I'm not?" Sims cocked an eye. She seemed calmer now. He stopped stacking the coins, and let them lie still in his palm.

"You know what I mean, Charlie. JT has turned this into a big business. This isn't a three card molly hustle, or some sleight of hand. There's nothing for you here."

Sims shrugged. "Tuck seems to think there might be. I think they still rob banks, railroads, and anything else they get their hands on. How does that strike you?"

"Don't be ridiculous." She waved her hand once more. "They own banks and interests in railroads. They're not outlaws anymore."

"Is that a fact? Then what was Tuck Priest doing out in the dirt getting his hands dirty, Kate?" Quick Charlie began spreading the stack of coins back and forth down three fingers, the motion of it silent and smooth as silk.

She watched, and started to say something. But then she caught herself as if changing her mind. "No, I won't do this." She shook her head. "I promised myself I wouldn't talk to you about JT, or their business . . . or anything that would get me involved with you again. So don't ask. *Los Pistoleros* is dead and gone, Charlie. They're an investment business now. JT and his associates saw times were changing, and they were smart enough to change with them.

Something you should have thought about doing. That's all I'll say."

"Don't kid yourself, Kate." The coins glinted, moving back and forth as Sims spread them along his fingers. "JT Priest might be legitimate on the surface, but underneath he's the same thieving, murdering scoundrel he always was. He still collects ears."

"I don't believe that." She looked away.

"Of course you don't." Quick Charlie set down the drink he had poured earlier. "Why was he out there?"

"He and William Mabrey just bought the Old English Spread, if you must know. JT is only here to make sure the transaction went smoothly. Once we leave here, we're headed back East—hopefully for good."

"William Mabrey, huh?" Sims studied the silver dollars as he spoke. "So Mad-dog Mabrey still has his hand in *Los Pistoleros* too."

"Nobody calls him Mad-dog anymore, Charlie. Bill Mabrey spends his time in Washington these days, rubbing shoulders with politicians. He doesn't even come west to check on his holdings anymore."

"I bet." Sims smiled. "That's what he's got ole Tuck Priest doing."

"Nobody calls him Tuck anymore, either." She raised a hand, stopping the conversation. "That's all I've got to say about it. You're not going to pry information out of me. I'm not going to be your dupe, Quick Charlie. Leave me out of whatever you're up to."

"You're right . . . I'm sorry, Kate." He stopped spreading the silver dollars, reaching out and placing them back down on the green felt tabletop. "I won't ask you anything else about them."

"Good." A silence passed while she finished her drink in two long sips and set the empty glass on the bar. She then turned to face him and touched a hand to the long ringlets of dark hair on her shoul-

ders, seeing how he was still watching her. She felt
uncomfortable and needed to say something, anything. She asked in a more gentle tone, "So . . . how
have you been? Or should I even bother to ask?"
Her eyes motioned to the money in front of him.

Quick Charlie lowered his eyes and let out a
breath. "I think I've already summed up how I've
been." He rattled the cuffs on his wrists. On the tabletop lay a deck of playing cards, a bottle of whiskey, and half a black cigar in a brass ashtray. For the
past three days he'd played poker with Priest's men,
always winning, but always at just the right place—
not too much all at once.

Kate McCorkle looked at the tabletop, then once
more at the handcuffs, and shook her head. "Don't
tell me Quick Charlie Sims is down on his luck. I
wouldn't believe it."

"There's luck, and there's *luck*, Kate. Things haven't
been right for me since Colorado. Somebody set me
up for that bank robbery in Creed, and I've been on
the dodge ever since." His voice lowered. "You know I
didn't rob that bank, Kate. People rob banks because
they're either desperate, or not sharp enough to do
anything else."

"I don't know what you're capable of doing, Charlie." She turned away. "But don't ever mention Colorado to me," her voice snapped. "It still gives me
bad dreams. That part of my life is over . . . and
good riddance." She reached out with a trembling
hand and poured whiskey into her glass and threw
it back in a one gulp.

"I understand, Kate," Sims whispered.

"Oh, you do?" When she lowered the glass to the
bar, she gripped the bar edge for a second, then spun
toward him. "I spent a miserable ten months in
prison there, Charlie, ten long, terrible months, just
because I wouldn't say the one name they wanted
me to say. Did you know that? Did you, Charlie?"

"No, I didn't." His voice remained low, almost

apologetic. "But I would never have expected that of you, Kate. You could have said whatever you wanted to . . . I was already in the jackpot. I wouldn't have held it against you."

"I'm certain you wouldn't." Kate McCorkle swallowed hard against the strong aftertaste of whiskey. "But I would have." She pressed a hand to her chest. "I would have held it against myself. Want to know why, Charlie? I'll tell you why—because I was a fool! But not anymore. From here on, Kate looks out for Kate, and nobody else. Do you understand that, Charlie? *Nobody* else."

He stared at her, and realized he had to let her know something. He couldn't leave her entirely in the dark, not after all she'd done for him. Not after all they'd once meant to each other. "Then listen close to what I'm telling you, Kate. It's time you gathered in whatever you can for yourself. Do you understand me?"

She settled herself and returned his stare, all business now, getting his message loud and clear. "This hasn't been a scam for me, Charlie."

"I understand. But nevertheless, it's time to strike your tent and load your wagon."

"I see. Then there's nothing I can do, or say, to stop you?"

"Nothing." Sims shook his head without taking his eyes from hers. "Not unless you put a bullet in my brain, or warn Tuck Priest about me. This goes back a long way, Kate. Nothing will stop it. It's old business between Priest and me."

"The bank robbery in Creed? Is that what this is about?"

He didn't answer.

"I see." She hesitated, then added, "Thanks for warning me. I'll be ready, as ready as I can be on short notice." She turned and gazed out through the window across the endless prairie.

* * *

Inside the engineer's compartment, the pressure of the steam beneath the boiler had died down to a slow, pulsing throb. But the heat had only worsened now that the train had sat motionless for the past half an hour in the scorching sunlight. "What the hell are they doing now?" the fireman asked the engineer as he swabbed a bandanna across his forehead.

"Beats me all to pieces," the engineer said, his voice testy and gruff, the heat starting to get to him. "Mister Priest wants to do some shooting. So that's that. He'll shoot or be damned, I expect."

Twenty yards out on a low rise, four men stood in a semicircle, studying the ground below. Each man held a rifle, either propped on his shoulder or hanging from his hand. In their midst, a tall man in a long pin-striped dress coat stooped down and ran his pearl gray glove back and forth across the dirt. "There now. That should do it." He stood up, took off his gloves, pulling at one finger at a time, and looked out across the endless roll of prairie toward a small herd of buffalo some seven hundred yards away.

"Oh . . . another thing, Deavers." He spoke over his shoulder at a small man who sat sobbing and trembling on the ground a few feet back from the others. "Don't forget to mention something about how sorry you are . . . how you've brought shame to your poor wife, your lovely daughter, and so forth and so on." He rolled a white ball around in his hand as he spoke, and chuckled under his breath. "People eat that stuff up, don't they, Kerns?" he added, smiling at the rifleman nearest him.

"Oh, *hell* yes, Mister Priest," Kenny Kerns replied. He returned his boss's smile. "It gives a really solid, personal sort of touch to it."

"Yep, that's what I thought." He nodded and spread a pale hand outward across the prairie. "Have you much experience in this?"

"Well, no sir, Tuck," Kerns said, shooting a proud

glance at the other three riflemen. "This is my first time . . . but I've always wanted to." There it was, another man calling him Tuck. He'd have to do something about that—but not right now. Right now he had to concentrate.

"Then just watch and learn, Kenny. Who knows, you may be called upon at some time." JT Priest held his black silk top hat in place against the strong wind blowing across the plains, and gazed at the distant small herd of buffalo. "A pitiful sight, that." He shook his head. "Soon, there will be none left to kill." He sighed and reached down once more. This time he pulled up a small plug of wild grass and let it blow from his hand.

"That's the truth, Tuck," Kerns said, looking off toward the milling herd.

Tuck, again . . . JT Priest settled himself. "You know, Kenny, wind is the single most important factor in making a good shot. I don't care how much you practice, or how good you are. Ignore the wind in a long shot like this, and you'll never hit squat." He looked out across the plains and shook his head in finality. "You just won't . . . and that's the truth."

"Yes sir, Tuck." Kerns took a step back and lowered his rifle from his shoulder. "I'll remember that."

"How's that letter coming, Deavers?" JT Priest demanded, not bothering to look back at the man.

"Mister Priest, in the name of God," Lyle Deavers sobbed. "Please don't do this! I'll never say a word, ever! Not to anyone!"

JT Priest rolled his eyes upward. "He's going to start in blubbering again, I bet." He finally turned and looked at Lyle Deavers, at the paper flapping beneath his thumb on the writing pad, the ink pen trembling in his hand. "Deavers, you pitiful wretch. We've been through all this. Now either write the note and sign it, or else forget all about it. I'm not going to argue with you. Can't you see I'm trying to concentrate here?"

"But . . . but, Mister Mabrey swore nothing like this would ever happen. He gave his word . . . for both of you!"

"Perhaps I should have mentioned this earlier on . . . it may have slipped my mind. But, you see," Priest said, raising a finger for emphasis, "my dear partner, Mister *Mad-dog* Mabrey, is a liar, a scoundrel, and a murdering thief. I have to say I'm a bit surprised you didn't notice that back when you first agreed to do business with us. It would have made this so much simpler!"

"*Mad-dog?*" Deavers shook uncontrollably. "I . . . I never heard Mister Mabrey called that."

Priest grinned at his riflemen. He tweaked his thin mustache, and nodded toward Lyle Deavers. "He never heard him called Mad-dog." Priest's eyes turned cold. "I've never heard him called *anything* else. I suppose one hears only what one chooses." He took a deep breath as if seeking to rein in his patience, and stooped down beside the trembling man. "Let's go through this one more time. Your bank signed for—and billed the government on our behalf—for tons of beef that were never delivered to the reservations, correct?"

"Well, yes, but I never thought—"

"Follow me on this," JT Priest cut him off. "Your bank handled over one million dollars in counterfeit cash and bearer bonds."

"Please, Mister Priest! Nobody will ever know! I swear to God!" He clutched at JT Priest's sleeve, but Priest shook him loose, and stood up and dusted himself off.

"Show some guts, man. They already know . . . that's why we have to kill you. You danced the dance!" Priest shrugged, his hands spread wide. "Now the fiddler *must* be paid. You don't want a man with a name like Mad-dog sending a few of his men to call on your wife and lovely daughter, now do you?"

"No! No, please, no!" Deavers shook his head quickly.

"There, then. It's all settled." JT Priest patted Deavers' trembling shoulder. "Get the letter finished and signed. And try to hurry—you're holding up a sporting event."

Priest walked back to his spot among the riflemen. "Now then, where was I?" He took off his top hat and dress coat and handed them to Kenny Kerns as he gazed out once more across the plains. The wind had lessened now, and he judged it again and smiled. "Perfect." He bent down, picked up the long driver club from the ground, tested its hickory shaft between his hands, then positioned himself above the gutta-percha golf ball he had placed on the ground. "Everyone quiet now. Deavers, don't you dare snivel back there whilst I shoot."

The riflemen stifled their laughter, then stood silent and still. Their eyes cut from the ground upward to the sky at the quick swish and solid whack of the golf ball. JT Priest followed the ball with his club, his head bending slightly when at sixty yards the ball began a slice to the right. "Uh-oh . . ." The ball sliced harder right until at one point, it may have intended to circle back like a boomerang. But then it drove away into the tall grass.

"Damn it to everlasting *hell*!" JT Priest pounded the club head to the ground, his easy, gentlemanly composure suddenly shattered. He turned wild-eyed to the riflemen. "Who brought the rest of the damn balls? Huh? Where are they? Give me a blasted ball!"

Three balls appeared quickly on Kenny Kerns's palm. Priest snatched one and looked at it and cursed it as if it were some living demon. "Lousy, rotten, little bastard!" He bent down, scraped up a short mound of earth, and stood the ball on it. He stood back up, turned to Lyle Deavers, and pointed at him with the club. "Get it *finished* and get it *signed*! How am I suppose to shoot with you back there carrying on, you sniveling coward!"

"Yes, sir," Deavers replied in a broken voice.

JT Priest glanced back at the windows of the Pullman car, then took a breath and adjusted the club in his hand. "All right," he whispered to himself, "remember the fundamentals . . ."

As he made his swing, the whistle from the train resounded in a deafening blast of steam. The ball looped high and landed less than fifty feet out. "Damn it! Damn it to bloody hell!" He shot a crazed, wild-eyed glare at the engine of the train as he slung the golf club to the ground and snatched Kenny Kerns's rifle from his hand. "Can anybody here drive a train? Huh? Can they?" He swung the barrel toward the engine.

"Easy, Tuck," Kerns said. "None of us are engineers. It's a long way to Abilene."

"Don't *Tuck* me, you punk!" Priest swung the rifle barrel back and poked it hard into Kerns's chest. "I'll blow your damn heart out. Understand?" The other riflemen stood frozen in place. Lyle Deavers cringed on the ground.

"Yes, sir, Mister Priest, I understand!" Kerns's face turned chalk white.

Priest turned to Deavers in a rage, his knuckles white on the rifle stock. "Is it finished? Is it signed?"

"Yes." Deavers shielded his hands above his lowered head as Priest stalked toward him. The letter fluttered in Deavers's fingertips.

Priest snatched it and looked it over, calming down some, then said in a quieter tone, "All right, now get up and get out of here. You're destroying my swing."

Deavers looked up at him. "You mean . . . go? Out there?"

"Yeah, out there. Get going."

"But, I . . . What about my buggy?" He gestured a

trembling hand toward his one-horse buggy waiting beside the train.

"I said get going. Don't worry about your horse and buggy. I am not going to kill you, fool! You've got my word. Now get out of my sight."

"My daughter, Ellen? My wife—"

"I'm going to count to three. If you're not out of here, I swear to God I'll shoot you where you sit!"

Lyle Deavers scooted sideways the first few feet, then came to his feet in a run, bounding out through the wild grass. The riflemen watched him for a second, then turned back to JT Priest. "Now then." Priest put the letter inside his vest, tugged the vest down into place, and walked back to where his golf club lay on the ground. "Maybe with that coward out of the way . . ." He took another ball from Kerns's hand, positioned it on the ground, and adjusted his stance.

This time, the ball sailed upward and away, a good strong shot that arced over a hundred yards out. "There, you see? I don't think I need some jake-leg like Quick Charlie Sims showing me how to hit a golf ball, eh? I've got the hang of it now, boys. Kerns, watch this." He mounded the ball, attended to his grip, adjusted his stance to exactly the same position, and brought the club back, precise and perfect.

He brought the club facedown, strong and powerful, and swung through with one smooth, even stroke. Yet even as his eyes went upward to follow the shot, the ball only streaked straight out across the ground, whipping through the grass like some snake gone berserk.

JT Priest stepped back and leaned on his golf club and shook his head. He took a deep breath, then stood up and pointed the club out toward Lyle Deavers, who was over a hundred yards away, bobbing up and down in the tall grass. "Will some of you, please, follow him out of sight, then kill that miserable wretch before he gets all the way to Texas on us! Get rid of the buggy too.''

As two of his men turned and trotted away, Priest grabbed Kenny Kerns's arm and stopped him from joining them. ''Kenny, go bring out some more golf balls . . . and bring Sims back with you.''

''Yes, sir,'' Kenny Kerns said. ''Want me to find a way to uncuff him first?''

''No . . . leave him cuffed. I just need him to give me a couple of pointers.'' He swung the golf club up under his arm and stalked back toward the shade of the waiting train. ''*God!* This game makes me *crazy!*''

Inside the Pullman car, Quick Charlie Sims had stood up, parted the curtains with his cuffed hands, and looked out at JT Priest and his men as they came walking back. ''Looks like Tuck is going to be needing my help any minute now.'' He smiled, and turned to face Kate across the car, keeping the curtains parted for her to see through.

''You be careful, Charlie,'' she said, stepping over closer to him, gazing past him and out the window of the car. ''JT Priest is not a man to take lightly.''

''Don't I know it,'' Sims said with gravity in his voice. He let the curtains close. ''But it looks as if he's inviting me to play.'' Quick Charlie smiled. A poker chip appeared in his hand as if out of thin air. ''And you know me, Kate.'' The poker chip turned back and forth from one knuckle to the next. ''I only play to win.''

Chapter 5

For the past two days, Sullivan Hart and Twojack Roth had been traveling on land belonging to the Old English Spread. It would still take another full day of riding before they reached the main house. At dusk they'd pitched a camp and struck up a low campfire for the night, when three cowhands came riding in from the north out of the gray light. The three riders caught sight of the low fire and moved closer with an air of caution until Twojack Roth raised his rifle above his head and waved them in. Each rider led a short string of horses behind him.

At the edge of the camp alongside a narrow creek, the three men stopped for a second until one of them, an elderly drover, recognized Roth and called out to him. "*Hola*, Twojack, can you spare some firelight?"

"Yep, come on in, Cooney. The coffee's hot." Twojack sat down and picked up his tin cup full of coffee and raised it toward the drovers as they moved their horses forward.

After they had swung off their saddles and led their strings of horses over to a downed sycamore to tie them there, Cooney stepped forward ahead of the other two, taking off his leather gloves. "Much obliged. I haven't seen you in the longest time, Twojack Roth." His eyes cut to Sullivan Hart, and upon recognizing his face beneath Hart's lowered hat brim, he added, "Good to see you too, Hart."

"Evening, Cooney," Roth said.

Sullivan Hart nodded and raised his hat brim.

The other two men moved in closer to Cooney now, each carrying their own tin cups from their saddlebags. "At least a man can still round himself up a cup of coffee out here, I reckon," one said.

Cooney gestured his thumb toward them. "These boys are Bob Robison and Hewey Clark." He gestured over toward Hart and Roth and finished the introductions. Then he said to Sullivan Hart in a lowered tone, "I heard what happened to your pa. A terrible thing. I never had nothing but respect for ole Coleman. I hated hearing about it."

"Thanks, Cooney," Hart replied. "How'd you hear about it so fast? It's been no more than a week."

"Word travels on the wind, I reckon." Cooney and the other two circled the fire and stooped down. Pouring himself a cup of coffee, Cooney said, "A feller rode through here past the main house three days ago. Said he was in Fort Smith the day you brought ole Coleman's body in." He shook his head and sipped the hot coffee as the other two men filled their cups. "I expect you're hunting the men what done it?" He looked back and forth between the two of them.

"Yep," said Roth. "We don't have much to go on. We're heading in now to talk to Tillford."

Cooney squinted beneath his thick tangle of eyebrows. "What for? Tillford ain't mixed up in it, is he?"

"No," said Sullivan Hart. "But his name came up. We think maybe he knows the men who did it."

"You won't be talking to Tillford," said Hewey Clark, a young man wearing a lizard-skin vest over his faded blue range shirt. "He's long gone up to Canada. Left here over a week ago."

Twojack Roth and Sullivan Hart looked at each other.

"Yep, it's the truth," Cooney added. "The English Spread sold out last month. Tillford was just waiting to get things settled up. He'll be headed all the way back to England before long, is my guess."

Robison sank back on the ground with both hands wrapped around his coffee cup. "For two cents I'd have gone with him. This is the first time I've been out of work since fifty-four. Might give up cattle for good and go to playing banjo for a living."

"The new owner let you go?" Twojack Roth asked.

"Aw-yeah, real quick," Robinson replied. "They've brought in their own cowhands." He shrugged. "If you want to call them cowhands. Looked more like a bunch of grifters and sporting men, if you ask me."

"Sporting men, huh?" Sullivan Hart leaned forward, suddenly more attentive. "You mean well-dressed?"

Cooney laughed under his breath. "Yep, too well dressed for drovers, I'd say, unless they's carrying work clothes in their spindles."

"Hell, it don't matter though," Robison said. "There ain't a lick of cattle on this place now. Mexican rustlers cleaned them out three weeks back."

"Ha, rustlers my Aunt Mabel's wooden leg," said Cooney. "They can call it rustling if they want to . . . but I know better."

Hart and Roth looked at each other again. "What are you saying, Cooney?"

Cooney passed a guarded glance at the other two men, then said in a lowered voice, "What happened is, Tillford cut a deal. He sold off the cattle to the new owners a week before the sale tally took place. I figure they bought them from him, then he declared them stolen. That way the new owners had to pay the shareholders in England for the land itself. Tillford cashed in on the cattle."

"Hush up, Cooney," Hewey Clark said. "You don't know that for a dead-level fact."

"I don't know for a dead-level fact that rain falls from the sky. But all the evidence I've ever seen sure points that way." Cooney sipped his coffee. "There ain't been no rustling of that size around here in years. Most we've lost is a few head now and then to some hungry Comanches what got tired of starving, waiting for government beef that never came—and can't say as I blame them. I know slick thieving when I see it, boys.''

"These new men you're talking about," Hart asked, "who's in charge of them?"

Cooney studied Hart's eyes for a second, then answered with a knowing expression, "Cleveland Phelps. Ever heard of him?"

Hart nodded. "I've heard of him. Never seen him, but if he's the one who shot Dan Trabold in Carson City . . . I've heard enough about him. He's a big gunfighter from the Wind River country."

"Well, there you are." Cooney smiled and tossed a callused hand for emphasis. "Need I say any more? He's the one in charge back there for now. Nothing more than a hired killer, is what he is. I heard of him years ago. He used to ride with a gang called *Los Pistoleros* right after the war. Ever heard of them?" He looked first at Roth, then at Sullivan Hart, but neither of them said anything. "Well, it don't matter . . . your daddy knew them."

"Why don't you hush, Cooney," Hewey Clark cut in. "You've said too much already. Sounds like you've just got a mad-on because we lost our jobs."

"I hate being out of work, that's true. But boys, with that kind of men running the Old English . . . I'd just as soon not be around."

"Who are the new owners?" Hart asked.

Cooney chuckled and shook his shaggy head. "That's anybody's guess. Owners don't have faces anymore—they've only got company names. Some speculators from back East bought the spread. They call themselves the Midwest Alliance. They play with trains like they was kids' toys. They're supposed to cut a rail spur out here all the way from Teesdale Sidings. If they do, it'll cut a cattle drive down to a hundred-mile jaunt. Then everybody'll be out of work. Fellow by the name of JT Priest is half-owner, best I could understand. He's just a thug in a white shirt, for my money."

"You met him?" Twojack Roth asked.

"Yeah, we met him," Cooney replied, "for all of about five minutes. I personally weren't all that impressed." He looked around at Clark and Robison. They nodded in agreement.

"So," Clark said, "with Tillford gone, are you still riding in to the main house?"

"We came this far," Roth said. "We'll go on in, have a look around. Maybe this Cleveland Phelps can tell us something."

"You're all welcome to pitch a blanket here," Sullivan Hart said, finishing his coffee and slinging the grounds from his cup.

"We was hoping you'd say so." Cooney grinned. He looked around at the horses, then asked, "Say . . . where's that big morgan cross you always ride, Sully?"

"That's a long story," Hart said. "I'd feel better talking about it after a good night's sleep."

By the time darkness had fully set in, the men had spread their blanket rolls and dropped their saddles, and had taken their positions for the night around the low flickering campfire. Yet sometime during the night, Hewey Clark slipped out from beneath his blanket, eased his saddle up onto his shoulder and silently made his way to the horses. In a few moments he'd led his riding horse out onto the flatland, then saddled it and faded away into the darkness.

Just before dawn, Sullivan Hart awoke, feeling Cooney's boot toe tapping him on his leg. "Sully, you best wake up. Come on now, ya hear me?"

Sullivan Hart raised his head from his saddle on the ground and blinked his eyes. "What is it, Cooney?"

"Hewey Clark's gone, Sully. I got up to take a jake, and he ain't to be seen."

"Gone? Gone where?" Hart rose to his feet now, rubbing both hands across his face.

"From the looks of his tracks, I'd say he's headed back toward the main house," Cooney said. "Must've been in a hurry. He didn't even take his string along with him." He pointed to Clark's three spare horses still hitched to the downed sycamore.

Sullivan Hart looked back, seeing Twojack Roth already rolling his blankets up on the ground. "Roth? Are you thinking what I'm thinking?"

"If you're thinking we might be in for an ambush up ahead, yep, I suppose so." Twojack Roth stood up with his rolled blanket underneath his arm. "I've already been ambushed once this month. I don't intend for it to happen again."

"Me neither." Sullivan Hart turned to Cooney. "We'll need to use Hewey Clark's spare horses."

"Help yourself." Cooney spread his callused hand toward the three-horse string. "It'd serve him right if you kept every one of them."

"Damn Hewey's hide," cursed Robison, standing up from his blanket in the circling glow of dim firelight. "He must've figured he'd run back and tell Cleveland Phelps you're coming—thinks it might get his job back for him."

Cooney spat in disgust. "I don't know what's wrong with Hewey. He ain't acted right ever since that big she-cat got his head in her mouth two winters back." He looked down at Sullivan Hart, who'd stooped and started rolling up his blanket. "Reckon me and Robison oughta ride along with you? Phelps might not like answering any questions from a lawman."

"Thanks, Cooney, but no. Roth and I will handle it from here. Phelps shouldn't mind us coming, unless he's got something to hide."

"That's what I'm getting at," Cooney said. "Men

like Cleveland Phelps have always got something
to hide."

Hewey Clark's horse staggered in place as he leaped
down from the saddle in the gray light of dawn and
hurried across the front yard toward the large house.
He was stopped at the front porch by two men with
rifles. "What are you doing back here, cowboy?" one
asked, levering a round into his rifle chamber. Behind
the riflemen, through the glow of a lamp in the front
window, Hewey saw the shadows of men moving
across the room toward the door.

"I need to speak to Mr. Phelps! It's important!"
Hewey replied with his breath pounding in his chest.

Before either man could answer, the door opened
and a big man wearing a dress suit and a wide flat-
brimmed hat stepped out on the porch. Silver gray
hair hung down to his shoulders. A short cigar
glowed beneath his wide mustache. "That's all right,
Barnes, I'm here. Let him talk." He turned his gaze
to Hewey Clark standing at the foot of the porch
steps. "What's on your mind? I thought you and
your friends headed for Texas yesterday."

Hewey Clark jerked his hat from his head and
stood gripping the brim hard. "We was . . . that is,
we did. But there's two federal deputies headed this
way. I wanted to warn you."

Cleveland Phelps allowed a thin smile.

"Well, that's thoughtful of you, Clark. Tell me
more . . . "

Clark swallowed back a dry lump in his throat and
told him everything. When he'd finished, Cleveland
Phelps nodded and gestured a thumb back toward
the house. "Bet you're hungry. Go on back to the
kitchen and get yourself some breakfast. See Virgil
after you've eaten. Maybe we can find you a job here
after all."

"Much obliged, Mister Phelps." Clark stepped up

on the porch, glancing nervously back and forth at the riflemen, then went on inside the house.

Once Hewey Clark was out of sight, one of the men said in a low tone, "Boss, you've got to be kidding . . . keeping some lop-eared cattle drover around, what with all we've got going on."

"Of course I'm kidding, Barnes. As soon as he's fed, tell a couple of the boys to take him out and shoot him somewhere away from the house. I can't have him hanging around, firing his mouth off about us killing two deputies, now can I?"

Barnes grinned. "That's what I thought. Are we going to catch the others out there, or let them ride on in?"

"Get our horses ready," Cleveland Phelps said. "Round up four more men. We'll hit them when they make their turn through the rock pass."

"Now you're talking my language, boss," Briley Barnes said, grinning and jiggling the rifle in his hands.

"Your language, huh?" Cleveland Phelps stopped walking and looked at him coldly before Briley Barnes could turn and leave.

Barnes shrugged. "I got no qualms about shooting a couple of no-good lawdogs, if that's what you're asking."

"Blood costs money, Barnes." Phelps stared at him.

"But it's a necessary expense, ain't it?"

Cleveland Phelps let out an exasperated breath. "That sounds like some of JT's thinking. Can't you see the kind of mess he stirs up every time he gets out here? All he had to do was let ol' Coleman and his partner ride through. They would have found the cattle, and gone on about their business. It might have cost us a couple hundred dollars." He shook his head. "But that would have been the end of it. Now we're going to have to kill two more lawmen. Then after that, I expect we'll have two or three more snooping around out here."

"So? I've got plenty of bullets."

Cleveland Phelps just stared at him for a second and controlled the urge to draw his pistol and smack Barnes across the face with it. "All right, Barnes. That's good to know. When we get out there, I'm putting you in charge of this business."

"Suits me," Barnes said, catching up to Cleveland Phelps as Phelps walked on toward the horse barn. "You won't be sorry, I can promise you that."

"Hell, I'm sorry already," Cleveland Phelps grumbled under his breath. He had no business with this bunch of second-rate thugs. Damn JT Priest for ever asking him to come out here with them.

Chapter 6

Instead of riding the flatland trail to the main house, Sullivan Hart and Twojack Roth swung wide of it, up into a stretch of rocky hills. They started out on the spare horses they had taken from Hewey Clark's string. When those two horses wore down, they turned them loose, saddled their rested mounts, and came down from the hills behind the house. Cleveland Phelps and his men waited in hiding for them three miles along the trail. Moving forward slow and still to keep down any rise of dust from their horses' hooves, Hart and Roth stopped a mile back from the house in the dark shade of a low cliff overhang.

"How long will it take, do you think?" Hart asked Twojack Roth.

The idea was for Hart to hold the horses back out of sight while Roth slipped the rest of the way in on foot. Once Roth found out how many men they would be up against, he would signal Hart. But now, as Twojack gazed through his telescope toward a dry wash a half mile to their left, he saw two men with shovels step over the edge and disappear from sight. "Not as long as we thought," he said. "Take a look at this."

Sullivan Hart took the telescope and adjusted it to his eye. The first thing he saw through the wavering lens was Hewey Clark's body lying stretched out along the edge of the wash. As he watched, one man stepped up from the dry wash and dragged the body over the edge. Hart scanned the distance over to the main house and across the empty yard. He noted the open doors to the horse barn, and the empty hitch rail in the broad shade of a white oak tree.

"If these two are the only ones here, we're in luck." He collapsed the telescope and handed it to Twojack Roth.

"For my money they are," Roth said. "But we better move quick before the others figure out we've swung around them."

"All right. Which do you want, those two or the house?"

Twojack scanned the terrain once more with his naked eye. "I'll get these two and bring them on in. You go make sure the house is empty first."

"Suits me." Sullivan Hart stepped back, took up the reins to his horse, and led it forward.

Once Roth had led his horse off in the other direction Hart slipped forward, keeping close to the shade of brush and scrub juniper, until he'd reached within a hundred yards of the main house. Then he tied the horse's reins to a stand of brush and moved the rest of the way forward in a crouch with his rifle across his chest. Twenty yards from the back door, Hart waited and listened. Twojack Roth was right—they didn't have any time to waste. In a moment, Hart slipped forward in a quiet trot, and didn't stop until he stood with his back against the wall beside the kitchen door.

At the edge of the dry wash, Twojack Roth stood up with his pistol drawn and cocked, then pointed it down at the backs of the two men digging a narrow grave. It took a second for the men to realize a slight shadow had just moved over them. When they did take note, they both turned as one, their hands snapping to the pistols on their hips. But they stopped, frozen in place, seeing the bore of a revolver pointed at them ten feet above. "An Injun . . ." the man on the right whispered. The shovel in his left hand fell to the ground.

"That's a bad choice of words," Twojack said. He motioned them up from the dry wash with this pistol barrel. After they stepped up over the edge, Twojack reached out and lifted their pistols, pitching them sidelong away. "I had a vision last night," he said. "And in my vision, I saw myself killing two men." He moved his pistol barrel back and forth as he spoke. "Now the question is—was it you two, right here and now? Or will be a couple of others later on today?"

"We don't want trouble," one man said. Both of them stood with their hands held chest-high. The one who spoke glanced at the badge on Twojack's chest. Then he nodded toward Hewey Clark's body on the ground. "We didn't do this either. We found this poor wretch alongside the road and—"

"That's enough, let's go," Twojack cut him off, waving them toward the house with his pistol barrel. "Anybody else in there?"

"No, sir, just us. I'm Cobb . . . he's Macklin. We're just traveling drummers happened by and found the place empty. That's the truth, so help me God." As the man spoke, Twojack took note of their dress suits, bowler hats, and high-topped dress shoes. But he also noted their tough-looking faces, rawboned and whiskey-seasoned.

"He's not lying, Inj—I mean, mister," the other man said. His hands eased down a bit.

But Twojack jerked his pistol barrel upward, causing the man's hands to raise with it. "I know you both work for Cleveland Phelps, and that him and some other *Los Pistoleros* are out there waiting for me and my partner right now."

The two men looked at each other, seemingly bemused. Macklin said, "*Los Pistoleros*? What's that?"

"I better warn you both, it's going to really disappoint my partner if you get in there and start lying.

He goes crazy when people lie to him." Twojack Roth motioned them toward the house with his pistol barrel and fell in behind them, leading his horse. "Move along now, Mister Cobb and Mister Macklin—and don't forget my vision."

Sullivan Hart pushed the back door open and stood to one side as the men filed past him with their hands still in the air. "There's nobody else here." Hart spoke in a lowered voice all the same.

Twojack Roth looked all round at the stacks of wooden crates on one side of the kitchen wall. One crate had been opened. A new Winchester rifle stood leaning against the wall where Hart had put it. "There's more throughout the house," Hart offered, seeing the curious look on Twojack's face. "Looks like *Los Pistoleros* was about to do a little gun-running."

Twojack nodded, then turned his gaze back to the men beside him. "Maybe these two can tell you something. They said their names are Cobb and Macklin. Claim they don't know anything about *Los Pistoleros*. But I warned them how crazy you get when somebody lies to you, so you might want to ask them again."

As soon as Sullivan Hart turned to them, the men's faces took on a frightened expression. "That really is our names, mister. I'm Cobb, he's Macklin. We came here with Briley Barnes out of Chicago. I admit we came here to run some guns across the border. But I swear I never heard nothing about *Los Pistoleros*— whatever that means!"

Sullivan Hart ignored him and stepped away, looking at crate after crate of rifles and ammunition. When he turned back to Cobb, he asked, "How many men are out there with Cleveland Phelps?"

"Four, five maybe?" Cobb offered a weak shrug. "I didn't really count, mister. That's the truth."

"You don't know how many men you're riding

with?'' Hart shook his head. ''That right there is enough to make me—''

''I swear, mister!'' Cobb interrupted, seeing Sullivan Hart raise a long knife from his bootwell. ''Men come and go here nearly every day. I can't keep track of them sometimes. This is a big outfit!''

Hart let the knife slide back down in his boot. He looked at Twojack. ''What do you say? Is he lying?''

Twojack Roth nodded. ''Yep, he's lying. I heard six horses when I put my ear to the ground.''

''Okay! Then it was six!'' Cobb and Macklin were both shaken by the sight of the big knife, and didn't want to see it again. ''I was mistaken! I didn't meant to lie, though! Ask me anything! I'll tell the truth.''

Beside him, Macklin spread a thin nervous smile. ''They're pulling our legs, Cobb. Nobody can count horses by listening to the ground—not that close anyway. And they're not going to kill us either. They're lawmen! Just running a bluff.''

''A bluff?'' Sullivan Hart jerked the knife from his bootwell once again, grabbed Macklin by his lapel, and yanked him forward, throwing the blade of the knife up against his throat. ''That was my father *Los Pistoleros* killed, you rotten—''

''Easy, Sully!'' Twojack Roth shouted, seeing the blood had left Hart's face, and that his eyes had turned killing cold. Roth moved in quick, grabbed Hart by his wrist, and held tight, the blade across Macklin's throat drawing a thin red line in the frightened man's skin. ''He's right! We're lawmen! Don't kill him, not like this!''

But Sullivan Hart would have none of it. He kept the blade pressed hard to Macklin's neck, Twojack's powerful hand barely able to hold him back.

''Mister! Please!'' Macklin's voice turned to jelly. ''I swear I had nothing to do with that! I only heard about it the other day when I first got here! I don't know nothing about *Los . . . Los* whatever you called it! I can't even speak Mexican!''

Sullivan Hart relented, but it took him a second to settle down and take the knife blade away from Macklin's throat. "That's it, nice and easy," Twojack said in a firm, level voice. Beside them Cobb stood wide-eyed, his mouth agape.

When Sullivan Hart finally lowered the knife, he shoved Macklin away from him. "Stay out of my sight, or I'll kill you!"

Twojack caught Macklin by his coat sleeve and pulled him over beside Cobb while saying to Hart, "I'll get them cuffed. You go keep an eye out for the others." He turned to Cobb and Macklin and added in lowered tone, "See what I mean about my partner? Let's go." He turned them around with their backs to him, took out a pair of handcuffs, and secured them around the long handrail of a winding staircase. "From now on, when I ask you something, you answer honest and fast. If not, I'll turn you over to him."

Sullivan Hart stood at the parlor window with his rifle cradled in his arm, keeping watch out across the open flatland in front of the house. When Twojack Roth came in from the other room where their two prisoners stood handcuffed, Hart saw the two brand-new Winchester rifles under his arm. "At least we've got plenty of firepower," Roth said. He set a large box of ammunition down on the table beside the lamp.

"Did you find out anything else?" Sullivan Hart said, turning back to gaze out the window.

"No. I think they've told me everything they know. The way you bluffed them, I don't think they're going to lie anymore." He paused, then asked, "You *were* bluffing, weren't you?"

Sullivan Hart didn't answer. Instead, he peered out the window and said over his shoulder, "Looks like this outfit is even bigger than we thought. It could take a long time getting to the men we want."

"I know." Twojack Roth leaned one of the new

rifles against the lamp table and checked the other, levering a round up into its chamber. "According to both Macklin and Cobb, nobody here even knew about it until the other day. So there's more than one branch to this *Los Pistoleros* gang. I think we've only scratched the surface here."

"Me too." Hart stared out across the land. "The ones that killed my father could be anywhere by now. How do you suppose Dad knew about them?"

"Probably just from the old days. Everybody we've talked to who knows anything at all about *Los Pistoleros* acts like the gang hasn't been around for years."

"That doesn't mean they haven't been in business, though. Just that they've been real careful maybe. One thing's for certain, we've come to the right place." He nodded over his shoulder at the crates of guns stacked throughout the house. "This is no small operation here. Whoever deals in this amount of weapons has to know what they're doing. They have to have some big connections to make this kind of thing work."

Twojack looked around once more. "Yep, this has Mexican *federales* written all over it. This is no two-bit gun-runner selling rifles to the local tribes."

Gazing out the window, Sullivan Hart said, "Well, maybe this Cleveland Phelps will tell us something." He stood tensed and ready. "Here he comes."

Five hundred yards away along the flat trail, Cleveland Phelps reined his horse to a halt and sat staring at the house. He'd been quiet and cross on the way back, having spent the past half day waiting in the harsh sun among the scorching rocks to ambush two men who hadn't shown up. Briley Barnes rode up and stilled his horse beside him. "What's wrong, boss?"

Cleveland Phelps glared at Barnes from beneath his wide hat brim. "I'll tell you what's wrong, Barnes," Cleveland snapped at him. "While we lay back there baking ourselves to the bone, they've circled around us. They're in there right now, just waiting for us." Under his breath, Phelps whispered to himself, "Damn you, JT Priest . . . "

"Naw, boss. Like I said earlier, they seen Clark had come to warn us. They got scared and hightailed it." He chuckled. "Isn't that the way you say it out here? *Hightailed* it?" He glanced around and saw one of the other men from Chicago stifle a short laugh. "If you thinks it a problem, I'll ride in myself and check things out." He started to heel his horse forward, but Phelps caught his horse by its bridle and stopped him.

"Listen to me, idiot! I should have thought of it before we left, but it's hard to think with a fool like you rattling in my ear. Those two are in there right now. So shut up and see if you can manage to stay alive long enough to get them out. If we lose that shipment of rifles, we'll not only have JT Priest down our shirts, we'll have a lot of Mexican brass wanting to see our heads on a post. Do you understand?"

"Okay, okay!" Briley Barnes turned serious, seeing the intense look in Cleveland Phelps's eyes. "Let's say they are in there—now what?"

Phelps looked around at the four men behind him then back at Briley Barnes. "Spread out, get some room between yas. If I'm right, we've got a fight on our hands."

"Time for some good sport, boys," Briley Barnes called back to the men, raising a pistol and firing two shots in the air before Cleveland Phelps could finish talking.

The men raced past Phelps, whooping and raising their rifles and pistols. Phelps had to steady his horse to keep it from rearing beneath him. He watched the five men spread out a little, but not enough, as they sped their horses forward in a rise of dust. He shook his head. Heeling his horse forward in a cautious trot, he saw the first rider fly backward out of his saddle as a rifle shot exploded from the front window of the house.

Chapter 7

At the end of a hard round of shooting, two of Cleveland Phelps's men lay dead in the dirt. The other three had scattered farther apart and dropped down from their saddles. They'd taken cover as best they could behind low clumps of brush and short uppropings of rock. Phelps himself had lingered back long enough to tie his horse to a downed oak tree. Then he'd moved forward in a crawl, taking position fifty yards out behind a pile of cedar fence posts and a few rolls of barbed wire.

Ten yards to Cleveland Phelps's right, Briley Barnes lay flat on the ground behind a low rise in the dirt. His horse, along with the others, had long since raced away from the gunfire.

"Cleveland Phelps," Hart called out from the shattered front-room window. "This is Federal Deputies Sullivan Hart and Twojack Roth. You and your men are under arrest. Throw out your weapons and come forward with your hands in the air."

"What's the charge, lawman?" Cleveland Phelps yelled in reply.

Twojack Roth called out, "Suspicion of smuggling firearms across the United States border."

One of the men started to stand up from behind a low-lying juniper, but Cleveland Phelps fired a shot from his rifle that thumped into the ground near the man's foot and sent him leaping sidelong back to the ground. "Everybody stay where you are!" Cleveland

Phelps bellowed. He glared back and forth at his men until they'd resumed their fighting positions, then yelled out toward the window of the house, "Let's cut the small talk, lawman. I know why you're here, and it ain't about gun-running. You're looking for the men who killed Coleman Hart!"

"You're right as rain, Phelps," Sullivan Hart replied.

"Nobody here had anything to do with killing him!" Phelps said, and leveled his rifle toward the window.

"Then come on up and we'll listen to what you have to say. We want to know about *Los Pistoleros*." Sullivan Hart ventured a glance out the window and across the yard as he spoke.

"I don't think so, Hart!" A shot from Phelps's rifle sent a spray of splinters flying from the window ledge across the room. Sullivan Hart jerked back out of the way. Phelps added, "I've never told the law about anything in my life! I'm not starting now!"

Another round of gunfire erupted back and forth. Ducking closer to the ground, Briley Barnes cut a glance over to Cleveland Phelps and saw him darting backward in the dirt. Barnes ventured a shot toward the window of the house, then hugged the ground and scrambled back in a low crouch, trying to keep up with Phelps. "Wait for me, boss! I'm going with you!"

"I don't think so!" Ahead of him, Cleveland Phelps turned and fired, the shot slamming Barnes in his thigh and knocking him to the dirt. At the window, Sullivan Hart managed to catch a glimpse of Phelps making his getaway, but the heavy firing kept him from taking a good aim at him.

Twojack Roth called out to Hart from the other window, "Phelps is cutting out! Cover me! I'll try to drop him from here!"

"No, wait! Don't risk it." Sullivan Hart stood flat against the wall beside the window, reloading his rifle. "Let him go. You heard him. He won't tell us

anything we don't already know." With his rifle reloaded, Sullivan Hart turned and punched two shots
out into the yard, then fell back out of sight. He
looked all around at the crates of rifles and ammunition. "We'll send *Los Pistoleros* a message with him."

Twojack Roth also cut a glance around the room.
"I hear you." He swung his rifle around the edge of
the window, fired, then dropped back just as a bullet
whistled past his head. "He's made it back to his
horse."

Sullivan Hart slumped against the wall beside the
window and pushed his hat brim up on his forehead.
"All right, let's give him a couple of minutes, then
we'll end this thing."

The firing stopped. Hart and Roth stood in silence.
When the shooting erupted again, neither of them
returned fire. They stood tense and waited. This time
when the firing lulled, the voice of one of the two
remaining gunmen called out across the yard,
"That's enough, Lutz. They're dead in there."

"You don't know that, Digger," the other man
shouted back to him. Another shot exploded.

"Damn it, Lutz, they're dead! Hold your fire."

Inside the house, Twojack Roth had stepped a few
feet across the floor to where he could level his rifle
on Cobb and Macklin. The two men stood huddled
down against the stairwell, their cuffed hands
stretched up over their heads. "Tell them they got
us," Twojack whispered, his thumb cocking the rifle
toward them, "and make them believe it."

"Lutz, it's true!" Macklin yelled out to the yard,
his eyes wide as he faced the pointed rifle. "They're
dead. Don't shoot! You'll hit me and Cobb!"

"Macklin? You're in there?"

"Yeah, I'm in here, and so is Cobb. Stop shooting."

"Then come on out," Lutz shouted.

"We can't! We're cuffed to the stairs banister."

"Are you sure they're dead?" The man's voice
sounded uncertain. "Can you see their bodies?"

"Oh, yes . . . plain as day." As Macklin spoke, he glared at Twojack Roth. Roth nodded to him, and Macklin added, "Now come get us out of here!"

The sound of footsteps came up onto the wooden porch, then Twojack Roth took a step back with his rifle pointed at the door as the doorknob turned.

"Whooie, that was something," Lutz said as he stepped in and looked over at Macklin and Cobb cuffed to the stair railing. Lutz wore a thin smile, but it faded fast as his eyes moved over to the sight of the big Cherokee aiming a rifle at his stomach from ten feet away. Behind him, the other man, Digger Stewart, froze in place, then almost turned to bolt back through the open door. But seeing Sullivan Hart step into view from the other room, also aiming a rifle, both men let their pistols slump in their hands and dropped to the floor.

"Macklin, you lousy jackpotting rat," Digger Stewart hissed, cutting a glance to the two cuffed men.

"You can't blame us," Cobb said. "What was we supposed to do, let him shoot us?"

Sullivan Hart stepped toward Digger and Lutz and said, "Kick your guns over here." When they did, he picked the pistols up, shoved them down into his belt and motioned toward the door. "Everybody outside now. Come on, before Cleveland Phelps gets too far away to see our message."

Twojack unlocked the handcuffs on Macklin and Cobb as the other two turned and started out the door ahead of Sullivan Hart. "You'll play hell catching up to Cleveland Phelps," Lutz said over his shoulder.

"We're not even going to try," Hart said. He walked the two men out across the yard and had them sit down in the dirt twenty yards from the porch. "From here on, instead of us hunting for *Los Pistoleros*, we're going to make them come looking for us." He gazed out across the stretch of flatland and saw Briley Barnes struggle to his feet and stagger in place. Barnes held his right hand pressed against his wounded left thigh.

"*Los* what?" Digger Stewart asked, looking up at Hart's face.

"*Los Pistoleros*, the people you're working for," Hart replied, watching the man's expression closely to see if he was lying.

The two men looked at each other, then back to Hart. "I never heard anybody called that." Digger Stewart looked to be telling the truth.

"Me neither," said Joe Lutz.

Beside them, Macklin and Cobb sat down on the ground and held their hands chest high. "I told them the same thing," Macklin offered. He turned his eyes up to Hart and Roth. "We're all just Chicago boys from the South Side. Briley Barnes said he had plenty of work for us out here if we didn't mind a little action."

"Briley Barnes, huh?" Hart's turned to watch the wounded man struggling across the rough terrain.

"That's right," Macklin acknowledged, "Barnes is the one who brought the deal to us. But he'll never tell you nothing. He's tough as a pine knot. What the hell does *Los Pistoleros* mean, anyway?"

"In Spanish it means, 'The Gunmen.'" Sullivan Hart studied each man's face in turn. They looked back at him with bewildered expressions. Hart cut another glance out to where Briley Barnes staggered a few feet farther away. "We'll have to see if Barnes tells us the same thing you have. If not, I'm going to be real upset all over again." His gaze leveled into Macklin's frightened eyes.

Twojack Roth nodded out toward Barnes and asked Hart, "Think we need to get out there and grab him?"

"He's not going anywhere." Once again, Hart looked hard at the men. "None of you have heard the name *Los Pistoleros* mentioned since you've been here?"

All four shrugged and shook their heads. "All I ever wanted to hear was when's payday, and how far it is to the nearest saloon," replied Digger Stewart.

"Well, payday's over. As far as the saloon, it's close to eighty miles in that direction," Hart said, nodding toward the north. Then he said to Twojack Roth, "Keep an eye on them. I'll gather some canteens and bring the horses on my way back."

Cleveland Phelps reined his horse up at the top of the stretch of hills and looked back at the black smoke curling upward from the burning house. *Damn JT Priest* . . . The smoke drifted sidelong on the breeze, nearly a half mile back and below him. He wasn't taking the blame for this mess, Phelps thought to himself. If JT Priest liked to get out in the wilderness and kick up his heels, causing trouble for everybody, then JT Priest could take responsibility for what happens.

As far as those jake-legged city thugs and barroom brawlers from Chicago went, Phelps didn't owe them a thing. He needed to get away from here and get a wire off to Mad-dog Mabrey. Then he needed to gather a few of his own men—the *real* members of *Los Pistoleros*.

Phelps turned the horse in place. The big animal was winded but still restless, wanting to run. For a moment he stared back at the smoke and thought about how much money the lawmen had sent up in flames. Then he shook his head and leveled his hat and gave heel to the horse's ribs. From what he'd heard about that big Cherokee Roth, the man could track a bird in flight. Phelps had to put some miles behind him.

In the front yard of the burning house, Twojack Roth stepped forward and took the reins from Sullivan Hart's hand. Fire and black smoke now billowed in a windy roar, causing the horses to shy back and nicker deep in their chests. Boxes of ammunition popped like firecrackers. Cobb looked up at Hart with a worried look on his face. "Are we safe sitting here?"

"You should have thought about being safe before you left Chicago," Hart replied.

"What's going to happen to us now?" Macklin asked Twojack Roth who stood near him.

"We're going to walk you to Little Red Springs and turn you over to the sheriff." Twojack Roth kept his eyes on the fire as he answered.

"We can't walk that far," Cobb moaned. "That'll kill everyone of us."

"You'll make it," said Hart. "Just walk slow and drink plenty of water." He spread a slight smile. "The next time you decide to take up a gunfight, maybe you'll remember to keep a horse close at hand."

Twojack Roth took out sets of handcuffs from his saddlebags, and once the men's hands were shackled behind their backs, the two deputies mounted their horses and followed the prisoners out toward the distant hills. When they started past Briley Barnes where he had sunk down onto his knees in the dirt, Barnes raised his head and called out, "Hey, lawman, I'm over here . . . I'm surrendering. Somebody want to give me a hand?" But as Macklin started to veer toward him, he stopped short at the sound of Sullivan Hart's levering a round into his rifle chamber.

"Get back in line, Macklin," Twojack Roth warned in a stern tone, "or we'll leave you sitting there beside him, in the same shape."

Macklin hurried back into line, then called back to Roth, "We can't just leave him here to die, can we? He's wounded bad."

Briley Barnes heard Macklin plead on his behalf, and he called out as the next three men filed past him with their heads lowered, only casting sidelong glances in his direction. "Boys, he's right! I'm in bad, *bad*, shape!" He looked expectantly at Hart and Roth as the two moved past him on their horses, their rifles propped straight up from their saddles. "Good Lord, man, please! Don't leave me here to die like this!"

Twojack Roth cut a guarded glance at Hart beside him and said loud enough for Briley Barnes and the others to hear, "They're right, Sully. We can't leave him here like this."

"Then drop back and put a bullet in his brain," Hart said, staring forward. Seeing the men slow down and glance back over their shoulders at him, Hart added, "If you men don't want the same, keep moving. We've got a long way to go, and barely enough water. Don't think we won't leave you for the buzzards, too."

"Sully, can't we make room for him someway?" Twojack Roth asked.

"No," Hart snapped at him. "He can't tell us any more than these others—he's no good to us. Shoot him."

"All right, Sully, you're in charge."

Terror filled Briley Barnes's eyes when Twojack Roth turned his horse toward him and lifted the rifle to his broad shoulder. "No! Please! All I need is a bandage! I can make it once I'm on my feet! Don't kill me!"

"Sorry . . . I've got no choice," said Roth, cocking his rifle and dropping his horse back to a halt. "He's in charge. You heard him." He shrugged and took aim.

"Wait! Please! What he said about me not knowing anything—he's wrong! I know plenty! Just don't kill me!"

Sullivan Hart smiled to himself and heeled his horse forward. Behind him, he heard Twojack say to Briley Barnes, "Aw, come on now . . . you don't know anything about *Los Pistoleros*. You're just saying that to save yourself."

"No, mister, you're wrong! I know plenty about

Los Pistoleros! I know all about Cleveland Phelps, JT Priest . . . where he hides out. I know most of the *Los Pistoleros* operation, the counterfeiting, the bank robbing. Ask me anything, anything at all!"

Twojack Roth lowered the rifle an inch and looked down at him over the barrel. He hesitated and shook his head. "I don't know. We're awfully short on water—"

"Hell! Then I won't drink any water . . . won't eat either! Give me a rag to hold against my leg and help me to my feet. I'll tell you everything, I swear!"

When Sullivan Hart heard Barnes' plea, he looked back to see Twojack Roth step down from his horse and move toward Briley Barnes with his hand out to him. Roth pulled the man to his feet and handed him a bandanna to tie off his wound. Hart brought the men to a halt. They waited until at length Twojack came riding up with Briley Barnes, who sat in front of the Cherokee in the saddle. Barnes weaved back and forth, cradled in Twojack's big arms.

"I thought I told you to kill that worthless peckerwood," Hart said in a tight, demanding voice. "Am I going to have to do it myself?" He jerked his pistol from his holster and cocked it.

"Wait, Sully! Give this man a chance. I think he might be able to help us."

Sullivan Hart turned an icy stare into Briley Barnes's eyes. "If he does, he better get to telling it." He leveled the pistol on Barnes's chest. "You know how I am, Roth, once I get in a killing mood . . ."

Twojack Roth lifted Barnes from the saddle and stepped down behind him; and for the next twenty minutes Barnes seemed unable to stop himself from talking. He told them how Cleveland Phelps and JT Priest had met him in Chicago. An old counterfeiter Barnes had been in prison with had given Phelps his name, and told Phelps that Briley Barnes was the one who could get some men together for him. Barnes told the two lawmen how this gun-running was just one more thing JT Priest and Phelps were involved in, and how they'd promised Barnes that if he did a good job for them, they might work him into one of their robbery jobs—show him where the real money was.

Briley Barnes went on to name names, and the dates of bank and train robberies the *Los Pistoleros* had been involved in. He told them of past schemes and schemes in the making. Lastly, Barnes told them how Phelps had once confided in him that JT Priest had been known as a hired killer called Tuck Javin years ago, who had kept a string of ears he collected from those he'd killed. And according to Cleveland Phelps, JT Priest had once killed a whole caravan of gypsies who'd pitched camp on the land of the man he'd been working for—that man being William Mad-dog Mabrey.

"Priest slaughtered them one and all alike," Briley Barnes concluded, "men, women . . . even children in arms. He took some thirty pair of ears that day, a few of them no bigger around than a Canadian quarter piece." Barnes paused now, catching his breath. He looked first at the men who'd sat down on the ground and listened. Then he looked back at Roth and Hart in turn, and added in a somber tone, "Cleveland Phelps laughed when he told me that story." Barnes's expression darkened. "That's the kind of man you're looking for, deputies."

"And that's the kind of man you've been working for." Sullivan Hart holstered his pistol and swung up on his horse without another word.

Barnes turned to Twojack Roth. "Does this mean you're not going to shoot me?"

"We'll see." Roth gave him a hand, shoved him into the saddle, and then stepped up behind him. "If I were you, I'd be on my best behavior this whole trip."

Chapter 8

In the evening Hart and Roth had the prisoners stop and make camp below a sparse grove of cedars that stretched up along a rocky hillside. They ran a long chain through each prisoner's handcuffs and wrapped it around a tree before locking it. After feeding the prisoners beans and flapjacks, then graining the horses and picketing them on a nearby pallet of grass, Twojack Roth and Sullivan Hart sat on the other side of the small campfire and watched the men sip weak coffee, sharing it back and forth in two spare tin cups.

"I should have connected JT Priest to Tuck Javin right away," Sullivan said just between Roth and himself. "Dad talked about an outlaw named Tuck Javin back when I was in my teens."

"Don't blame yourself. I heard of Tuck Javin too," Twojack offered. "But for some reason I thought he'd died in Mexico a few years back." He sipped his coffee and added, "We're both learning as we go. It's not like most times—the judge hands us names and sends us out to hunt them down. So far this has been like hunting the wind. We've got some work cut out for us with this bunch. And there's no telling where this will end up. There's nothing back there to connect Priest or Mabrey to anything. They might own the land, but that doesn't make them guilty of anything. Besides, we can't prove where the guns were going. We could spend our lives sifting through a bunch of *Los Pistoleros's* hired help if we're not careful."

"Yep, it's a big country. This Priest and Mabrey could be anywhere in it. That's why I'm hoping they'll be coming for us now . . . give us a chance to gather the head men in one spot."

"I hope you're right," Twojack said. "As big as this operation is, they could just take their loss on the guns and go on to something else."

"Then we'll get them again." Hart took his pistol from his holster and inspected it as they talked. "Every time they stick their heads up, we'll hit them hard. Sooner or later they'll have to reckon with us. They can't afford not to. Like any business, they've got expenses. They won't stand for us costing them money." He paused in reflection, then asked Roth, "Do you get the feeling Quick Charlie Sims ties into this someway?"

"It crossed my mind a time or two," said Roth, "but I put it aside. I kept thinking about the strange look Sims had on his face when he saw the name *Los Pistoleros* written in blood. After Barnes's story about the caravan of gypsies, I'm thinking about it again. Could be it wasn't so much the name in blood as it was him seeing what they did." His voice softened as if touching an open wound. "I mean about Coleman's ears being missing."

Hart winced at the memory, but didn't let it stop him. "Because of what some say about Sims being a gypsy?" He looked at Twojack and shook his head. "I always thought that was just an expression. I don't think anybody really knows where Sims comes from. Besides, Sims is Irish, isn't he?"

"Who knows?" Twojack shrugged. "Even so, maybe Sims is his real name. Or, maybe Sims is short for something else. Since we don't know where he's really from, there's room for all sorts of possibilities."

"Well, whatever the case . . ." Sullivan Hart let out a breath and slipped his pistol back in his holster.

"The main thing for now is that we get these men to town, then see what our next move is going to be. We've got plenty to keep us busy without worrying about Quick Charlie Sims."

Kenny Kerns, Ned Norris, Stanley Lane, and Quick Charlie Sims stood for a moment looking out through the wide boards of the stock car at the rolling Missouri countryside speeding past them. Behind them in the stalls, the horses had been unsaddled and wiped down with handfuls of straw. Quick Charlie looked down at his severed handcuffs, only an inch of chain dangling from each wrist now. Moments ago JT Priest had taken a pair of long-handled bolt cutters and snipped the short chain connecting the handcuffs.

Sims smiled, jiggling the two short chains, then asked Priest why didn't he go ahead and get the two steel cuffs off his wrists. "Don't push it, Quick Charlie," Priest had told him. "I like the looks of those cuffs on you—lets you know right off who's in charge here."

But it was important to Sims that JT Priest had gone this far in setting him free. It meant he'd gained some ground. It meant even more to him that a couple of the men had asked JT Priest in a roundabout way the night before why he hadn't already taken the cuffs off Quick Charlie. Slowly but surely, Sims had put himself in good standing with the men, even as he took their money from them night after night across the card table.

Last night had been his best night ever. JT Priest had even sat in for a few hands, taking the big heavy high-backed chair in which no one else was allowed to sit. Rather than go at Priest head on, Sims had handled the deck in a way to make sure that Kerns, Norris, and Lane all won pretty much equally. Then once JT Priest had thrown in his last hand and retired from the game—after losing close to four hundred dollars—Sims took back about half of each man's winnings. Everybody came out ahead and happy except Priest.

But today even Priest had gotten into a good mood as soon as the train stopped long enough to let the three horsemen aboard. Priest saw the thick bag full of money, and his eyes had lit up instantly. That's when he'd taken off Sims's cuff. When the train gathered speed once more, Priest had taken the bag of money from Kenny Kerns and walked out toward the Pullman car with it.

"Boys," said Sims, now that Priest was gone, "this is the only way to rob a bank. How long have you been operating this way?"

The three men looked at one another first, as if leery of answering. But then Kenny Kerns grinned, ducked a glance to the door at the end of the stock car, and said, "For me, the past two months." He turned his gaze to Norris and Lane. They hesitated.

Quick Charlie shrugged. "If you rather not say, forget it, fellows. I'm just making conversation."

"Geez, you two," Kerns said to Norris and Lane, "the man is one of us now." He nodded at the broken handcuffs chain link on the straw-covered floor. "JT's taking him in . . . we've been playing cards with him every night. So far he ain't exactly been the card-sharking devil JT warned us about. Hell, Stanley, you even said yourself that you've beat him some at checkers."

"Beat me?" Sims managed a short laugh. "Yesterday, he would have gutted me if I hadn't quit on him."

"I grew up with a checkerboard in my hand," Stanley Lane said, giving a proud little jut of his chin. "I just don't brag about it." He turned his gaze to Sims. "Me and Norris have been taking banks this way the past two years. Usually Cleveland Phelps and a couple of his gunmen ride with us. But he's busy doing some other things right now."

Sims shook his head slowly in admiration. "It's slick! Ride in, take the money, get on board, and forget about the law."

"Yeah, and get a load of this," Norris cut in. "Most times we hit a bank, it's right after a big government deposit was just made. We don't rob nothing small."

Quick Charlie looked taken aback by Norris's words. "Whoa! So you boys are cutting up some big shares."

"Well, we get paid good, let's put it that way."

"But not full shares?" Sims looked surprised.

"No, not yet. But look at it this way," said Kerns. "The way this is set up, we'll never get caught neither."

"But still, you take a big risk while you're in town." Sims spread his hands. "None of my business . . . but who gets the bullet in the back if some posse ever manages to get to you before you make it to the train? What happens if you get to a meeting spot and the train's not there?"

Stanley Norris scratched his head up under his hat brim. "That's never been a problem."

"No, and it won't ever be . . . but *once.*" Sims raised a finger for emphasis and smiled at each of them in turn. He watched it cross their minds for a second, but then before any of the three could comment, he added, "But, hey, forget about it. You're happy, JT Priest is happy—it's none of my business. Forget I ever mentioned it."

"You'll be riding with us on a job before long, I figure," said Kerns.

Quick Charlie rubbed his chin. "I don't know. How much are we talking about making for pulling a job?"

Lane said, "We just made five hundred apiece, and for what? Four hours work, at the most."

"That's not bad." Sims allowed himself to look interested again. "Of course, that's more than you made the last time—having Phelps and some others with you, right?"

"No, we made the same last time." As Kenny Kerns answered, Sims could already see he had set the wheels turning in Kerns's mind. "But it seems like maybe we should make something extra this time, just being the three of us." Kerns passed a curious glance back and forth between the other two men. "Don't you think so, Norris? Lane?"

"Yeah, come to think of it." Stanley Lane picked up on the thought. "Last time there was six of us, this time there was only three—"

"But don't forget, men," Sims put in, "when you don't work for an equal share, it makes no difference. Somebody just made an extra fifteen hundred dollars this time." He tossed it off with the turn of a hand. "But that's life . . . so long as that same somebody never gets too greedy, decides why send six men when three does the job just fine. Of course, if three can do it, why not two? That's saving even more money."

"Yeah, but the risk is worse for three than for six," Kerns threw in. He looked at the others, his expression turning a bit tight.

"So, what say we go have a couple of drinks, relax, and play some poker?" Sims grinned and rubbed his hands together.

The three men moved into a closer circle together. Norris said over his shoulder to Sims, "You go on ahead . . . we'll be there in a few minutes." Quick Charlie Sims smiled and turned to walk to the door at the far end of the stock car. He glanced back for only a second and saw Kerns shaking his head about something as the three of them began speaking in lowered voices.

The stock car rode at the end of the three-car train, not counting the small red caboose that rumbled and rocked along behind. The car between the stock car and the Pullman was partitioned by long pine board

walls in such a way that it provided only a narrow
aisle down the middle. As Sims walked along that
aisle he cast a curious gaze along the thick wooden
doors that stood every few feet. Each door had a
large lock hanging in its hasp. He stopped beside the
largest door long enough to peep through a crack
between the boards.

In the darkness he saw a big steel safe facing him,
and he felt his blood race. He smiled to himself. The
safe had to be there for a reason. With a good piece
of wire he could jimmy the lock and get inside the
room. Then with a little luck and some concentration
he knew he could crack the safe. But now wasn't the
time to do it. The safe would have to wait. He
stepped back from the wall and continued on, jiggling the short chains on his freed wrists.

When he stepped across the coupling platform and
into the back half of the Pullman, JT Priest looked
up from the stacks of money on top of the card table.
Seeing it was Sims, Priest smiled and waved him
forward with a thick black cigar in his hand. Sims
noted that the door was closed to the front half of
the car. Kate McCorkle spent most of her time beyond that door, in the living quarters and the master
bedroom. Sims wondered if Priest had locked the
door to keep her from seeing the bank money. Did
Kate McCorkle know that somewhere back there a
bank had been robbed? And if she knew . . . did
she care?

"Kate's asleep," JT Priest said. Quick Charlie was
stunned, as if Priest had just read his mind. "So why
don't you pour us a drink." It wasn't a request—it
was an order.

"Sure." Sims stopped and turned to the bar. He
picked up a full bottle of Kentucky bourbon and two
shot glasses and took them to the table. He sat down
across from JT Priest without being invited, pulled
the cork from the bottle, and filled both glasses.

JT Priest just stared at him for a moment as if on

the verge of saying something. But then he chuckled and let it pass, and drank the shot of bourbon, setting the glass down without taking his fingers from around it. He bumped it on the tabletop and gestured his cigar toward the money as Sims refilled his glass.

"Isn't this a beautiful sight, Sims? Something about money all stacked up like that before me nearly brings tears to my eyes." He spread a smile and sipped the bourbon.

Quick Charlie Sims nodded. "I know what you mean. I'm getting a little misty-eyed myself." He raised his own shot glass in a toast. He threw back the drink, let out a bourbon hiss, and refilled his glass. "Are you going to give me a chance to get out there and make some money for myself? Or are you going to keep teasing me with it? If I didn't know better, I'd think you were still holding it over me— what I said that time about never being anybody's lackey?"

"Ah, would I do something like that, Sims?" Priest said with a sly grin. "Don't worry. I'm short a couple of men right now. Next job comes up, you're in on it." He widened his grin and drew on the black cigar. "So much to do . . . so little help." He exhaled a curl of gray smoke through his pursed lips.

"I hope you plan on getting these two bracelets off my wrists before I ride out on a job." Sims held his right hand up and shook the one-inch chain back and forth.

"Sure, when the time comes. Tell me, Sims, what do you think of this kind of setup?" JT Priest beamed, gesturing again at the stacks of stolen money.

"I think it's a shame I didn't think of it first." Sims grinned and offered his shot glass in salute.

"Aw, but you see . . . to do it you have to first own a bank, your own rail car, and a few other things." Priest tapped a finger on his forehead, the cigar between his fingers. "What is it they say, Sims?

The rich get richer, and the poor get . . . oh, well, you know how all that works." Arrogance glowed high and shiny in his eyes.

Sims nodded. "Yeah, I know."

Priest went on. "Not only is this a fast getaway, but who is actually going to stop us and ask any questions?" His brows arched. "And if they should stop us . . . why on earth would I have anything to do with robbing a bank that I might well own an interest in?"

"You're the whole thing, Tuck. I give you that." Sims threw back his drink. He wanted to ask how that worked—Priest owning an interest in the banks he robbed. But now wasn't the time for questions. Priest was giving him quite a bit of information on his own. So Sims smiled and put his glass down and said, "This next job—when are you talking about pulling it? I need the money."

"Don't get too anxious," JT Priest cautioned. "It won't be long. Meanwhile, we're headed for Little Red Springs. We'll take on plenty of wood and water there. Then we're going to make ourselves a run all the way to Memphis. You and I are going to show a couple of fine-haired gentlemen there how easy it is to lose a vulgar amount of money playing golf, eh?" He winked and smiled again. "How does that sound to you?"

"It sounds to me like maybe I created a monster, showing you how to square up your club head and getting your left shoulder behind the ball."

"Ha . . . all you did was correct my stance a little, give me some pointers. I used to always shoot that way, Sims. Just got into a bad habit of late, I suppose."

"I know how that goes, Tuck." Quick Charlie tossed back another drink. "Everybody needs a little correcting now and then."

"Yeah." Priest stared at him through eyes that were hazing over behind a deep bourbon cloud.

"Speaking of correcting something, don't be calling me *Tuck*. I don't go by that name anymore. I haven't for a long time."

"Sorry. I didn't know," Sims lied, returning his stare. "Hope I haven't started something among the men."

"Just don't be doing it, all right? I dropped the name right after some things I did up near Cayenne Pass . . . some things I don't care to talk about right now." He downed his drink and blew out a hot breath. "If you keep your nose clean, Sims, and do like you're told, you'll look back a short while from now and realize you've become a rich man. If you don't . . ." JT Priest leveled a menacing bourbon-lit grin. "You won't be looking back at all."

PART 2

Chapter 9

JT Priest watched from the window of his Pullman car and saw the lawmen, Sullivan Hart and Twojack Roth, bring the prisoners into Little Red Springs and guide them to the sheriff's office. "Sims, get over here," Priest called out to the bar, where Sims stood staring down at the checkerboard, considering his next move. Across from Sims, Stanley Lane and the others looked up at the urgency of Priest's voice.

"Yeah, what is it?" Sims moved over beside him at the window and looked out. At the sight of the prisoners stepping up onto the boardwalk with Roth and Hart behind them, Sims managed to stifle a smile. "Oh, it's them, the ones you weren't worried about. I told you they would be hard to shake off your tail."

Priest shot Sims a sidelong glance, then looked back out the window. "Well . . . at least they don't have Cleveland Phelps on that chain. Those boys are just some hired help out of Chicago. Phelps was too much for them, I imagine." Yet even as Priest spoke in an unconcerned manner, he thought about the big shipment of rifles and ammunition, and wondered what had become of it.

"Maybe so," said Sims, "but either way, Hart and Roth are getting closer to you. I told you before, they're no light piece of work. Maybe you need to let me take care of them for you? It's the least I can do." Sims made the offer, hoping that Priest wasn't about to take him up on it.

"No, Sims, we're going to lay low and get out of town while they don't have the slightest idea we've even been here."

"Yeah, I suppose you're right," Quick Charlie said. "Why take a chance on a couple of lawmen like that ruining everything."

"I'm not worried about them, Sims, if that's what you're thinking." Priest gave him a harsh glare.

"Not at all, JT." Sims smiled. "But even if you were, I couldn't blame you. Those two are a real handful."

"Like hell." JT glared at Sims and called out over his shoulder to the others, "All three of you, get over here. I've got something that needs taking care of."

Quick Charlie Sims stepped back to give the other men room as they moved in and Priest pointed out toward the sheriff's office a block away. "I want the three of you to get off here with your horses and rifles. When those two deputies come out of that office, blow the hell out of them. Show Sims here what happens when the law comes snooping around our neck of the woods."

The three men stood looking at one another for a tense second. At the door to the sleeping quarters, Sims caught a glimpse of Kate McCorkle looking out at the others gathered around JT Priest. Sims caught her eyes for only a second before she withdrew and closed the door.

Inside the sheriff's office, Sullivan Hart stepped forward ahead of the prisoners with his rifle across his chest. Sheriff Bud Kay stood up as they began to file in. He placed his hands on the edge of his desk and shook his gray head slowly back and forth. "Lord, Sully, I've got no room for these knotheads. Ever since that rail spur cut into town I've had to deal with every drifter and drunk from here to the panhandle."

"We had to jail them somewhere, Sheriff," Hart replied. "You happened to be the closest place." As he spoke to the sheriff, Hart looked to his left at the row of jail cells and saw dirty faces pressed to the bars. "Are all your prisoners going to be here for a while?"

"Yep, leastwise until the circuit judge comes back through. That could be another week." Sheriff Kay let out a breath. "But hell, we'll stack them up some way, I reckon." He picked up the set of keys from his desk and pitched them to Twojack Roth. "How bad is that one wounded?"

"It's clean," Hart said. "He'll need a doctor to take a look at it though."

"I'll see to it," Sheriff Kay replied. "What're you charging them with?"

Hart told him the whole story as Roth unlocked a cell and moved the prisoners inside. Once he'd unlocked their cuffs and chain, he stepped back out through the steel door and closed it with a solid clang. Sheriff Bud Kay looked Hart and Roth up and down with a bemused smile and motioned them away from the cells.

Once they were out of hearing distance from the prisoners, Sheriff Kay rubbed his long gray mustache and said in a lowered voice, "You wasted your time bringing them in. Unless you can prove the gun-running charge, the most you've got on them is resisting arrest, and firing on officers of the law. Any lawyer with half a mind will have them out of here before the dust settles when the judge arrives."

"We know that, Sheriff," Hart replied. "The thing is, we couldn't leave them out there with no horses and no way to take care of themselves." He gestured back toward the cell. "Look at them. They're all thugs. But they're city boys, every one of them. We hoped if you kept them here awhile and let that one heal up a little, maybe by the time you turn them loose they'll be sick of this place and want to get on back to Chicago."

Sheriff Kay looked over at the prisoners in the cell just in time to see Macklin shove one of the older prisoners off a bunk and sit down on it. The older prisoner grumbled under his breath, but moved away, dusting his knee. "That's just wishful thinking in my opinion," Sheriff Kay said. "But I'll help you boys out the best I can."

"Thanks," Twojack Roth said. "That's all we ask."

"I hated hearing about Coleman getting killed. This whole territory lost a good man there." Sheriff Kay looked back and forth at them. "I expect you're on the trail of the ones who did it?"

"Yep." Hart and Roth exchanged glances. "Ever heard of a gang called *Los Pistoleros*?" Hart watched Sheriff Kay's expression as he spoke.

Kay winced and nodded. "Oh, yes, I've heard of them. But it's been years. If they're anything like they were in the old days, you two need to get some other deputies along with you."

"If it comes to that, we will," Twojack Roth said. "So far, all we've been able to do is piece some things together about them. Anything more you can tell us?"

Sheriff Kay thought about it, scratching his head. "No, only that they got started good and strong right after the war. Nobody got close enough to know who the leader was back then. They were more like a secret society, best I recall."

"Ever heard of Cleveland Phelps?" Roth asked.

"You better believe I've heard of that murderer." Sheriff Kay's expression darkened. "At some time or other, he's rode with every band of outlaws you can name—even the James Younger Gang. If he's part of this, you boys have your hands full."

"He's part of it, all right," Hart said. "He's not the one who killed Pa, but he might be the one who runs things out here."

"Out here?" Sheriff Kay gave him a curious look. "You make it sound like they're everywhere. Just how widespread are they?"

"We still have no idea," said Hart. He nodded toward the men in the cell across the room. "Evidently *Los Pistoleros* pulls in men from everywhere to do their dirty work. The main crew has a way of disappearing at just the right time. I've never seen anything this well organized."

"Then how in the world do you expect to catch up to them? What's your plan?"

"We'll keep dogging them," Twojack Roth offered. "That's all we can do. Sooner or later they'll get tired of us and come looking."

"We need to get resupplied and get moving, Sheriff Kay," Sullivan Hart said, pushing his hat up on his forehead. "We need to telegraph Judge Parker and let him know our whereabouts."

"I understand. Telegraph office is right down the street by the rail depot. Get yourselves collected. Don't worry about these prisoners or about saying good-bye before you leave. You boys are doing some serious manhunting . . . I'll help you any way I can."

Quick Charlie Sims stood to one side of the stock car and watched Kenny Kerns, Ned Norris, and Stanley Lane ease their horses down the wooden boarding ramp on the opposite side of the loading platform. Each of them carried a rifle in his hands. Lane was the last one to lead his horse out, and he stopped and looked back up at Sims with a slight leer. "Don't worry, Sims. As soon as this is over, we'll be back. I'll give you a chance to get even on the checkerboard."

"Thank you, Stanley." Sims returned the smile, leaning out closer to him. "I never doubted you for a minute." Before Stanley Lane could turn away, Quick Charlie Sims caught him by his coat sleeve. "But tell me one thing before you leave. When and how often does Priest and Mabrey get together . . . you know, to divvy up any proceeds?"

Stanley Lane's eyes turned cold on him. "Hey, that's dangerous stuff for me to be telling you. He'd kill me."

"He'll never know. You're into me for over fifty dollars. Think I'd say something and risk getting you killed before I get a chance to win some of my money back?"

Stanley Lane pulled his arm free of Sims's grasp and looked in both directions to make sure no one was near. "They meet up about once every three months—it could be anywhere. Mabrey pops up whenever he chooses. But it won't be long. Priest has a lot of cash on hand. Mabrey will be wanting his share." Lane stopped and gave Sims a skeptical look. "How do you know I won't tell Priest about you asking me this?"

Quick Charlie's good-natured smile became wider. "Oh . . . let's just say I trust you, Stanley. Now you be careful out there, you hear?" He stepped back and guided the loading ramp in as the men pushed it to him. Then he closed the stock car door and dusted his hands together, the one-inch cuff chains swinging at each wrist. On his way back toward the Pullman car, Sims felt the train lurch forward beneath him, starting its slow departure from the Little Red Springs siding rails near the loading platform and onto the main tracks leading out across the prairie. As he passed through the car carrying the large safe behind its locked door, he patted the door for luck.

As soon as Sims closed the door to the Pullman car behind himself, he saw Kate McCorkle standing at the bar with JT Priest. He couldn't help but notice the red welt on Kate's face. As he walked up to Priest, he pretended not to see the anger in Kate's eyes before she turned away from Priest and stalked off to the open door of the sleeping area. Sims looked surprised when she slammed the door behind her. "Hope I'm not barging in on something."

"Not at all." JT Priest shot an angry glance toward the door, then looked back at Sims. "Women . . . who can please them?" he added in a flat tone. "Did the boys get off all right?"

"Oh, yes. But getting back on board might be harder than they think."

"We'll wait for them out on the flatland," Priest said with a shrug of his thick shoulders.

"If they make it back." Sims gave him a dubious look.

"Ha. You overestimate those two lawmen, Sims." Priest raised a cigar in his left hand and placed it between his teeth. "A hundred dollars says my boys kill them both dead in the street before this train is out of sight. What do you say? Is it a bet?" Priest's eyes searched his.

Quick Charlie chose his words with care. "Sorry, Priest. I'd be betting against my own interest. I want those two dead as bad as you do."

Priest nodded, seeming satisfied. "Right you are." He raised a heavy arm and placed it across Sims's shoulder. "So let's just pour ourselves a drink and watch the show . . . on our way out of town, of course."

"This is slick, Tuck." Sims grinned and managed to get out from under Priest's arm by reaching for two shot glasses and a bottle of bourbon on the bar. "I've got to hand it to you. This is the only way to live . . . give an order, then get of town before the lead starts flying."

"Don't call me Tuck," Priest reminded him.

"Sorry," Sims replied.

"Not that I'm afraid to face those two lawdogs myself, you understand." Priest raised a thick finger for emphasis, his diamond ring sparkling. "It's simply that a smart man must delegate certain tasks to his underlings. It keeps them knowing who's the top dog, wouldn't you agree."

"Certainly. Although I've never been a top dog." Sims grinned as he poured the shot glasses full and handed one to Priest. "It must be a good feeling to know there's nobody above you, pulling your strings." He left his own drink sitting and idly picked up a golf club that stood leaning against the bar. He toyed with the club, making a few short practice swings before propping it back over his shoulder. "Why don't we both go watch this from the rear platform . . . enjoy a little fresh air?"

"Naw, you go ahead." Priest waved him away. "I'll see it from the window."

"Suit yourself." Sims walked toward the door at the rear of the Pullman car, the golf club still resting on his shoulder. Beneath his feet he felt the train lumbering forward, slow and steady.

On the crowded dirt street, Sullivan Hart and Two-jack Roth walked toward the telegraph office, leading their horses. When Stanley Lane fired the first shot from around the corner of a building, the street began to clear in a flurry of skidding buggy wheels and rearing horses. A woman's flowered hat sailed high and seemed to hang suspended in air for a second before sailing to the ground, only to be trampled by a pair of fleeing boots. A pedestrian jerked backward in mid-step, then fell to the ground with a red stream of blood spilling from his chest.

"Get down!" Sullivan Hart shouted as he dropped to one knee, the reins flying from his hand while his pistol flashed upward from his holster. The next shot came from a different direction, followed by another, then another, until Hart and Roth both saw they were kneeling and returning fire amid a hail of bullets. Hart drove away in one direction. Twojack Roth rolled off in the opposite direction, firing toward the puffs of rifle smoke over the roof of the telegraph office.

Atop the telegraph office Kenny Kerns let out a long yell as a bullet sliced through his shoulder. He fell forward over the eaves of the tin roof, dropping twelve feet and landing hard on the ground. The fall knocked him cold. Beyond the telegraph office, the short train rolled slowly forward past the station's platform. Sullivan Hart caught only a glimpse of a man standing on the rear deck of the train, but there was not enough time to recognize him. He swung his pistol toward the rifle fire coming from the corner of a building, and fired twice as Stanley Lane ducked back out of sight.

Twojack Roth had fired two shots at Ned Norris when Norris gave up his position behind a rain barrel and went running back along the street toward a water trough. Twojack's shots thumped into the trough. Roth stood up and ran forward, hoping to get into a better position before the rifle came over the edge of the trough and fired. But as he moved forward, Stanley Lane jumped from his cover behind the edge of the building and got off a good straight shot before Sullivan Hart's pistol fire spun him in place and slammed him to the boardwalk.

Twojack went down with a wound spreading blood across his chest. He struggled halfway to his feet, but fell back down when a bullet from behind the water trough grazed the side of his head. Sullivan Hart stood to fire as Ned Norris came up from behind the water trough, taking a sure, straight aim at him. Hart squeezed the trigger, but heard the sickening hollow sound of the hammer dropping on an empty chamber. Norris saw it as he aimed, and almost smiled. Yet something distracted his aim at the last second as the rifle fired; and Sullivan Hart heard the bullet whistle past his face as he dove for Twojack's pistol where Twojack lay facedown in the red dirt.

Norris jerked around in surprise and glanced back
and forth behind him. Then as he levered a fast
round and raised the rifle to aim, Hart had come up
with the pistol from Twojack's holster and fired. The
bullet punched a hole in the center of Ned Norris's
chest and sent him backward, the rifle flying out of
his hands. Hart stalked forward in a crouch, sweeping the pistol back and forth. A woman screamed
from her hiding spot on the boardwalk, and Sullivan
Hart spun back toward her.

"Shut up, lady!" Sheriff Bud Kay yelled at her as
he ran forward, his pistol drawn, making his way
through the tight group of people huddled together
on the boardwalk.

Sullivan Hart stopped him with a raised hand,
then moved forward with caution until he was close
enough to look over the trough and see the gunman
lying dead in a pool of dark blood. "He's dead, Sheriff!" Hart called back over his shoulder. He hurried
around the trough, looking out toward the short train
as it gained speed and shrank away toward the prairie. Hart could just make out the man's face on the
rear platform more clearly now. He clenched his
teeth at the sight of Quick Charlie Sims, leaning on
something. *A cane perhaps?* Sims wore a wide, taunting smile and waved a hand back and forth at him.

"Damn you, Sims." Sullivan Hart seethed under
his breath, gripping the pistol in his gloved hand. He
turned and looked back at his horse milling to one
side in the street, its reins hanging in the dust. He'd
never catch the train by the time he got mounted and
on his way. Already, above the rooflines of buildings,
he could see the stream of engine smoke streaking
backward as the train gained speed. He looked behind him and saw Twojack roll over onto his back
and try to sit up. A man and a woman had kneeled
beside him. Hart turned and ran back, sliding down
beside his wounded partner.

"Take it easy, Twojack." Hart pressed Roth back to

the ground as the big Cherokee tried to struggle to his feet. Hart turned away long enough to call out to the townsfolk who had just begun to rise from their cover. "Somebody give me a hand! Let's get this man to a doctor!"

"No. Get me up on a horse. I'll be all right," Two-jack rasped in a strained voice. Yet even as he spoke, Hart could see he wasn't going anywhere for a while. A bloody graze streaked back along his hairline. His eyes had a dazed look.

"Lie still," Hart said. "You took a bullet in the chest. We've got to get you taken care of."

The sheriff came forward, half dragging Kenny Kerns by his coat collar. "This one is still alive." Kerns staggered in place, blood running freely from his shoulder wound.

"Make sure he stays that way, Sheriff," Hart said as two townsmen moved in, helping him with Roth. "I'll be wanting to question that bird first chance I get."

"Hear that?" Sheriff Kay shoved Kerns toward the jail. "This ain't exactly your lucky day, boy."

Hart and the two townsmen carried Roth over to the doctor's office, where a young red-haired doctor in a long white apron stood holding the door open for him. "Take him straight back to the surgery room," the doctor said, already falling in beside Two-jack Roth to examine the chest wound as the men moved across the waiting room.

Once Roth was on the surgery table and the young doctor had shooed everyone from the room, Hart stepped out on the boardwalk and looked at the two bodies on the ground. Sheriff Bud Kay had returned from putting Kerns in a cell. He stepped down into the street as some townsmen laid the bodies out in a row. "What about that wounded prisoner, Sheriff?" Hart asked. "Is he going to be all right?"

"I gave him a wet rag to put against his shoulder. That's more than he deserved." Sheriff Kay looked up at Hart, pointing at the two dead gunmen. "Recognize either of them?"

Sullivan Hart shook his head. "But I recognized the man on the end of that train headed out of town. That was Quick Charlie Sims."

"Quick Charlie Sims?" The sheriff looked surprised. "You never mentioned him having anything to do with any of this. Last I heard, Sims was wanted for bank robbery up in Creed."

"It was Sims," Hart said.

"Maybe that explains this," Sheriff Kay said and pitched a gutta-percha gold ball to him. "I found it on the ground near the man behind the water trough. What do you make of it?"

Hart caught the golf ball and rolled it back and forth in his gloved hand. "I have no idea, Sheriff." He shook his head and gazed once more out across the flatland.

"Well, something distracted that man from shooting you. I saw it," Sheriff Kay said. "Surely, Quick Charlie didn't hit him with a golf ball . . . did he? From the back of a moving train? Nobody could do something like that, could they?" Sheriff Kay looked stunned by the prospect.

"I doubt it, Sheriff. But I'd put nothing past Quick Charlie Sims." Sullivan Hart gripped the ball tightly in his hand, still looking out toward the distant rails. "If he did something like that, the question is, *why* would he? He's on the run. There's no reason I can think of for him wanting to help us. If anything, he'd be more likely to take their side."

Sheriff Bud Kay raised his battered Stetson and blotted a forearm against his moist brow. "All I know is, if he hit that gunman with a golf ball, you might just have to thank him for saving your life back there."

Hart ran it through his mind as he palmed the golf ball and studied the distant land. Surely, hitting the gunman had been a mere fluke of luck. Yet Sullivan

Hart had to wonder why Quick Charlie Sims would have done such a thing in the first place. Was Sims sending him a message, making it a point to let Hart know where he was and what he was up to? Hart dropped the golf ball into his duster pocket. "Sheriff, how far does this rail spur go before cutting into the main line?"

Sheriff Kay looked out across the land. "Oh, thirty miles, more or less. Why? You'll never catch that train on horseback. And there's not a telegraph line hooked in yet. You can't even wire ahead to the rail junction to have it stopped."

"I see." Hart turned and walked toward the jail, Sheriff Kay following at his heels. "Sheriff, I want to question that new prisoner. Once I see that Twojack's going to be all right, I've got to get going. We're too hot on the trail to pull back now."

"Don't worry, we'll take care of Roth for as long as it takes. As far as questioning the prisoner, you can do that with a pick handle for all I care."

"Thanks, Sheriff." Once he was inside the sheriff's office, Hart stopped and stood in the middle of the dusty floor. He took off his hat and ran a hand through his hair. He needed some rest, but sleep was out of the question right now. Quick Charlie Sims wanted Hart and Roth on his trail. Sullivan Hart had to find out why.

"He's in the first cell there by himself." The sheriff pointed toward the row of cells across the rear of the building.

Kenny Kerns sat hollow-eyed and trembling, a blood-soaked rag pressed gingerly to his shoulder. Three cells away, Briley Barnes looked out through the bars, a smug look on his face, and a dirty cloth bandage wrapped around his wounded leg.

"I'm bleeding real bad," Kenny Kearns called out to Hart and the sheriff as they walked over to his cell. "Is the doctor coming?"

"We'll see," Sullivan Hart said. He took the cell key from the sheriff's hand and unlocked the door.

"You'll see? Is that all? You'll *see*?" Kerns's voice turned shakier. "I'm bleeding something awful here!"

Sullivan Hart gestured for Sheriff Kay to leave them alone. When Kay turned and walked away, Hart stepped inside the cell and stood before Kerns. "I'm betting you can tell me everything I want to know before you bleed to death. If you talk, I'll have the doctor patch you up. If not, we'll have to take you out of here in a sponge and a bucket."

Kenny Kerns swallowed hard. His eyes dropped to the flow of blood seeping between his fingers. "All right . . . what do you want to know?"

Chapter 10

"I wanted to be there . . . when you questioned him," Twojack Roth said. He struggled to raise himself up, but couldn't quite manage it. He looked up at Sullivan Hart standing beside the bloodstained operating table and forced himself upward again. This time Hart's hand pressed him back down.

"Take it easy, Twojack. You're not going anywhere for a while," Hart said. Three hours had passed before Roth fully regained consciousness. His eyes and demeanor still looked unsteady.

"I . . . can ride," Twojack said, raising an arm and letting it lie down on his bandaged chest. "All I need is for somebody to give me a hand."

"It's out of the question," the young doctor said, leaning in before Sullivan Hart could answer. "You won't be traveling for at least a week, and that's really pushing it. You may have a fracture in your forehead, not to mention a drastic bullet wound in your chest that has shattered a rib and came dangerously close to—"

"Did you get the bullet out?" Twojack Roth cut the doctor short, managing to get a handhold on the doctor's dangling necktie and jerking it down. Roth glared at him nose to nose.

"Yes," the young doctor rasped. "It's out . . . it deflected off a rib and came out your side."

Twojack Roth released the doctor's necktie. "Then your job is done."

The doctor staggered back a step and tugged at his necktie, his face red, his manner shaken.

"Settle down," Hart said. "You're in no shape to ride, and that's all there is to it."

Twojack Roth slumped back on the table. "Sorry, Doctor." Then he looked at Hart and asked in a halting voice, "What did you find out from Kerns?"

Hart turned to the doctor and the sheriff and gestured toward the door. "Maybe you better go take a look at the prisoner, Doctor. He's bleeding pretty bad."

Once the doctor and Sheriff Kay had left the room, Hart turned back to Roth. "According to this fellow Kerns, the train is headed for Memphis. And it seems that Quick Charlie Sims is in *Los Pistoleros* up to his elbows."

"Then let's get to Memphis." Twojack Roth almost managed to raise himself up this time. But again, Hart stopped him.

"Not yet. Besides, by the time we get there, the train could be anywhere. We can't keep up with it, and we've got no legal reason to have it detained."

"You've got the prisoner's admission," Twojack said.

"And that's not worth spit in this case. These men will have a lawyer rip his statement to pieces." Hart shook his head. "We've got a big snake by the tail here, Twojack. The only way we're going to kill it is to get our boots on its head. There's no help for us out there. As far as any legal authorities are concerned, until we can prove everything in a courtroom, we're just a couple of Wild West lawmen chasing shadows."

"I'm not about to give it up," Twojack said.

"Neither am I," Hart replied. "I've thought it over. With everything that's hanging over Sims's head, he wouldn't have let me seen him if he didn't want to keep us on his trail. I would have had no way of knowing that train was even connected to the shooting if it hadn't been for him. He's up to something. He doesn't make a move unless it suits his purpose."

"You're saying we should *trust* Quick Charlie Sims?" Twojack looked dubious at the prospect.

"I'm saying unless we can outthink him, maybe we better start following his lead on this thing. See what he's trying to tell us."

Twojack thought about it for a second. "You say he grinned and waved at you?"

"Yep, bold as brass. Like he was daring us to follow him."

"I don't think so." Twojack offered a weak smile. "I think he was telling you we *couldn't* follow him. You said yourself, by the time we get to Memphis, the train could be anywhere."

"I know . . ." Hart let out a deep breath. "So where does that leave us? What's our next move?"

A silence passed between them as they considered what to do. Finally, Twojack Roth raised a weak hand. "I hate to say it, but if you're right . . . our next move is up to Quick Charlie Sims. Give him some time. I expect we'll hear from him."

The train bored across the prairie at what seemed like lightning speed, Quick Charlie Sims thought as he walked back once more through the swaying caboose. Now standing on the rear platform, he spread both hands along the iron safety rail and looked back across the land as it fell away into the purple glow of evening. He puffed a cigar and watched the smoke spiral away from him in a draft of air.

Somewhere back there, over two hundred miles away, he estimated, Sullivan Hart would have gotten the message and taken pursuit. Sims hoped so, anyway. He smiled to himself. This was a dangerous game he was playing with Hart, but Sims wasn't worried. He wanted Hart and Roth to keep the pressure on JT Priest, and on Mad-dog Mabrey too. So far, the two lawmen had done a good job of clearing away some of Priest's gunmen. When the time came, Sims had every intention of handing Priest and Mabrey to the lawmen facedown across their saddles.

Of course he first had to get Priest down off his private train and into a saddle. *Mabrey?* He had no idea how to deal with Mabrey yet. But it would come to him, once he worked everybody into the position he wanted them in. He'd caught a glimpse of Twojack Roth going down in the dirt street at Little Red Springs, but he had no idea if the big Cherokee had been shot or was only leaping for cover. There was no question that Lane, Kerns, and Norris were dead though. Sims had seen the bullets fly. Luckily, JT Priest hadn't seen his little trick with the golf shot, Quick Charlie thought.

He let go of a long stream of cigar smoke, then turned as he heard the door open behind him. Kate McCorkle stepped out onto the platform. "Good evening, Kate." Sims motioned for her to join him at the rail. She did so, yet she kept what appeared to be a guarded distance from him. "Twilight on the rolling prairie," Sims said with a smile. "It's always been my favorite time of day."

She looked at him without responding, then pulled back a dark strand of hair that played wildly in the rushing wind. Taking out a flat silver case from a pocket in her long dress, she opened it and took out a short, thin Lady Finger cigar, and then held it out for Sims. He took it, cupped his hands around it, and lit it off his own cigar. He moved a step closer as he handed it back to her.

"Thanks," she said softly.

"Is he asleep?" Sims asked.

She drew on the thin cigar, tossed her hair back, and answered in a flat tone. "No . . . he's passed out, Charlie. There's a difference, you know." She looked back to the west where the horizon glowed red on the darkening shadows of coming night.

"He's been drinking more and more ever since you got here."

"Losing three men back in Little Red Springs didn't seem to bother him any." Sims looked her in the eye. "How'd he explain that to you? Did he say they accidentally shot one another?"

She didn't answer.

Quick Charlie stood silent too, looking down at the steel cuff on each of his wrists, their short chains dangling. Above the wide dome of the earth, stars seemed to dance in place. Beneath their feet the platform creaked and swayed with the motion of the train. After a pause, she exhaled another breath of smoke and said in a gentle voice without facing him, "This is my favorite time of day also." She shrugged. "If I still have a favorite time of day."

Sims puffed on his cigar and said nothing. She saw what was going on now. He was convinced of it. Finally, Kate turned, facing him with a paper money band on her finger. Sims knew at a glance it had come from one of the stacks of money from the bank robbery. "I found this on the floor last night," Kate said. "So I suppose you can gloat now—tell me what a fool I've been."

"I'm sorry, Kate." Sims closed his hand over hers, crumpling the paper band. "But you had to see it. *Los Pistoleros* is the same gang of killers and thieves, only in better clothes these days."

She nodded. "At first I told myself this could have come from anywhere. Why couldn't it? JT has plenty of money." She stopped and stared down at Sims's hand resting on hers. "But I know better. Perhaps I knew better all along."

"You saw what you needed to see, Kate. That's not easy to do with *Los Pistoleros*. They're invisible men unless you look close. But once you look at them for what they really are, it becomes as clear as the nose on your face." He smiled and squeezed her hand gently. "Not all outlaws spit and cuss and ride horses."

"I know . . ." Her words trailed off. She took her hand from his and said, "Why did you have to show up here, Quick Charlie?"

"Kate, I didn't cause any of this. I just pointed it out to you—made you think about it."

"But you complicate things, Charlie. You always did."

"If I make you *think* complicated things, I won't apologize for it, Kate."

"You know what I mean," she said. "Everywhere you go, there's trouble. People are drawn to you. They can't help it. You reel them in, then you use them. JT Priest warned Kerns and the others to keep their distance. Still, you sucked them in, won all their money. All the while you had them thinking they were getting ahead somehow—as if they were the ones winning."

"I didn't twist anybody's arm." Sims lowered his gaze.

"No, of course not, you never do. You stand back and let them flock to you. I don't know how, but even JT is drawn to you, and he *knows* not to get tangled up with you in any way shape or form! It's as if he has to prove something to you. I know he hates you. I know he's afraid of you—would probably love to kill you, I'm sure. Yet here you are, riding his train, drinking his whiskey." She tossed a hand to the wind. "I can't believe I'm even standing here talking to you! How did you know that I wouldn't go right to him—tell him everything you told me?"

"I didn't want to see you come out of this with nothing. I owe you more than that. I had to tell you."

"But how did you know I wouldn't tell? Am I that predictable, Charlie?"

"I took a chance on you, Kate. If I had been wrong, Priest would have killed me and the rest wouldn't have mattered. I took my chances, and you didn't let me down. For that, I owe you even more."

"There, you see? See how you just did that?" She raised a finger for emphasis. "You turned everything I'm saying around, and now, for some *insane* reason, I'm obligated to not let you down! I don't want to talk to you, Charlie." She took a deep breath as if to clear her head. "I'm sorry . . . but it's like talking to a chessboard. I feel like every word you say is your way of setting up the next move."

"All right, Kate. I'm a player, but so are you. We don't have to talk—we don't have to prove anything to one another." Sims took a step back from her along the safety rail. "No games, no sleight of hand. Just one question. Are you going to come out of this thing in good shape?"

Her gaze turned cool, businesslike, Sims thought. "No, probably not," she said. "I have no access to anything. JT keeps a tight hand on the money. He has a safe. I can't get to it. If I'm lucky, I'll walk away with what's on my back. But you're not going to let that stop you, I'm sure."

Sims searched her eyes in the growing darkness. Now who was being a player? he thought. "No," he said. "I wouldn't let that stop me if that were the case. But I already know about the safe. Do you want what's in it?"

She stood silent, gazing back into his eyes.

"A simple yes or no, Kate. This is no trick question."

"Yes. I mean, of course I want whatever is coming to me—"

"No games." Sims cut her short. "This has nothing to do with money for me. Not this time. When I start this ball rolling, you can walk away with the money, free and clear. You'll owe me nothing, and you'll never have to see me again. Fair enough?"

"If you mean it . . ." As she spoke, Sims saw hesitancy. It was about something more than the money in the safe, he thought.

"I mean it, Kate. Be ready to move fast. Once you have the money, drop out of sight. Get down south somewhere and stay out of sight until I finish with Priest and Mabrey. Then you can do as you please."

"And that's it?"

"That's it. I promise." Sims put his cigar back into his mouth and gazed out into the gathering darkness. He felt her move closer beside him, felt her hand on the back of his hand. Then she touched the metal cuff on his wrist. "Why are you still wearing these? I know you can drop them both anytime you please."

He didn't answer, and he didn't face her. Instead, he said over his shoulder, "Go on inside, Kate. Keep an eye on JT. Give me some time to work."

She stood quietly for a moment longer, as if searching for something more to say. But when Sims still wouldn't face her, she turned and opened the door to the caboose. Sims heard her close the door. He waited. When he finished with his cigar, he threw it out onto the tracks, then turned and went inside. In the caboose, he picked up a lantern, checked it for fuel, then stepped out across the walk ramp and into the next car.

In the darkness, Sims stood at the large wooden door, his feet spread to steady himself against the sway of the train. He took the flat narrow strip of steel he'd fashioned into a jimmy out of his trouser pocket and in a moment stood inside the door with the opened lock hanging from his hand. He closed the large wooden door and slipped over to the safe.

Kneeling in front of the huge steel safe Sims lit the lantern and trimmed the wick into a low glowing circle of light. He looked around on both sides of the safe and saw stacks of small wooden dynamite crates against the wall of the car. He reached out and shook one, just enough to be able to tell it was full. A reckless thing to do, he thought. Was this JT Priest's way of destroying any evidence should the going get tough? Sims turned his attention back to the safe.

He took note that the safe's dial was set on the number seven. It would have to be set back on the same number when he finished, in case this was something JT Priest did out of habit. He took out a strip of rawhide from his pocket, laid it over the top of the dial, took it in both hands, and using a motion similar to shining a shoe, began spinning the dial back and forth—racing the tumblers it was called—limbering and warming the inner mechanism.

Then he stopped and rubbed his palm in a circular motion on the safe door near the combination lock. He placed his ear against the spot, shut out all the clacking rails and creaking wooden car beams from his mind, and concentrated on the dull metallic clicks as his fingertips turned the dial, listening for the tumblers to fall into place.

For well over an hour Sims listened to the click and fall of metal safe tumblers, stopping only now and then to blot the dampness from his ear, then going right back to his task. He memorized short sequences of numbers, remembering each of their distinct sounds until he was certain he had the correct first four numbers of the five-digit combination. He stopped again, wiped his brow, took a few deep breaths, and started all over, going through each of the first four numbers in turn. This time he stopped before trying for the last number.

He held a firm outward grasp on the brass door handle and turned the dial as slowly as possible from one mark to the next, giving the tumbler a chance to fall into place and catch there once he reached the correct number. When the dial stiffened a bit in its turning, he stopped dead still and let the tumbler slip into place, at the same time keeping smooth, firm pressure on the brass door handle. Sims watched the big safe door swing open in his hand.

Holding the lantern inside the safe, Sims smiled

and ran his free hand across stack after stack of crisp new bearer bonds that lay on the center shelf. *Counterfeit?* Of course they were, what with that many unsigned and undesignated. They had never even been folded! He took out a half dozen from the stack—not enough to be missed—looked at them, then folded them and put them inside his shirt. He would look them over later.

From the top shelf he took out a folded legal document, studied it for a moment, then smiled to himself and put it back in the exact same spot. Everything in its right time, he thought to himself. On the floor of the safe, he noticed a bulging carpetbag. Reaching and peeping down into it he saw banded stacks of paper money, along with some loose bills—the stolen bank money JT Priest had counted the other day, no doubt. Only there was obviously more than just the money from the one bank. A scrap of paper lay atop the money. Sims picked it up and looked at it. The figure 322,000 had been scribbled in pencil—Priest's total count. This was a whole cache of money, perhaps the proceeds from several other robberies or schemes.

"The treasure of *Los Pistoleros's* kingdom," he whispered to himself, sitting back on his haunches, taking it all in. He took a deep breath and closed his eyes for a second, like a man giving thanks. Finally, he leaned forward and went to work. He shook out the carpetbag on the floor of the safe and began switching bands from one stack to another, taking larger denomination bills and placing them atop smaller ones, then rebanding them until he'd gathered what he calculated to be over fifty thousand dollars.

He started to put the rest of the money back into the bag, but a thought struck him and he stopped. This was a risky move, but he was betting that JT Priest wasn't about to count the money again. If he was going this far, he might as well go for broke.

Sims looked at the tall stacks of bearer bonds with satisfaction. He reached into the safe, took out a four-inch stack of the flat bonds, and filled the bottom of the carpetbag with them. Then he shrugged. What the hell . . . if Priest saw what he'd done, he was dead anyway.

He took only a few stacks of dollar bills, just enough to cover the top of the bearer bonds he'd stacked in the carpetbag, and began shoving the largest part of the money—some three hundred thousand, he estimated—down inside his shirt. The phony bearer bonds should make for some interesting conversation when the time came, he thought. Sims closed the safe, spun the dial, and redialed the combination to make sure he had it right. When he locked the safe this time, he set the dial on the number seven. With one hand holding the lantern, he stood and backed away from the safe, looking all around the floor to make sure he'd left no sign of having been there.

Moving to the steady sway of the train, Sims stepped back, shoved the stacks of bills farther down into his shirt, and slipped out the wooden door. *Not a bad night's work* . . . He locked the wooden door, raised the globe of the lantern, and blew out the short flame.

Chapter 11

The train pulled into a town in Missouri the following morning, and JT Priest had arranged for breakfast to be brought on board from a small restaurant. Now that Priest had no gunmen to do his bidding, the train's old fireman brought the food into the car and helped Kate McCorkle set it out on the table. Sims gathered three china coffee cups from behind the bar, and as he sat them on the table, Kate cast him a guarded glance. He saw the question in her eyes, nodded, and whispered close to her ear, "Everything went fine. Be ready when we get to Memphis."

Once the table was set and the old fireman had gone grumbling back toward the engine, JT Priest stepped out of the sleeping quarters, his face hangover gray, his eyes red-rimmed and weak. Sims stood at the table, pouring coffee for the three of them from a fresh pot Kate had made only moments before. He took note of the pistol in a holster strapped to Priest's hip. Without his hired guns around him, JT Priest didn't seem so cocksure of himself.

Sims liked that.

"Good morning, boss." Sims spread a beaming smile. "I trust you slept well?"

"Don't good morning me," Priest growled. "I've been up over an hour." He cursed under his breath and took a seat at the table.

"Sorry . . ." Sims already knew that. He'd watched Priest step off the train earlier and head to the telegraph office at one end of the platform. Sims set the cup of steaming coffee in front of Priest. "With a little luck, I suppose we should be in Memphis by this time tomorrow. Maybe shooting a little golf by the afternoon?"

"Yeah, Sims," Priest said in a sour voice. "We'll be there by tomorrow." Gazing down at his plate of ham, eggs, and potatoes, he added, "We'll have to wait and see about the golf game though. Things haven't gone quite the way I wanted them to." He looked across the table at Kate McCorkle, saw her eyes on him, and avoided her stare. "After what happened in Little Red Springs, I need to take on some new men. I've also got a meeting to attend."

Kate McCorkle touched a napkin to her lips. "What *exactly* happened in Little Red Springs?" Sims knew she was only asking to put Priest on the spot. He seated himself, picked up his coffee cup, and glanced back and forth between them, enjoying this.

"It was an unfortunate misunderstanding, Kate," Priest offered in a begrudging tone, "nothing more." He sipped his coffee, then looked up at her and leveled a malevolent, bloodshot glare. "Now can I eat my breakfast in a little peace and quiet? I don't need all this noise and commotion."

A tense second passed as Kate McCorkle sat braced forward in her seat, her fingernails tapping out a hard, almost military-sounding rhythm on the table-top beside her plate. Sims saw something coming, but he wasn't sure what, until the plate hurled forward toward JT Priest's face.

"You liar!" Priest had no time to duck away. Eggs, ham, and potatoes splattered on his chest. Kate McCorkle sprang up from her seat and with the swing of a forearm sent dishes and cups flying across the Pullman car. Priest jerked back in his seat, his hands wiping grease and egg yolk from his eyes.

Jesus! Kate! Not now . . . ! Quick Charlie Sims leaped forward, catching her around her waist as she clawed at Priest across the table. Priest rose from his seat, slinging his napkin away. His pistol came up from his holster in his right hand and cocked toward her. "You rotten little trollop! I'll kill you!"

"No! Priest, don't shoot!" Sims spun Kate around, shielding her behind him, and stood facing JT Priest. "For God sakes, control yourself!"

Kate McCorkle struggled against Sims's shoulder as she raged at JT Priest. "Liar! Dog! That's right, pull a gun! You coward! You won't dare face me without one—"

"Get out of the way, Sims!" Priest snarled, "or I'll kill you too!" His hand trembled; his face swelled red. Egg dripped from his chin.

"Easy, JT." Sims freed a hand from Kate and raised it out toward Priest. "Think this through—clear your head! This is crazy! It isn't worth it!" As he spoke, he inched past JT Priest, moving toward the door to the sleeping quarters, forcing Kate McCorkle along, as she struggled against him.

"No four-flushing bitch treats me this way! I'll kill her!" A string of saliva swung from Priest's lips as he shouted. "Now get out of the way!"

"Bitch?" Kate McCorkle clawed forward. "You dare call me a bitch?" Her arms flailed past Sims, desperately trying to get a hold of Priest's throat from twelve feet away. Sims pressed her back. He felt behind his back for the doorknob, and threw the door open as he yelled, "JT, you're both out of control! She's talking crazy!" He shoved Kate backward into the sleeping quarters and pulled the door shut. Kate banged her fists on the other side, shouting and cursing. "Both of you calm down," Sims shouted, and faced JT Priest with his back against the door.

With Kate out of sight, JT Priest relented a little, his pistol barrel lowering. He ran a hand across his chin, smearing egg yolk.

"That's it, take a couple of breaths." Keeping one hand on the doorknob, Sims leaned forward toward

him with his hand raised. "You don't want to do
something like this. Not here. Not in the middle of
a rail station." He gestured toward the open window
to where people filed back and forth along the
platform.

Behind Sims, Kate McCorkle stopped beating on
the door. Sims heard her move away, her ranting
now reduced to a stream of low curses. "You're right,
Sims." JT Priest breathed deep. "I don't know what's
come over her lately." He holstered the pistol, shaking his head. "I'm going out back to get some air.
See if you can settle her down—or I really will put
a bullet in her." He walked to the door at the far
end of the car, snatching a bottle of bourbon from
the bar top on his way. Then he turned before opening the door and said, "Women, huh? Nothing ever
pleases them . . ."

Quick Charlie Sims walked into the sleeping quarters and leaned back against the door, collecting himself. He looked at Kate and shook his head. "Are you
out of your mind, Kate? You can't fly off like that.
Do you realize what we're about to do here?"

Kate wrung a small handkerchief in her hands. "I
couldn't help it, Charlie. I looked at his pig face, realized what a fool I've been, and I just wanted to rip
his heart out. Can you blame me?"

Sims stepped toward her. "Kate, listen to me.
Don't you think I feel the same way? I know now
that he was behind the bank robbery in Creed. Look
at this." He pulled the bearer certificate from his
pocket and unfolded it before her. "There's too many
of these in the safe to even count! I see now what he
meant about *Los Pistoleros* robbing banks he owns an
interest in."

Kate looked the certificate over with a puzzled
expression.

"Can't you see?" Sims shook the certificate in his
hand. "These are phony—not worth the paper
they're written on."

"What's that got to do with bank robbery?" she asked in a lowered tone.

"It works like this, Kate." Sims spoke barely above a whisper. "Priest and Mabrey are getting inside information on when a bank gets a government reimbursement for such things as Indian beef and supplies. They know the right time to rob the bank. But before hitting it, JT Priest cashes one of these in, for say twenty, thirty thousand dollars or more. The next day, or sometime before the bank sends it back to the bank of issue to redeem their money, *Los Pistoleros* robs the bank! Now the phony bond is gone. Clever, huh?"

Realization came into her eyes. "My gosh, Charlie. Do you think this is something JT is doing on his own? Something Mabrey doesn't even know about?"

"I've got a feeling that if Mabrey ever found out, JT would be a dead man. The amount of the bond he cashes at a bank before they rob it is going to cause the whole job to come up short by that amount. But all Priest has to do is jerk the bond from the money bag once he gets it. Traceable bonds get destroyed. So, nobody ever knows what he did."

"It's a great scheme, Charlie. Why didn't *you* think of it first?"

"I did," he replied, "about five years ago . . . that's how I figured this out as soon as I laid eyes on the phony bearer bonds. I gave this scheme to JT Priest one night up in Creed before the bank robbery there."

"But . . . ?" she urged him on.

"But since I'm not a bank robber, it was only talk. That's the night I turned Priest down—told him I was nobody's lackey. Now look what it has grown into." His eyes turned cold. "He set me up for that robbery, Kate. I know he did. He wanted me in jail, and he wanted you all to himself. So how hard do you suppose it would be for me to put a bullet in him now?" He took back the certificate, folded it, and put it away. "But I can't. I've got to get proof on him for that bank in Creed. If not, it's the end of me."

"I'm sorry, Charlie. You know how I lose my temper." She reached out with a hand and gently brushed a lock of hair back off his forehead. "Priest and Mabrey used both of us. He framed you for the bank job, then let me sit in jail until he knew I'd welcome help of any kind, even his." She added with bitterness, "He got everything he wanted."

"Yep . . . he did." Quick Charlie took her hand and looked straight into her eyes. "Until now."

"But why on earth has he risked having you around, Charlie? He would have been better off killing you the day you met out on the prairie."

Sims shrugged. "Why does anybody want me around?"

"Seriously, Charlie." She brushed a hand across his cheek.

"Okay. Because he's grown rich and arrogant, Kate. Tuck Priest was never anything but a thug. He got on a streak of luck, and it's changed him. He misses the old days. Running into me was a blessing for him. It gave him a chance to gloat to himself, get a little private laugh, knowing what he did to me—to both of us. That's why he likes having you with him, too. He's not that smart. Mad-dog Mabrey is the brains behind all this. Priest knows he's just an errand boy for Mabrey, the same way those three gunmen were errand boys for him. Having us around boosts him up in his own eyes. He likes to think he can shoot golf, play poker, be part of a sporting world—but it's not in him, Kate. He's all suit and no shoulders."

"But you'll never prove anything on him or Mabrey, either. They're too big, too well connected. They can't be touched."

"Really? He's packing a pistol on his hip now, Kate. How long since he's had to do that?"

"Not since I've been with him," she said, thinking about it.

"Exactly." Sims nodded. "He's lost his three personal gunmen. He's having to light his own cigars." Sims spread a vindictive grin. "I'm whittling him down, Kate. I won't stop until him and Mad-dog Mabrey are both back where they belong—in a saddle, looking over their shoulder as they slink their way out of town."

"All right, then I'm staying to help you." She gripped his shirtsleeve.

"No, you're not. You're clearing out once we get to Memphis."

"But you need help!"

"I'll have help when the time comes. That's why I've kept Sullivan Hart and Twojack Roth in this game. The worst mistake Priest ever made was killing old Coleman and cutting his ears off. All I've got to do is get Priest and Mabrey together with Roth and Hart in the same spot. Once I do that, I'll make them admit what they did in front of witnesses."

"And if they don't admit to it?" She searched his eyes, already dreading, yet knowing, what his answer would be.

"Then I won't wrongfully hang for shooting that bank guard—I'll *rightfully* hang for killing Priest and Mabrey."

On the platform behind the caboose, JT Priest leaned on the rail in the morning light, his necktie undone, the now half-empty bottle of bourbon in his hand. His red eyes turned to Quick Charlie Sims in a liquor-induced swirl as Sims stepped out onto the platform and closed the door. Sims tried a cautious smile. "You two play rough, JT," he said, stepping over closer to the rail beside him.

"Yeah?" Priest leered at him, drunk and angry. "Let me tell you something, Quick Charlie Sims. I've been standing here thinking, and it seems to me everything was going just right until you showed your face." Priest's free hand fell to the pistol at his hip, and he drew it and let it hang at his side. He wobbled in place on the swaying platform and almost fell. But Sims moved in, caught him, and steadied him against the safety rail.

As soon as Priest had gathered his balance, he swung his gun hand, sending Sims back a step to avoid the barrel. "Whoa, easy, JT. Surely, you're not blaming me for that little blowup back there?"

"All I know is she didn't act this way before you came along. I don't know what kind of line you've been feeding her."

Sims looked hurt. "JT, how can you say that? You've been with me nearly every minute of every day." He spread his hands. "Look at me. I'm down and out. I'm grateful you even took me in. Neither of us has mentioned it, but let's face it, I didn't have a roof over my head or any idea were my next meal was coming from."

Sims could tell JT liked hearing that. "Not to mention you had the law down your shirt." A flat, sarcastic smile spread on JT's drunken face.

"There you are," said Sims. "And you think I would do something to cause you trouble, especially after you treated me so kind? I'd have to be a fool."

"But there's been other things too," Priest said in a drunken slur. "I can't put my finger on them . . . but when you showed up, my luck started running bad."

"I can't believe you're saying this, JT. Seems to me your luck is running pretty good." Sims pointed a finger up and down Priest's finely tailored suit and the diamond ring on his finger. "Your trouble started when you ran into old Coleman Hart if you ask me. I just happened to be there at the time. Don't blame me for that. It wasn't my choice."

Priest shrugged, giving it some thought. "All right, forget it, Sims. I never should have brought Kate

along on a business trip. Women always get in the
way. Losing those three gunmen was a bad break . . ."
As he talked, he slid the pistol back down in his
holster.

"Aw, come on, JT. You said yourself these gunmen
are a dime a dozen. You'll get straightened out.
Looks to me like you made a wise choice. You gave
up three men to get rid of two lawmen. Anybody
would have done the same thing."

"You think so?"

"Of course. I warned you about those two, didn't
I?"

JT Priest didn't answer for a moment. He took a
long slug of bourbon, then wiped a hand across his
mouth. "Gunmen *are* a dime a dozen, Sims—those
kind anyway. They were what you might call the
scrub team."

"Oh?" Sims wanted to keep him talking. "Then
thanks a lot, JT," he said, feigning offense. "You were
going to send me out with the scrubs?"

JT chuckled. "Just on a couple of jobs, Sims . . .
just long enough to see if you had the talent to ride
with Cleveland Phelps and the real *Los Pistoleros*."

"Send me out with Phelps and his boys anytime,
JT. I can hold my own."

"Naw, it doesn't work that way." Priest dismissed
him with a toss of his hand. "First you gotta prove
yourself. Then we kick you up a notch." He took
another drink and turned facing Sims. "See, this
whole operation is set up in different groups." He
tapped a finger to his forehead. "I did it this way to
protect myself."

"Really?" Sims leaned closer, paying attention,
knowing that Priest was bragging now, taking credit
for what Mad-dog Mabrey had done.

"That's right. Me and Mabrey sit at the top. Those
guys beneath us like Kerns, Norris, and the others,
they just go out on the simple stuff. When we need
some real experts, I snap my fingers and we bring

in Cleveland Phelps, Raymond Cloud, Otis Farnsworth, the Mallony brothers." He spread a crooked grin. "Any of those names ring a bell?"

Sims whistled under his breath. "I'll say so. Maybe I better be careful saying I can hold my own. That's a tough bunch."

"Yeah, and they're all in the palm of my hand, Sims. Don't ever forget that."

"I won't, JT . . . believe me, I won't." Sims took the bottle of bourbon from Priest's hand when he extended it to him. He took a short sip and handed it back.

"Want to hear more, Sims, since you're going to be part of our gang?"

"Sure, JT. I mean, so long as you don't think Mabrey would mind your telling me." He lowered his eyes. "I wouldn't want to get you in any trouble with the main boss."

"Main boss?" Priest stared at him, his eyes red-rimmed and wild. "I tell you any damn thing I see fit to." He thumped the bottle of bourbon against his chest. "Sims, when you looking at me, you're *looking* at the main boss."

Chapter 12

Gray streaks of morning fog clung low along the line of steel shelter columns at the Memphis railway station. Quick Charlie Sims stood at the window of the Pullman car, expressionless, idly turning a silver dollar back and forth across the knuckles of his right hand. He watched JT Priest as he walked away through the flow of travelers who moved forward with their bags in hand, and stepped onto a waiting train.

As soon as JT Priest was out of sight, Quick Charlie Sims looked toward the telegraph office sign at the other end of the station. He shoved each steel cuff up under his sleeve, making sure the short chains were out of sight. Then he flipped the silver dollar, snatched it sideways out of the air, and pocketed it. He stepped over to the door of the sleeping area, knocked softly on the door, and spoke through it in a whisper to Kate McCorkle on the other side. "Get ready, Kate," Sims whispered. "I'll be back in ten minutes."

"Please hurry, Charlie," she replied. She had begun packing her things into a large trunk as soon as JT Priest had left a few minutes before. She hefted the heavy trunk, shoving it to the door, and waited. Ten minutes passed. *Where was Charlie?* She sat on the side of the bed with her silk purse lying on her lap, her foot nervously tapping on the floor. *Had he left her? Because if he had . . .*

Another soft knock on the door caused her to let out a breath of relief. "Come on, Kate, hurry up," Sims whispered through the door.

She sprang up from the side of the bed, unlocked the door, and swung it open. "Where did you go? I was getting worried." She struggled, hefting the big awkward trunk toward the open door. "Give me a hand!"

"Uh-uh, Kate. It's not that kind of trip." He raised a boot and placed it flat against the trunk, stopping her from dragging it forward. She turned and saw a bulging leather bag in his right hand. "This is all you'll have time for." He held it out to her.

Instead of taking it, she took a step back. Her eyes brightened. "My God, Charlie. How much is in there?"

"Close to three hundred thousand—I kept some for expenses." He smiled and jiggled the bag in his hand. "Take it, it's yours."

"All of it? But—?" She reached out with both hands, still not taking the bag, but rather seeming to feel the aura of it, the way a person might caress the glow surrounding a lantern. Her eyes turned up to his in question. "He'll kill you, for sure!"

"There you go, doubting me. No questions, Kate." He held the bag farther out until she was compelled to take it. "It's for all the things I promised, but never gave you." He turned the bag loose and let his hand drop to his side. "Do me a favor . . . spend lots of it on the most foolish things you can imagine." He winked. "And think of us when you do it."

"Oh, Jesus, Charlie." She looked down and shook her head slowly. A baggage tag was still tied to the leather handle, as he'd stolen the bag from a railway cart on his way back from the telegraph office. She smiled, tore the tag off, shoved it down into her pocket, then patted it into place. "When this is over, Charlie, promise you'll come to me. I'll be in—"

"Sssh." He gently placed his finger to her lips. "No

promises, Kate. Head south, but don't tell me where you'll be. If something goes wrong . . . well." He shrugged. "I might not be as good at keeping my mouth shut as you were in Colorado." His eyes studied hers. "Besides, I don't need to know where you are in order to find you. You know me, I travel on thin air and instinct."

"Take care, Charlie." They moved out of the sleeping area, Kate with the bag of money hanging heavy down her side.

"I plan to." He picked up a corked bottle of bourbon from the bar and handed it to her neck first.

She looked at it, then looked up into his eyes. "Do I have to, Charlie?"

"Yep." He smiled and nodded. "Call it one for the road."

William Mabrey looked up from his thoughts at the sound of the door opening. From behind the polished mahogany desk in his hotel suite, he watched Red Lohman step inside. Red Lohman stopped and stood like an officer at attention, his suit coat lapel slightly open on one side, revealing the pistol in the shoulder holster under his arm. "Mister Mabrey," Lohman said, "Mister Priest is here. Shall I send him in?"

"Yes, by all means, Red." Mabrey nodded, catching a glimpse of JT Priest already stepping in behind Loman. JT Priest had not yet gotten used to going through others to get to see his old partner, William Mad-dog Mabrey. But that was how things had to be from now on. "That will be all, Red," Mabrey said in a quiet tone, seeing Red Lohman cut a sharp glance toward JT Priest as he sidestepped around him and came forward. The familiar bulging carpetbag swung back and forth in JT Priest's hand. A similar empty carpetbag sat at one end of Mabrey's desk.

"Yes, sir." Lohman's cold stare lingered for a second on JT Priest. Priest returned his gaze until Loman turned, stepped out, and closed the door.

"What do you feed him, Mabrey, raw meat and gunpowder?" JT Priest offered a faltering, half-hearted laugh, coming to a halt at the edge of the mahogany desktop.

"He's well paid to act that way." Mabrey showed a thin smile and rose up from his seat, offering his hand across the desk. "How are you, Tuck?"

"I'm good." William Mabrey was the only person he still allowed to call him by his old name. Priest didn't like it, but what could he do? He turned Mabrey's hand loose and looked around the suite at the plush furnishings and décor as he backed to a leather-cushioned chair and sat down. "Not *this* good, but good." He set the carpetbag beside his chair and placed the side of his boot against it to keep it upright.

"Trappings," William Mabrey offered, "simply trappings." He moved around from behind the desk to the small bar, picked up a bottle of bonded Kentucky bourbon and two glasses, and approached the chair near Priest's. He handed Priest one of the glasses and sat down in the chair beside him. Priest inspected the glass, tapped a fingernail against its rim, and smiled at the ringing sound of the fine crystal. Mabrey broke the seal on the bourbon and filled both of their glasses as he spoke. "I've found that one must look successful in order to be successful."

"I'm sure that's true." JT Priest smiled. They clinked their glasses in toast and watched each other's eyes as they sipped.

When they'd settled back into their chairs with their glasses in hand, Mabrey looked down at the carpetbag, then back up at JT Priest and said, "All right, talk to me, Tuck."

JT Priest shoved the carpetbag over beside Mabrey's feet with a casual sweep of his boot. "Three hundred and twenty-two thousand, all right there. That's thirty more than we'd anticipated."

"Oh?" Mabrey looked pleasantly surprised, but he

already knew how much should be there. He was curious as to whether or not JT Priest would mention it. "Well, that is a bit of a bonus then." He leaned forward and pulled the empty carpetbag from beside the desk and slid it over to Priest, to be used for their next get-together.

"Yes, I knew you'd be glad to hear it." JT Priest swirled the bourbon in the glass and sipped it slowly, savoring the taste. He was certain Mabrey already knew about the extra thirty thousand. Mabrey had a way of knowing most things. "Apparently the bank had issued more credit to the government for Indian beef supply than we thought over the past year." Priest grinned, settling down some now that the bourbon started to warm him. "I love getting paid for beef we never delivered."

"So do I, especially after the last few jobs had brought in less than we thought." Mabrey let his words hang for a moment. Then he asked, "I trust we won't be hearing any more from our friend, Lyle Deavers, then?"

"I took care of him." Priest then nodded. "You needn't worry."

"I'm afraid we're going to be out of the government beef business for a while," Mabrey said. "Only until the Senate investigations are concluded. According to my source in the Bureau of Indian Affairs, some heads are going to roll over beef that was paid for and never received—not *our* heads of course, now that Lyle Deavers won't have a chance to tell them anything." Mabrey tipped his glass in salute. "You see, Tuck, information like that costs us plenty, but it's worth it. The more important people we have in our pockets, the larger our pockets grow. So I've always got to have plenty of cash money to take care of our friends in Washington."

"Yes, I understand," Priest replied. Any half-wit would understand by now, he thought to himself. He resented Mabrey always reminding him of the same things over and over, as if he were some kind of second-rate delivery boy. "The money will always be here. You can count on it."

"Yes, I'm sure I can." Mabrey took another sip. "But let's be careful. We don't ever want to be over-confident, or let ourselves grow lax. This is still a risky business, Tuck. I'd hate to see you back in a saddle, beating a trail out of town with nothing but the shirt on your back."

"That will never happen, Mabrey." JT Priest leveled his gaze on him, wondering just how much news had gotten back to him. "Is everything all right? It's been a while since we've met in person. You seem distracted."

"Distracted . . ." Mabrey nodded, allowing himself a slim, tight smile. "Things were going very well, very well indeed." Mabrey studied the glass in his hand, then reached out and set it on the desktop. He then took out a handful of folded telegrams from inside his jacket pocket. "Then last week I started getting these." As he tapped the telegrams against the palm of his other hand, his eyes betrayed a controlled, smoldering rage.

Mabrey spread the first telegram open. "Cleveland Phelps," he said, holding the leaf of paper up, shaking it. "He says here that you killed Coleman Hart. Brought two lawmen down on the Old English Spread, and caused us to lose the arms shipment in a fire."

JT Priest's eyes widened. "He said that? In an open telegram?"

"Don't be absurd." Mabrey wadded up the telegram and tossed it away. "He told me Coleman Hart was dead, that his killer took his ears. I knew what he meant. Then he told me about the fire at the Old English—and in his own way, how it all came about." Mabrey stared at JT Priest, waiting for an answer.

Priest felt the bourbon grow heavy inside his stomach. "I did kill Coleman Hart. He rode in on us—I had to. But I had no idea about the arms shipment burning up. Why didn't somebody get in touch with me? We can't stand losses like that!"

"Exactly. I couldn't agree more. I've made arrangements to have another load of guns delivered to the Old English Spread. Believe me, we don't dare disappoint the Mexican *federales*." Mabrey stared at him, opening another telegram. "From Cleveland Phelps." He shook it open, then looked at it. "Says here that three men were shot down in the street at Little Red Springs. I get his drift. He's telling me you sent three men out to die when all you had to do was slip out of town. Why would you do something like that?"

"Phelps knew about that?" JT Priest looked stunned. "How did he know what happened? I didn't see him there!"

"Of course you didn't see him," Mabrey snapped sarcastically. "Because he's not an idiot. He laid low, then got out of there. He lined up three local shooters to take care of those two lawmen. Do you realize what all this is going to cost us, hiring outside gunmen? Now Phelps is gathering his own men together in case something goes wrong." Mad-dog Mabrey shook his head. "The tab on this keeps growing higher and higher."

"Mabrey, I—"

Mad-dog Mabrey cut him off, raising the next telegram. "Finally, this one from you . . . the other day. You confirmed the part about the three men in Little Red Springs. You tell me you're traveling with Quick Charlie Sims?" He wadded the telegram and tossed it. "Quick Charlie? Charlie the Wizard, of all people? Have you lost your mind? After what you did to him in Creed, why on earth would you take a chance having him around you? For God sakes, Tuck, you're sleeping with Kate McCorkle!"

"Hold it, boss." Priest raised a shaky hand. "Sims has no idea that I set him up. As far as him and Kate, there's nothing there. He told me so himself."

William Mabrey squinted his eyes shut and pinched the bridge of his nose. "He . . . told you so."

Priest shrugged. "We're always needing good men. Sims is good at what he does . . . you can't deny that."

"Oh, yes, he's good at what he does all right." Mabrey somehow managed to hold his rage in check. "But what exactly is it that he *does*? He's not a bank robber—he made that clear enough to you in Colorado!" He leaned closer to JT Priest, so close that Priest shied back from him. "I'll tell you what he does, Tuck. He finds a way to weasel himself into anybody's business who's fool enough to have anything to do with him."

"I can see through his every move," JT Priest offered, his voice sounding a bit unsteady. "Sims is down and out and trying to scheme his way into something. You can't blame him for that. He's not so slick anymore, either. He lost fifty bucks to one of the boys playing checkers—hell, I even saw him lose at poker! He's not so hard to handle."

"Down and out?" Mabrey shook his head in exasperation. "Nobody can handle Sims, Tuck! Not me, not you, *nobody*! Of course you see through his every move—anybody can if he lets them! That's part of his illusion—his way of drawing you in. He shows you what you want to see, just to make you think you're a step ahead of him. But what you see is never quite what's really going on! There's always some poor fool who comes forward thinking they've got Sims pegged." Mabrey pounded his fist on his chair arm for emphasis. "And that's the kind of person he feeds on!"

"Jesus, boss! You're saying I don't know my job?" JT Priest protested, rounding a nervous finger inside

his damp shirt collar. "That I don't have enough
sense to handle my end of things?"

William Mabrey stopped short and stared at him
in silence for a second, thinking things over. When
he spoke, his voice sounded calmer. "Okay, Tuck. I
see what it is now. I see why you let that grifter into
things. It's not about Sims. This is about you and me,
and how we've set this thing up." He pointed a finger at Priest. "Being around Sims has made you start
thinking maybe you should be bigger in all this than
you are. Am I right?"

"Hey, boss, come on." Priest looked embarrassed.
"I'm not complaining. We've got a good operation
going on here. I've got my own Pullman car, plenty
of money."

"Right," Mabrey said, "but something's missing.
You didn't even realize it until Sims showed up,
right? Now somehow he's gotten under your skin . . .
you need to impress this two-bit grifter someway?"
Mabrey watched Priest run the words through his
mind, then he tapped his temple with his finger and
added, "See, Tuck, that's the way this guy works.
Are you starting to get the picture?"

JT Priest didn't answer. Instead, he adjusted himself in the chair. "Maybe you're right—we've got no
place for Quick Charlie Sims. I'll get rid of him in
Chicago, once I pick up some more men."

Mabrey stared at him hard. "Get rid of him how?"

"You know . . . have one of the boys put a bullet
in his head and drop him in the river."

"Good idea." Mabrey nodded. "Then you get with
Cleveland Phelps and his men and deal with these
two lawmen before we get them any farther down
our shirts. Whatever mess is out there, I want it
cleaned up, understand? And no more fooling
around. Your job is to keep cash coming into this
operation. We're only as big as our bankroll."

"Sure." Priest finished his bourbon. "We shouldn't
be too worried the two lawmen, though. They'd have

a long, hard climb to get to us. We've got ourselves pretty well insulated."

"Yes . . ." William Mabrey let his words trail off and paused for a moment. "And I have every intention of keeping us that way. I'm going to have Red Lohman ride along with you to Chicago, just to see if he can be of any help."

"What?" Priest looked stunned, offended. "I don't need some hired gun looking over my shoulder!"

"Of course you don't." Mabrey played it down. "But Red's a good man. It's time someone showed him how we operate in the field."

"Why? So he can take over my job someday?" Priest glared at Mabrey, wanting to put more bite into his words, but reminding himself whom he was talking to.

"No . . . let's just say that two heads are better than one right now. Let him be the one who puts a bullet in Quick Charlie Sims. Once things are cleaned up out there, Red Lohman will come on back here."

"I don't like the man, boss. I don't want him with me."

"He's going with you, Tuck. And that's that. I'll fill him in on our plans for Quick Charlie Sims. He'll meet you at the train within one hour. Wait for him." Mabrey's tone turned firmer. He looked at JT Priest's empty glass, but made no move to refill it. "Is there anything else we need to talk about? If not, I need to get that money up to our friends in Washington— keep the gears of government well greased."

Priest held his gaze for a second without wavering. But seeing there was no room for any further discussion in Mabrey's cold stare, he relented. "No." He set the empty glass on the desk and stood up. "I'll keep you informed, and I'm sure Red Lohman will do the same." He pointed at the carpetbag on the floor as he leaned forward and picked up the empty bag beside Mabrey's chair. "Aren't you going to count it?'' he asked with a trace of sarcasm. ''Make sure I'm doing my job?''

William Mabrey stood up, ignoring Priest's tone. He tugged his vest into place and extended his hand. ''Nonsense, Tuck. When did I ever have to count any money you handed me?''

Chapter 13

She wouldn't have had to hit him that hard, Quick Charlie Sims thought, trying to lift his head from the floor through a drifting haze of consciousness. The pain in the back of his head thumped like a mallet on a hollow log. When he heard footsteps and felt something poke him in the chest, his first thought was that she'd returned, perhaps to hit him again. But when the poking continued and he heard unfamiliar voices talking back and forth above him, he batted his eyes and managed to keep them open.

"You, there," a voice asked. "I say, can you hear me?"

Sims looked up the shaft of a long hickory golf club. Beyond the far end of the golf club and the hand holding it, he saw an inquisitive face leering down at him. "Yes . . . I hear you." Sims tried to push the golf club to one side.

"Apparently someone has thwacked this poor devil senseless," another voice said. A second face came into view, this one wearing a white walrus mustache, and a thick monocle raised to an inspecting eye. "Oh, my. I hope this isn't going to interfere with our foursome this afternoon."

The two sporty-dressed gentlemen—one of them held the golf club as if it were a walking cane— moved back as Quick Charlie Sims sat up and shook his head back and forth. Sims smelled the strong odor of bourbon and felt drops of it run down the

side of his face. Looking around the wet floor at the
scattered broken glass, he asked in a weak voice,
"Who . . . are you people?"

"Here, poor fellow. Let's get you up from there."
The older man with the white mustache bent down
with a grunt as the one with the golf club stepped
in, assisting him. "I'm Bradford Hines," said the
older man as the two of them helped Sims to a chair
by the felt-topped table. "This is my links partner, J.
Rudolph Flynn. There now." They lowered Sims into
the chair, and Bradford Hines patted a hand on
Sims's bourbon-soaked shoulder. "If I might ask,
what has happened here, sir? Should we send for a
police officer?"

Sims raised a hand. "No, please, that's not necessary." He batted his eyes and looked back and forth
at them. "I'm Charles Simpson. This was just an accident, gentlemen. I hope we can be discreet—"

"An accident?" Bradford Hines stepped in, placing
both hands on his hips. He took note of the steel
cuffs on each of Sims's wrists. "Now see here, sir. If
something untoward has taken place, I think we need
to do something about it."

J. Rudolph Flynn, a younger man around Sims's
age, caught a glimpse of the large trunk sitting inside
the open door to the sleeping quarters. In an ashtray
on the bar he saw the stub of a lady finger cigar, a
trace of women's lip gloss circling the end of it. He
tapped the end of the golf club on the floor. "Excuse
me, Mister Hines." He turned his eyes toward the
steel cuff with its snipped chain dangling on one of
Sims's wrists. "Isn't it obvious there's been some
rough sport here? If Mister Simpson says this was
an accident . . ."

"Oh? Rough sport?" Bradford Hines looked at him
through his raised monocle.

J. Rudolph Flynn made the slightest gesture about
the room with the golf club. Bradford Hines's face
reddened. He made a polite show of clearing his

throat. "Why, yes, of course . . . an accident of some sort." He caught the knowing glance that passed between Sims and Flynn and added, "I have some ice in the cooling chest, out on the carriage. Why don't I step out there and get some?"

"Thanks." Sims nodded, cupping a hand to the back of his throbbing head.

As soon as Bradford Hines left the Pullman car, J. Rudolph Flynn stepped closer and bent down beside Sims. His voice dropped almost to a whisper. "You don't remember me, do you, Quick Charlie?"

Sims only stared at him.

"I'm Rudy . . . Rudy Flynn? We both played in the Yonkers tournament up in New York, remember?"

Sims let out a breath. "Rudy the Fly . . . of course. How's your game, Rudy?"

Rudy shrugged, grinning. "We came here today to find out. A fellow by the name of Priest wired Hines the other day, said he had a real hot-shot player he wanted to introduce. I'm shooting for Hines these days. Hines had us booked for eighteen holes out on the Archibald Estate. He's real excited about it. You know how it goes these days, every rich ol' fart has to own his own golf coach—show ponies is what I call us. I suppose you're past all that, eh?"

"We all do what we have to, Rudy," Sims sighed, "for the sake of the game."

Rudy the Fly glanced about the Pullman car, then looked back to Sims. "Speaking of games . . ." He nodded at the cuff on Sims's right wrist. "I take it we've caught you right in the middle of one here?" When Quick Charlie Sims didn't answer, Rudy nodded, saying, "Never mind. But I owe you one for giving me a couple of breaks in New York. Anything I can do to help?"

Sims held his pounding head and considered. "Yeah, as a matter of fact. Did you see which way the woman ran when she left here?"

At first Rudy looked blank. But then a sly smile

came to his face as he realized what Sims was asking
him to do. "Which woman was that, the one wearing the . . . ?"

"The long brown day coat," Sims said, filling him
in. "The dark-haired woman carrying nothing but a
thin silk purse . . . headed for the northbound on the
far side of the station, wasn't she?"

"Yep . . . that's the one I saw, all right." Rudy
picked right up on it. "I'm pretty sure Bradford
Hines saw her too, come to think of it." Rudy
grinned.

"Thanks, Rudy. Now I owe you one."

"Call us even, Quick Charlie. Us golfers have to
stick together." Rudy winked. "For the sake of the
game." He tapped the club head on the floor and
stepped back as Bradford Hines returned with a
handful of ice wrapped in a white linen napkin.

"Here, Mister Flynn, perhaps this will ease his
pain." Bradford handed the ice pack over to Rudy
the Fly, who in turn passed it to Quick Charlie Sims.

"Mister Simpson was just telling me that the
woman we saw in the brown coat did this to him,"
Rudy said to Bradford Hines as Sims held the ice
pack to the back of his head.

"What woman?" Hines asked.

"You know, the one carrying a thin silk purse? Dark
hair? Hurrying toward the northbound platform?"

Bradford Hines touched his fingers to his walrus
mustache. "I'm afraid I didn't see a—"

"Come now, Mister Hines," said Rudy the Fly.
"How do you expect to see a ball a hundred yards
away if you can't see a woman breeze right past us?
You're not the kind of man who doesn't notice
women, are you?"

Bradford Hines looked embarrassed. "I . . . that
is . . . well of course I notice women, sir! And yes, I
saw her, I simply didn't recall the color of her coat.
Now that you mention it, though, it was brown,
I'm sure."

Rudy gave Sims a slight smile.

"My," Hines continued. "And that woman did this to you? May I dare ask why?"

"I'd rather not talk about it," Sims said. "Like I said, it was an accident."

"Of course, sir." Bradford Hines started to say something more, but the sound of JT Priest's footsteps caused the three of them to turn toward him as he stepped into view.

"What accident?" Priest's eyes went to the broken bottle and the puddle of bourbon, then to the trunk sitting inside the open doorway, then to Sims with the ice pack pressed to his head.

"Thank heaven you're back, Mister Priest!" Bradford Hines clasped JT Priest's hand as he moved into their midst. "Poor Simpson here has had a terrible misfortune. Luckily, Mister Flynn and I happened by to chat with you before the game."

Priest managed to shake Hines's hand away. He stared straight at Sims. "What's gone on here, Mister *Simpson*?"

"I got hit from behind," Quick Charlie replied, putting a little more pain into his voice than he actually felt. He ventured a glance about the room, past the trunk, then back to Priest. "She's gone," he added. "I wouldn't have even known what hit me if it hadn't been for these two. They saw her leaving . . . in a hurry, they said." He glanced at Hines and Flynn for affirmation.

"It's true," said J. Rudolph Flynn.

"Oh . . . yes, the woman in the brown coat," Hines offered, still seeming to struggle with his recollection of her.

"She must've really been in a big hurry." Flynn nodded toward the trunk. "All she carried was a small purse."

"That's not all she was carrying," Sims added. His hand had gone to his trouser pocket, then came back out, pulling on the empty white pocket lining. "I had almost eighty dollars in poker winnings—it's gone."

JT Priest looked back and forth between them. "Which way did she go?"

Sims ducked his head and smiled to himself as J. Rudolph Flynn answered, pointing in the direction of the northbound loading platform. JT Priest stalked out of the car.

"Well, I suppose this means our game is off this afternoon?" Bradford Hines asked Sims, crestfallen.

Quick Charlie held the ice pack to the back of his head. "Yes, I'm afraid so. My vision is blurry. I feel like I've been hit by a road wagon. I couldn't walk the course."

"Oh . . . well, what if you simply took along plenty of ice, perhaps if we looped our arms and carried you—?"

"For crying out loud! Can't you see he's in no shape to play golf?" J. Rudolph Flynn interrupted. He turned to Sims and winked, speaking to Hines over his shoulder. "I hope we'll get together somewhere in the near future, Mister Simpson. Mister Priest has told us so much about you." He backed away a step, ready to turn and leave.

"Thank you, I'll be looking forward to it." Quick Charlie nodded.

As Hines left, Rudy the Fly leaned in closer. "I've also heard you're quite a hand at chess and checkers."

"I've enjoyed those games on occasion." Sims smiled, adding, "I appreciate your help, Rudy."

"Don't mention it. Let's keep in touch. It's always good to get away from these gentlemen players and get into some *real* competition." Rudy turned and left, the golf club making casual little sidelong sweeps across the floor as he walked.

Moments later, JT Priest stalked back into the car, his tie undone and his breath heaving in his chest. Rage glowed hot in his eyes. Seeing that Hines and

Flynn were gone, he jerked the pistol from his holster
and cocked it. "All right, Sims, start talking and talk
fast! Where is she? I know this is some kind of
scheme and you're in on it!"

"Scheme?" Sims looked drained, defeated. "JT,
look at me. Do I look like I'm in any position to—"

"Cut the bull! I'm not falling for it!" JT Priest
raised the pistol with a shaky hand and leveled it
on Sims's forehead. "I'll blow your head off, here
and now!"

Quick Charlie looked down the pistol barrel, playing it for all he was worth. He sighed. "Go ahead
and shoot, JT. You'd be doing me a favor." He lowered his eyes and let the ice pack down from the
back of his head. "Throwing in with *you* and *Los
Pistoleros* was my last chance. If that's over . . .
well"—he shrugged—"just put me out of my misery.
I've never had such bad luck in my life. I couldn't
even keep from getting my pockets robbed."

JT Priest hesitated. The pistol barrel slumped a bit.
"You say she hit you while you weren't looking?"

"Yeah, but it was my fault. I *should* have been looking. Now I feel like I've let you down, JT. I can't
blame you for not believing it—hell, I can't believe
it myself."

JT Priest showed a condescending smirk. "Quick
Charlie, not as quick as you should be, eh?"

Sims just stared at him. "You don't have to rub
it in."

"Where do you suppose she went, Sims? She give
you any clue lately?"

"Me? Why would she? She used to talk about Minnesota a lot."

"Jesus, Minnesota? Why on earth there?" Priest
furrowed his brow.

"I don't know why, the accordion music maybe?"
Sims tried to look baffled. "Maybe she likes playing
in the snow? Maybe she wasn't really headed north.

Could be she just mentioned Minnesota to throw us off."

"Naw, Hines and Flynn said she was headed for the northbound, so it makes sense. It doesn't matter. I've been expecting something like this—the way she's been acting the past few days. When I run into her, she's dead."

"Looks like we've got something in common, JT. We're both a couple of her used-to-bes." Sims took on a dejected expression.

"You, maybe. But I'm not going to be treated this way by no damn woman."

"Well . . . if you're really going to shoot me, JT, go ahead. I'm tired of sitting here feeling like a fool."

JT Priest thought things over. "No, I'm not going to shoot you, Quick Charlie Sims. Not yet anyway." He uncocked the pistol and let it hang in his hand. "Instead, I've got something for you to do."

Sims looked at him, appearing surprised. "After all that's happened? You still trust me?"

"Ha! I've never trusted you. But if you're on the up-and-up about what happened here, I'll give you one more chance. Blow it, and you're finished for good."

"Anything you say, JT." Sims raised the ice pack to the back of his head.

Priest looked back at the car door as if to make sure no one could hear him. Then he whispered, "There's a gunman called Red Lohman coming with us to Chicago. He'll be here any minute. I want you to get rid of him for me. Do that, and you'll be my right-hand man. We might even branch out on our own down the road, start our own operation. How would that play for you?"

"That would be great, JT." Sims stopped as if just realizing what Priest had asked him to do. "Wait a minute, JT! Surely you don't mean . . . ?"

"Yeah, that's what I mean. Kill him. Any problem with it?"

"Damn, JT. I'm no assassin. I've never killed a man in my life." Sims fidgeted with one of his steel cuffs.

"What about the guard you're accused of killing in Creed?" JT Priest asked in a cutting, taunting tone.

There it was, Sims thought, Priest playing a twisted game. He knew full well that Sims hadn't killed that guard. Sims stared at him and said the unexpected. "That was different, JT. I had to kill him in the midst of a robbery. I had no choice."

Sims watched Priest's eyes take on a strange, puzzled glow, as if stuck for a reply. If there had ever been any doubt before in Sims's mind that Priest had set him up for the bank robbery, Priest's expression just confirmed things for him. Sims went on, saying, "But as far as an assassination? I wouldn't know how to handle something like that."

JT Priest collected himself. "First time for everything, Sims. Besides, I'm not asking you, I'm *telling* you. Get rid of him before we reach Chicago, or I'll get rid of you."

"All right, I'll do it." Sims's shoulders slumped in submission. "I can't believe Kate McCorkle would put me in a spot like this."

JT Priest grinned. "For a man with a reputation for being sharp, you sure have a lot to learn, Sims. I knew the day you joined us that it was only a matter of time before she did something to you. You can't treat people the way you treated her and expect them to just forget all about it. With that temper of hers, you're lucky she didn't cut your throat."

"Yeah, I guess you're right, boss." He looked up at JT Priest, realizing that Priest was feeling bigger by the second. "I'll try to remember that from now on," Sims murmured.

They'd begun straightening up the room when Red Lohman stepped on board and walked into the room, carrying a small black leather traveling bag. Priest stood with a dustpan full of broken bottle glass. Sims held a handful of towels, ready to swab the puddles and streaks of bourbon from the floor. An awkward moment of silence passed as Red Lohman looked at the mess on the floor. But then JT Priest took charge, saying, "Well, Lohman, don't just stand there. Take some of these towels and give us a hand." He nodded toward Sims. "This is Quick Charlie."

"Yeah, I've heard of you, Sims." Red Lohman looked at the cuffs on Sims's wrists, then appraised Sims with no offer of introducing himself. Sims noted the high-riding shoulder harness up under Lohman's left arm beneath his dress coat. The butt of a pistol showed through his coat as he turned back and forth looking the Pullman car over. "Mister Mabrey didn't send me here to be your chambermaid, JT. We might as well get that straight from the start."

JT Priest stiffened. "You're riding *my* train . . . you'll follow *my* orders!"

"I'm riding the *corporation's* train, not yours," Lohman shot right back. "I was sent here to keep an eye on things until you get some more men . . . and that's exactly what I'll be doing. If you've got any problems, take it up with the boss. Far as I'm concerned, you're just the delivery boy, Priest. Don't make yourself sound bigger than you are."

JT Priest's face looked as if he'd been slapped. He seethed, his hand trembling in rage and humiliation. Sims saw he was ready to drop the dustpan and go for his pistol. "Well, now." Sims stepped in between the two men's icy glare. "Looks like all that's left here is a little spilled liquor. I'm sure I can manage. You boys go have yourselves a drink. Cool out a little." He smiled back and forth between them.

"Do I look like a *boy* to you, Sims?" Red Lohman cocked his head slightly, a cruel grin snaking beneath his bristly red-gray mustache. Sims froze in place, stuck for an answer, carefully sizing Red Lohman up. The man had come in strong, letting everybody know to keep their distance—a real tough guy. Sims liked that. Before he could respond, Lohman asked Priest, "Now where do I stow my grip bag?"

"Back in the crummy, with the engineer and fireman's gear." Priest jerked his head toward the rear of the train. "There's beds and a cookstove back there."

"The crummy?" Red Lohman looked incensed.

"Yeah, the caboose," Quick Charlie cut in, getting a kick out of Red Lohman's attitude.

"I know what a crummy is, Sims." Lohman turned and stared back at Priest. "Why am I sleeping in one?"

"Because that's where the hired help sleeps, Lohman!" JT Priest moved over and laid the dustpan down on the table as he spoke. "You either sleep there, or get the hell off here right now. We'll go right back to Mabrey and ask him about it!"

Quick Sims loved it—two dogs growling over a bone.

Finally, Red Lohman relented. "All right." He threw his leather grip bag to Sims. "Come on, Quick Charlie . . . let's see how quick you can carry my grip back to the caboose."

JT Priest stood glowering, his fists clenched tightly at his sides.

Sims caught the bag, rocking back a step. "Sure thing, Mister Lohman." He moved past JT Priest, giving him a meek shrug and a helpless expression. "Anything I can do to help us all get along."

Chapter 14

The doctor had told Twojack Roth that it would be at least a week before he'd be up and around. But by the end of the third day, Roth had grown restless and began forcing himself up from his bed and pacing the floor of the doctor's office in his long white convalescent gown. On the evening of the fourth day, Sullivan Hart came to see him with a big tray full of food from the restaurant down the street, and a large bag under his arm. Roth met him inside the door, his long black braid undone and his hair glistening wild and unkept.

"Where's my clothes, Sully?" Roth asked, his broad shoulders filling the doorway, one hand behind his back holding his gown together. "If I don't get dressed and out of here, somebody's going to get hurt—"

"Take it easy, Twojack." Sullivan Hart managed to get past him and set the tray down on the stand beside the bed. He pitched the bag onto the bed. "There's your clothes and gun belt." He took a telegram from inside the bib of his shirt and handed it to Roth. "I was going to show you this after you ate. This came in earlier today, from Memphis. Looks like we're headed for Chicago."

Twojack Roth read the telegram aloud: "YOUR MORGAN HORSE IS IN CHICAGO STOP. COME AND GET IT STOP. SIGNED, CHARLES SIMS. PS, HE MISSES YOU." Roth looked up from the telegram with a curious expression and crumpled the paper in his thick hand.

"I know the horse is not there yet, and neither is Quick Charlie Sims," Hart said. "This is his way of telling us where he's headed. I say we move on it."

"Chicago is a big place, Sully." As Roth spoke, he ripped open the bag, shook out his washed trousers and put them on.

"Does that bother you?" Hart folded the telegram and put it away.

"No . . . as far as I'm concerned, it's only one more cow town, only bigger, with more horse droppings in the street. It could take us some time finding our way around." Roth threw on his shirt, the bullet hole now mended by a small patch, buttoned the shirt across his bandaged chest, and shoved the tails down into his trousers.

Hart nodded. "We'll have some help. Sheriff Kay checked with the Chicago police. There's a warrant on Briley Barnes for some old minor theft charge. I doubt if Chicago is that concerned with getting him back. But we're within our rights to transport him there. Nothing says we can't hold him a couple of days and make him show us around. He's already told me that he and these other thugs came from a labor contractor—a company called Hughes & Lindsay. I say that's a good place to start . . . beats sitting around waiting for Quick Charlie Sims to show his hand. I'd feel better if we weren't following Sims's lead on this."

"Me too." Roth shook out his washed socks, then sat down stiffly on the side of his bed and put them on. "But for now I'd follow the devil himself if it gets us to *Los Pistoleros*." He unrolled his high-topped moccasins and pulled them on. "What about the rest of the prisoners?"

"Sheriff Kay still has some inquiries out on them. I wired Judge Parker. He said to leave them here. He'll charge them with whatever he can come up with. He's sending out a circuit wagon for them, but it'll be sometime next week before it gets here. I told him we're moving on."

"So he approves?" Roth stood up and stamped his moccasins into place.

Sullivan Hart looked a little embarrassed. "Yes . . . only he has no expense money to send us. I talked to the mercantile owner here. He'll lend us some money against our rifles."

"That's just great." Roth shook his head. "We have to pawn our shooting gear to afford to track down criminals? This gets better by the minute."

Hart continued, "I've also got thirty dollars of my own. Sheriff Kay will lend us some money from his town discretionary fund. We can sign for our train fare and bill the government. We'll make out."

"Yeah . . ." Roth let out a breath. "Chicago. That seems to be the source, all right."

"Kerns said the only people left on the train are Sims, JT Priest, and a woman named Kate McCorkle. If they need more men, where would they go?"

"Anywhere they want to," said Roth. "Gunmen aren't that hard to find. But so far, Chicago seems to be where most of these men are from. By the way, I've got eighteen dollars in my saddlebags." Roth picked up his gun belt from the bed and strapped it on.

"Not anymore you don't." Hart smiled.

Twojack Roth took his pistol from his holster, checked it, spun the cylinder, and put it away. "What about my horse? I hope you didn't sell it out from under me." Roth turned to the tray of food without waiting for an answer and picked up two pieces of fried chicken. "Here, dinner is on me." He pitched a piece to Sullivan Hart, then turned and headed out the door.

After they'd picked up their horses from the livery barn, they walked them to the hitch rail out in front of the sheriff's office. As they stepped up onto the boardwalk, Roth asked Hart, "Do you remember a hardcase by the name of Hook Stevins? From over in the panhandle? Runs with the Bristol brothers, Ernie and Bob-boy?"

"Yep, I remember them. Arrested Hook Stevins my first year on the job for shooting an ol' boy in a card game."

Roth asked in lowered voice, "Think he'd still be mad at you over it?"

Hart gave him a curious look. "I don't know, why?"

"Don't look around, but him and the Bristols have had their eyes on us from an alley ever since we passed the mercantile."

Without turning, Sullivan Hart adjusted his hat and placed one hand on the doorknob. "Maybe we better ease over there and see what's on their minds." He opened the door, and they both stepped inside the office.

"Wasn't expecting you so soon," Sheriff Kay said, standing from behind his desk. He picked up the ring of cell keys and started toward the cell where he'd placed Briley Barnes by himself. "I'll get him ready to go."

"Hang on, Sheriff Kay," Sullivan Hart said, stopping him. "We need to use the rear door. We'll be right back." They walked past Sheriff Kay.

"What's up, Deputies?" He started to fall in behind Twojack Roth, but Roth turned and stopped him.

"We're not sure, Sheriff," Roth said. "But stay inside here while we find out."

"Dang it, Roth," Sheriff Kay called out, "you're in no condition to be getting involved in—" His words stopped short when the back door closed with a solid thump.

In the alley alongside the mercantile store, Bob Bristol looked at his older brother, Ernie, then at Hook Stevins, who stood between them in the shadows, loading a double-barrel shotgun that lay in the crook of his right arm. "I don't know about you two," said Bob Bristol, "but this makes no sense to me. We've already gotten paid for doing this. Why don't we just skedaddle? If we ever run into Cleveland Phelps, we'll tell him we chased them but they got away."

Brother Ernie smiled, liking the idea. But Hook Stevins gave them both a stern look and snapped the shotgun shut. "I'm gonna pretend I didn't hear you say that, Bob-boy. You don't want the likes of Cleveland Phelps catching up to you somewhere down the road, you having to explain why you didn't kill these two."

"It was just a thought, Hook," Bob Bristol said. "I meant no harm."

"Yeah, right." Hook Stevins reached up with the steel hook that served in place of his missing left hand, and scratched the point of it against his beard stubble. "Besides, for me this is the chance I've been waiting for. We get in good with Phelps and that bunch he rides for, and we'll be rich in no time." As he spoke, his eyes kept darting back toward the sheriff's office across the street.

Bob and Ernie Bristol looked at each other. Ernie shrugged, his rifle hanging in his hand, a big pistol standing in the waist of his trousers. "Well, I say we don't wait here all damn evening for them," Bob said. "What's taking them so long anyway?"

"Paperwork, more than likely," Hook Stevins grinned. "It's getting to where lawmen sling more lead from a pencil than from a firearm. That ain't bothering me a bit, though." He cast a sidelong glance at Ernie Bristol. "What about you, Ernie?"

"I ain't thinking about it. All I want is to say I'm the one shot that big Indian sucker."

"Then you better not quit on him once you start," Hook Stevins threw in. "You heard how he took that bullet the other day. That big hoss is already up and around."

Ernie Bristol spat and ran a hand across his mouth. "That's because the shooter had no experience shooting Indians. See, I grew up shooting them."

"I wish they'd come on if they're coming," Bob Bristol whispered almost to himself.

Ernie elaborated. "What you have to do with a big sucker like him is put that first shot right straight in his chest, knock him back a step." Ernie Bristol gestured with his free hand, showing them. "Now he's hit, his arms fly out like this . . . leaves him wide open. Second shot, *bang*! Same place, maybe a little higher, before he can gain his balance. Now he ain't dead yet, but he's getting there." Ernie grinned. "Third shot, right here, *pow*!" He tapped his forehead. "And that'll do it. All that's left to do is draw up that ol' scalping knife—"

"Ernie Bristol!" Twojack Roth's voice boomed along the alleyway, cutting Bristol off. Bristol froze with his free hand up as if it were holding a knife blade to his hairline.

"Oh, Jesus," Ernie Bristol whispered, seeing the two lawmen with the evening sun to their backs— Twojack on the left, his big frame seeming to fill the alley.

Hook Stevins gave Ernie a quick wild-eyed glance. "Thank you, you loud-mouth son of a bitch!"

Bob-boy Bristol managed to step to one side, his pistol already out, but still held down close to his thigh.

Twojack said to Sullivan Hart in a low tone, his eyes still fixed on the three gunmen, "How do you want them?"

"Alive if we can," said Hart, "one of them anyway." He stood with a pistol in each hand. "Ready when you are."

"I've got Ernie." Twojack raised his voice loud enough for Ernie Bristol to hear him.

"All right, boys," Sullivan Hart called out, "either drop 'em or make 'em sing!"

"Wait!" Ernie Bristol shouted, but it was too late. Bob-Boy and Hook swung their weapons up.

Hart would take no chance on Hook Stevins's big shotgun in a narrow alley. Before Stevins got the ten-gauge up and leveled, two shots hit him in the chest, spinning him around. The shotgun swung sideways as it fired and went off beneath Bob-boy's chin, blasting him high into the air. The pistol in Bob-boy's hand fired a shot straight down his thigh, and flames licked along his leg as he flew backward.

Beside Bob-boy, Ernie Bristol jerked back a step, Twojack's first shot hitting him square in the chest, making his arms spread wide. Twojack's second shot hit him a little higher. The third shot lifted Ernie's hat from his head, spinning it backward above a rise of blood and brain matter. From the street, a woman who'd just stepped down from the boardwalk screamed and jumped back. Ernie Bristol's body slammed to the ground at her feet. Blood splattered her dress. She screamed louder, until an arm reached as if from out of nowhere and jerked her out of sight.

"Are you all right, Roth?" Sullivan Hart asked without taking his eyes off Hook Stevins, who lay against the side of the mercantile wall, the shotgun only inches from his quivering hook-hand.

"I'm all right. You?" Twojack reloaded his pistol as they stepped forward.

"I'm good." Stepping forward, Hart raised the pistol in his right hand, leveling it at Hook Stevins. "Get your hook away from the scattergun, Stevins."

"Hell . . ." Hook Stevins gasped, blood running from his lips. "I can't . . . do nothing, with it . . ."

Hart stepped in and kicked the shotgun away. On the street, above the sound of the woman still screaming, horses nickered and stirred at the hitch rail. "Don't tell me this was because I arrested you that time way back," Hart said, stooping down over Stevins.

"Naw . . . it was for hire. Cleveland . . . Phelps paid us."

Roth and Hart looked at each other. "I hate to ask you this, Hook," Hart said, "but do you have any of that money left?"

Hook Stevins saw the embarrassed expression on Sullivan Hart's face. He coughed up a weak trickle of blood. "In . . . my vest. Go on, take it . . . I won't be needing it. Them either . . ." He tried nodding at the Bristol brothers. His eyes lingered on Bob-boy for a second. "Lord . . . I blew his head . . . plumb off." He coughed again and muttered under his breath, "Damn . . . *Los Pistoleros*. That's what I get for trying to . . . better myself." His eyes glazed over then, and his head slumped lifeless onto his shoulder.

Hart stood up, the money from Hook Stevins's vest pocket in his hand. He folded the money and shoved it inside his bibbed shirt. "This feels wrong, Twojack."

"You asked him, he agreed," Roth said. "There's something that seems fair about it to me, us using Cleveland Phelps's money to track down him and *Los Pistoleros*."

As they stood looking at the bodies, Sheriff Kay crept around the corner of the building with a rifle trained at them. When they saw his figure, they swung their pistols at him. Kay's face turned chalk white. "Boys, it's me!"

"Come on in, Sheriff." Sullivan faced him as Twojack bent down and, careful to not get his hands bloody, fished a handful of dollar bills from Bob Bristol's vest pocket. "You've caught us in the midst of robbing the dead."

"If they're not complaining, neither am I." Sheriff Kay stepped into the alley, lowering his rifle. His eyes scanned the bodies on the ground. "Do you deputies always live like this?"

"No, Sheriff Kay. Just since we got on this case." Hart nodded down at Hook Stevins. "He said Cleveland Phelps hired them to kill us. So maybe we're starting to get on the right people's nerves."

At the edge of the alley a crowd started to form around the body of Ernie Bristol. A lank hound squeezed its way through a forest of legs, poked its nose down to Ernie's wet bloody chest, and licked it. "I best break them up," Sheriff Kay said to Sullivan Hart. "The prisoner's ready when you are." He turned and raised his voice to the crowd, stepping toward them as he shooed them on with his hands. "All right . . . it's all over. A couple of you give me a hand hauling these bodies out of here. The rest of you, go on about your business."

Twojack Roth shook his head as the sheriff cleared the crowd away. When they were gone, he handed Hart the money he'd taken from Bob Bristol's vest pocket. "I've never seen a manhunt like this in my life. Do you suppose Quick Charlie Sims is having this much trouble on his end?"

Hart smiled slightly. "I hope he is." Hart shoved the money down into his shirt pocket. "You know when Judge Parker sent him out with me, I swore to myself I wouldn't get caught up in anything Sims said or did." He spread his gloved hands. "Now look at me . . . scraping together money to get to Chicago just because he sends us a telegram."

"Don't feel too bad, Sully. Everybody swears they're going to have nothing to do with Sims . . . but they always do. It's just how he is. I've never figured out if he plans things this way or if they just happen."

"Well, either way, he's the only lead we've got." Sullivan Hart straightened his Stetson. "Let's get Barnes and head to the station and get the horses on board. We'll be traveling all night . . . at least we can get some rest on the way."

Chapter 15

Quick Charlie Sims stepped into the caboose and closed the door, muffling the sound of the clacking rails as the train sped north through the night. Red Lohman looked up from the table where his personal weapons, a big Colt pistol, a leather-bound blackjack, and a small derringer lay out in a row. He'd been cleaning the big Colt but upon seeing Sims, he stopped and loaded it, then laid it close to his right hand as he looked up. "Something I can do for you, Quick Charlie?" His tone was less than receptive.

"I live here too, remember?" Sims steadied himself against the sway of the caboose and stepped over to the back door.

"I thought maybe you slept on the card table, a two-bit gambler like you." Red Lohman kept his eyes on him, no humor in his thin grin.

"I'm no gambler, Lohman. A gambler plays the game of chance. I play the game of skill." He stood with his hand on the rear door handle and added, "Things like chess, billiards, poker, golf. But I guess you wouldn't know one from the other."

"Ha! Poker's strictly a game of chance, Sims."

"If you believe that, Red, I'd love to play some draw with you sometime."

"You don't want no part of me, playing poker! I'll tell you something else—you don't ever want to try me on a chessboard either, Quick Charlie."

"Is that a fact? I'm ready to play right now if you are."

"I've got no time for your games, grifter," Red Lohman said.

"Why don't I give you a couple of minutes, let you get yourself ready?" Sims pointed a finger at him and winked.

"The hell is that supposed to mean?" Red Lohman tapped his fingers on the table beside his pistol, making sure Sims got a good look at the gleaming Colt.

Quick Charlie didn't answer. Instead, he opened the door and stepped out onto the rear platform of the caboose. He reached up to the glowing lantern hanging from the edge of the roof and raised the wick as high as it could go, the light growing wider and brighter around him. He found a spare lantern hanging on the back wall of the caboose, and after checking to make sure it was full of fuel, carried it back inside the caboose.

"The hell are you doing with that?" Red Lohman asked, eyeing the lantern. "Don't tell me you're afraid of the dark." He gave Sims a hateful sneer.

Sims ignored him. He stepped to the end of the table, pulled out a wobbly stool, and sat down, keeping his left hand down on one of the three wooden legs to steady it. He set the lantern down on the tabletop and watched the steel wire handle tremble with the vibration on the rails. "We've got to talk about something, Lohman."

"I didn't ask you to join me, Sims. Go talk to your buddy, JT. He might listen to your line. Not me."

"See? That's the very thing we need to discuss—this bad attitude of yours." He leaned a bit closer. "No wonder JT wants me to kill you."

Red Lohman was not taken aback by Sims's words. He only braced himself, the butt of his big Colt an inch from his fingertips. Sims wasn't going to make a move on him. If he was, he'd never have given him that kind of warning. Red Lohman realized it, and settled back on his short stool, glaring at him. "What kind of trick is this, Sims? I'm ready for your move any time you feel like making it."

"It's no trick, Lohman." As Sims spoke, he slowly opened his coat with his left hand. "And I'm not making a move. I'm unarmed." He slowly ran his hand inside his lapel, keeping his eyes on Lohman's, and pulled out a folded bearer bond and laid his hand down over it on the table. "Priest has me on a bad spot. I'm trying to get off it. Hoping maybe you'll help me out." He moved his hand back off the bearer bond, unfolded it, and let Red Lohman get a good look at it.

Lohman's eyes gleamed. "Fifty thousand dollars?" He looked back up at Sims. "This thing can't be real . . . it's not even made out to anybody."

"Of course it's not real, Lohman. But that's not keeping JT Priest from making me cash it for him. Get my drift? He's got a blue million of these things in his safe . . . all ready and waiting to be signed and cashed."

Red Lohman studied the bond, not touching it yet, but his eyes gleaming more and more as they passed across the blank signature line. "Hell, anybody can sign one of these and cash it." He stared closer as if to confirm it to himself. Sims saw that his mind was already thinking of the staggering possibilities. "Does Mister Mabrey know about this?"

"Are you kidding, Lohman? Think I'd be coming to you if this was something Mabrey was in on?" He shook his head. "Uh-uh. This is JT Priest, by himself, getting rich. Why do you think he's letting things get out of hand. What does he care? He tells me he's ready to drop *Los Pistoleros* and go his own way with these babies."

Lohman gave him a wary, puzzled look. "What's this got to do with him wanting you to kill me?"

"Use your head, Lohman. He's afraid you're going to find out and tell Mabrey."

"Oh?" Lohman studied his eyes. Sims could see the wheels in his head turning faster and faster.

"Yeah, but me, I *want* Mabrey to know. Priest is going to get me thrown into prison doing this—or worse! I don't want Mabrey thinking I had a part in anything that's going to come back and cause him trouble. I know he'll kill me."

"So you want me to get word to Mabrey? Not let Priest know you've sold him out to me?"

"Exactly." Sims started to fold the bond. He hesitated just long enough to give Red Lohman time to stop him from picking it up.

"Not so fast, Sims." Lohman's hand came out and pressed down on the bond. "You say he's got how many of these?" He picked the bond up and turned it back and forth in his hands.

Sims gave him a flat, level stare. "More than I'd care to sit and count. How many would you have if you ever got started printing them?" Sims shrugged. "There's a million or two at least. But that's not important. The main thing is, I don't want to be involved. I enjoy living too much."

Red Lohman grinned. "Too scared to get rich? That doesn't sound like the Quick Charlie I heard about. Mabrey says you would snake the devil out of hell. What do you want from me?"

"If I were that slick, I wouldn't be wanting anything from you, would I? If this gets to Mabrey, Priest is dead. That puts you up a notch, into his place. All I want in return is *out*. Can you give me that?"

Sims watched Red Lohman work it over in his mind—take the news to Mabrey, or keep quiet about the bonds, jump in and make himself a fortune? Sims could almost hear Lohman asking himself as he studied the bond. "Is it a deal, Lohman?" He watched Red Lohman keep his eyes on the bond. A small muscle twitched in his bearded jaw.

"Well, is it, Lohman?" Sims reached out with his

right hand to shake on it, having to nudge Red Lohman to get his attention.

"Huh?" Lohman cut his gaze from the bearer bond to Sims's extended hand. His guard was down now and Sims knew it. "Oh, sure. Why not?" Lohman raised his right hand to shake on the deal, moving it up away from the pistol butt—the very thing Sims wanted him to do.

Lohman knew he'd made a mistake the split second Sims's hand clamped onto his. He tried to jerk his hand back, but Sims had him. "Check!" Sims grinned, his left hand snatching the short stool from beneath him as he rose up. "And mate." The stool flashed in a wide circle and broke apart across the side of Red Lohman's head.

Quick Charlie Sims stepped back and straightened his lapels. "See? You weren't ready for chess at all." He picked up the folded bearer bond and shoved it down into Red Lohman's shirt pocket. Lohman lay knocked out cold across the table, a trickle of blood running from a rising welt above his right ear. This ought to get Mad-dog Mabrey out on the prowl, Sims thought, picturing Mabrey's face when he saw the phony bonds instead of money in the carpetbag Priest had taken to him. Now Red Lohman would show up with another bond, telling Mabrey about JT's plans.

Sims reached inside his belt and took out the key to his severed handcuffs. He unlocked each of them and dropped them on the table, then stepped over to the tool cabinet in the front corner of the car. He took out a small wrench along with a nut and bolt he spotted a few days ago. At the table, Sims slipped the bolt through the two cuff chains and tightened it to the steel nut with the wrench. He tested the repaired handcuffs, then put them in his pocket.

Sims picked up the lantern, lit it with a match, and turning the wick up high, stepped through the door and onto the platform between the caboose and the next car forward. He steadied himself to the sway of the train, hung the glowing safety lantern on the front of the caboose, then stepped to the other platform, bending down below the platform and placing both hands on the coupling lever. Maintaining a firm pressure on the lever, Sims waited until the tension on the coupling slackened with the bump and sway of the caboose, then he jerked hard on the lever.

"And there you go, Red," Sims whispered to himself, watching the caboose fall back away from the train, the glowing lantern growing dimmer until it became a small diamond in the dark night. He turned, stepped inside the car, and picked up the pistol JT Priest had given him to kill Red Lohman with from atop a wooden crate where he'd laid it. He cocked the pistol, then reached out through the open door and fired a shot into the air before closing the door behind him.

In the engine, the fireman yelled at the engineer above the roar of the train, "Was that a gunshot?"

"A what?" the engineer yelled back without taking his eyes off the darkness ahead.

"Gunshot, damn it! Did you hear a gunshot coming from back there?"

"I don't know. I might have. You're apt to hear most anything, this bunch we're railing for."

"Well, I know I heard it," the fireman shouted.

The train bored on through the gloom. Finally, the engineer yelled over his shoulder, "I think when we get to the roundhouse in Chicago, I'm dragging up off this job."

"I been thinking it for a while myself," shouted the fireman. He moved closer to the engineer's ear. "Just between us, I been getting a sneaking suspicion that these boys might be outlaws."

At the sound of the pistol shot, JT Priest had stood up and waited for a tense second before walking out of the Pullman and through the big freight car. Half-

way along the aisle he spotted Quick Charlie Sims
swaying toward him, a ghastly expression on his
face. JT Priest recognized the look and chuckled.
"What's the matter, Sims? Have you got no stomach
for killing?"

Without answering, Sims held the pistol out to him
butt first and shook his head. "I need a drink, JT."

"In a minute." Priest caught Sims's arm as Sims
tried to walk on to the Pullman car. "First, let's go
make sure that sucker's dead."

"Believe me, JT, you don't want to see it. It's pretty
messy." Sims tried to pull away from him. But JT
shook him to a halt.

"Let me straighten you out on something, Sims.
You work for me now. I say jump, you get to jump-
ing." He shoved the pistol Sims had handed him
down into his empty holster and gave Sims a smug
look. "I put the gun in your hand and made you use
it. I'm in charge. You're mine now. You got that?"

Sims spread his hands in submission. "Whatever
you say, boss. I'll go back there with you, but I don't
want to look at him."

"Jesus, Sims. Is there something wrong with you?"
JT Priest walked back through the swaying car with
Sims right behind him. "What kind of sporting man
are you, you can't stand the sight of a little blood?"

"Just weak I suppose."

Sims dropped back a step when Priest reached out
and swung the door open. He started to step out and
cross over onto the platform of the caboose. But the
sight of the caboose not being where it should startled him, and he grabbed both sides of the door
frame and held on. "What the hell has happened
here?" He looked back and forth in the rush of open
air as if the caboose might yet appear.

"Bad news, *Tuck*," Sims said behind him. "Looks
like you've just landed in the rough."

"Why you double-crossing son of a bitch!" JT
Priest swung around facing him. "I'll kill you!" His

hand went to the pistol at his hip. But his expression turned from rage to stunned disbelief as his hand slapped against an empty holster.

Priest's pistol was in Sims's hand, leveled only inches away from his face. "More bad news, Tuck." The pistol cocked and pressed up under Priest's sweaty chin. "You're working for *me* now." There was no smile on Quick Charlie Sims's face, only a cold killing stare full of deadly resolve. Sims held the newly repaired handcuffs up with his other hand and let them swing back and forth on his finger.

Chapter 16

The passenger car of the Missouri & Illinois Night-hawk Express was not crowded when Sullivan Hart and Twojack Roth led their prisoner aboard at Little Red Springs. A thin man wearing a gaily striped suit looked up at Briley Barnes, saw the handcuffs linking him to Sullivan Hart, and stiffened upright. "Oh, my," he whispered. He fidgeted in his seat, then stood up and moved farther away from them. Hart and Roth looked back at the few other passengers as they took seats across the aisle from one another, Hart nudging Barnes into the window seat, then sitting down beside him.

"What if I said I have to go to the jake?" Barnes asked, the train still building steam before leaving the station.

"Not until we're well under way, Barnes," Sullivan Hart replied, settling into his seat. "This is going to be a long ride. Don't start aggravating me now."

When the train conductor passed by and took their tickets, Hart looked back over his shoulder and made a mental note of the other passengers. The thin man in the striped suit sat five empty seats away. Behind him, three seats farther back, sat an elderly clergyman with a Bible raised to his face. Beside him was an elderly woman who attended a lap full of knitting. At the rear of the car sat a young woman wearing a broad flowered hat, her face obscured behind a delicate lace veil. She held a bundled infant to her bosom and modestly breast-fed it, a wide linen cloth draped down from her shoulder for privacy. She seemed to blush, Hart thought, as her eyes met his through the lace veil. Then she drew the bundled infant closer, adjusted the linen cloth, and lowered her face as Hart touched the brim of his hat toward her, then looked away.

"So how long you figure we'll be, getting to Chicago?" Briley Barnes asked.

"You should know, Barnes." Sullivan Hart settled farther down in his seat and lowered his hat brim over his eyes. "You've made this trip before."

"Nope. We came on horseback and in wagons." Barnes settled down as well.

"You brought the shipment of firearms by wagon?" Hart asked without raising his face. "You never mentioned that."

"Didn't figure it was important." Barnes shrugged.

The train made a short lurch forward, then halted and squeaked. A blast of steam resounded. A bumping sound rumbled along the rails, the slack between nine freight cars, six stock cars, and the passenger coach stretching into a taut line and crawling forward, slow and steady. "From here on, Barnes, you make a tally of everything you didn't think was important and tell me every one of them. You understand?"

Briley Barnes only nodded, his mind already making an attempt at it. Hart and Roth had both told him they would speak to the judge in Chicago on his behalf if he cooperated with them. Barnes was eager to help.

When the train gained speed and leveled out across the prairie at over thirty miles per hour, Roth walked back and stood guard while Hart allowed Barnes to relieve himself down off the platform of the Pullman car. Returning to their seats, the two deputies took turns sleeping, one of them keeping an eye on the prisoner at all times. At midnight, the train stopped long enough to take on water and let the clergyman and the elderly woman off. Then in moments, the train was barreling once more through the velvet night, Twojack Roth awake, but with his head bowed to his chest, his pistol in his hand across his lap.

Three hours passed before Red Lohman lifted his swollen head from the tabletop and looked all around the quiet caboose. It took him a moment to realize the floor was not swaying beneath him. The sound of crickets chirping caught his attention, and he struggled to his feet, staggered to the door, and threw it open. Darkness stretched long past the glow of the safety lantern, and in the vastness of the prairie night he shouted a hollow curse.

When he turned back inside the door and closed it, he began to recall what had happened to him, and his memory became even more clear as his hand rubbed his chest and found the folded bearer bond in his coat pocket. *Damn Quick Charlie Sims!* Lohman staggered to the table and picked up his pistol. Why in the hell had he ever let Sims sit down and begin running his mouth? He should have killed Sims right then, right there. Now he was in big trouble with Mabrey if he didn't straighten this mess out. Lohman pressed a hand to his throbbing head.

He holstered his pistol, took the bearer bond out, and looked at it, then put it away again, this time inside his coat. *Damn Sims and JT Priest too.* He'd find them. Once he got word to Mabrey what they were up to, Mabrey would want him to kill them both. He couldn't think of anything that would please him more. Lohman looked around the caboose. But what was he going to do right now, stuck out here—God knows where—on the Illinois prairie?

Standing there collecting his wits, he cocked his head sideways, taking note that the sound of the crickets had lessened. In the distant darkness behind him he heard the long, low whine of a train whistle. The floor of the caboose began to vibrate slightly. His eyes widened. He hurried back to the rear door and threw it open. The light of the oncoming train seemed to spring up out of the ground, boring toward him, much closer than the whistle had led him to believe.

In the cab of the Missouri & Illinois Nighthawk Express, the engineer had spotted the glow of the safety lantern from a distance of two thousand yards as his engine topped a long low rise and sped forward. His right hand went instinctively to the whistle chain and yanked down. "Uh-oh! Brake 'em down tight, boys!" he yelled aloud, although there was no one there to hear him. His left hand slammed the throttle closed and pulled back hard on the engine brake.

Steel engine wheels screamed in the night beneath the long blast of the steam whistle. Back along the freight cars, the heads of the brakemen sprang up like pigeons from their nests at the sound of the whistle. Brakemen scrambled atop the cars, grabbing the brake wheels and turning them down, the sound of metal on metal shrieking like tortured beasts. "We'll never stop her in time!" one brakeman yelled to himself as he spun the steel brake wheel as fast as he could.

Inside the passenger car, Roth, Hart, and Briley Barnes all rose up at the same time, startled by the noise and the sudden forward lunge of the passenger car. They looked across the aisle at one another, Barnes already trying to sink down to the floor, Hart pulling him back by his cuffed wrist. "What's going on?" Hart shouted above the sound of the whistle blast and screaming steel.

But there was no reply to his words, only the low rumble of cars bumping forward against one another until the slack caught up to the car they were on and jarred them forward, then slamming them back in their seats. In the aisle between them the thin man let out a scream as he sailed forward. His striped suit flashing in the dim light gave him the appearance of some clown gone berserk, doing cartwheels of his own design. Roth and Hart both shot a glance back at the young woman. She sat bowed over the infant, one arm out, bracing herself against the seat in front of her.

The passenger car slid and swayed, and for a long, tense second seemed dangerously close to toppling over on its side. But then it slammed back down onto the tracks, Hart and Roth bouncing high in their seats, clutching the backs of the seats in front of them. A hail of broken boards from the shattered caboose thumped down and skidded back along the car roof. Twojack Roth caught a glimpse of broken red boards sailing past his window in the darkness. Then the whole train came to a shuddering halt.

"Lord God!" Briley Barnes cowered, his free arm shielding his head.

"We've hit something!" Twojack Roth stepped out into the aisle, looking back and forth. At the front of the car, the striped dandy turned facing them, a trickle of blood running down from his flattened nose. He staggered in place, his arms out as if now steadying himself to walk a tightrope.

Sullivan Hart struggled from his seat and stepped out beside Roth, dragging Barnes behind him. "Take it easy," Barnes whined. They hurried to the rear of the car, seeing the young woman rise up from the floor and sink back into her seat, hugging the bundled infant tight against her chest. "Ma'am! Are you all right?" Hart asked, leaning down closer. He heard her sobbing and reached a hand out to the blanket.

But she jerked sideways, pulling the infant away from him, her hat down, her shoulders huddled over her baby like a protecting mountain cat. "Don't touch him! Leave him alone! Get away from us!" she screamed at Hart. She sobbed quietly, the bundle lying crushed against her, as silent as stone.

Hart pulled back from her and cast a glance at Twojack Roth as the Cherokee slid to a halt beside him and Barnes. Roth caught his expression and winced. "Oh, no . . ."

"Ma'am, here now," Twojack coaxed. "Let me have him." He leaned in past Hart and Barnes and as gently as possible tried to pry the bundle from her arms.

"No!" She screamed, pulling away again, this time swinging up from the seat as if to run past them. But Twojack caught her by her cradled arms, stopping her. "Get off! Turn me loose, you son of a bitch!" She slung herself back and forth, still trying to flee. Her hat flew from her head. In her struggle the bundle came halfway out of her arms. She groped for it with one hand as Twojack tried catching it. Then the whole bundle came apart and spilled at her feet between her and Twojack Roth.

"Oh, my God!" Briley Barnes stared down at a floor full of money. So did Hart and Roth, but only for a second until the cocking of a pistol caught their attention. They looked up to see the woman shaking out her long dark hair as she leveled the double-barrel derringer pistol an inch from Twojack's eye.

"All of you, get back!" Kate McCorkle stepped back herself as she hissed at them, "I'll shoot you both! Don't try me!"

"Easy, ma'am. We're both federal deputies." Sullivan Hart raised his free hand in a show of peace, Briley Barnes beside him staring at the bound stacks of money.

"I know what you are! I know *who* you are!" She flashed the pistol back and forth between them in an effort to keep them both covered. "You're the two lawmen hunting Charlie Sims and JT Priest." She gestured the derringer toward the bound stacks of money on the floor. "Now pick it up and give it here. I'm getting off—don't try to stop me!"

Roth and Hart stood stunned, letting the realization sink in. Finally, Sullivan shook his head to clear it. "Ma'am, a lot of things can happen here . . . but your leaving isn't one of them."

"Then you're both going to die," she said in a firm tone.

Twojack Roth pressed closer. "Lady, if I had a dollar for every time I've been shot by one of those peashooters, I could retire on my own ranch." He turned to Sullivan Hart without taking his eyes off Kate McCorkle. "What do you want me to do, Sully?"

"Everybody hold still." Hart turned his head slightly toward Briley Barnes. "Barnes, do you know this woman?"

"Yep . . . I saw her in Chicago with JT Priest. She's his woman. Her name's Kate something-or-other."

"McCorkle," Kate said, "and I'm my own woman." Her eyes and derringer fixed on Twojack Roth. "I used to be with JT Priest. Next time I see him, though, he's a dead man."

"You're the woman who was on the train when the three gunmen ambushed us in Little Red Springs, aren't you?"

"I was there. I didn't have anything to do with it—neither did Charlie. I'm not going to see you hunt him down like a dog, either."

"Ma'am," said Hart, "we are not hunting Quick Charlie Sims."

"Yes, you are. I knew who you two were the minute you got on the train last night."

"Lady," Roth cut in, "if you have any sense at all, listen to what he's trying to tell you—"

His words stopped as the conductor stepped into the far end of the car and called out, "Is everybody all right back here?"

Kate McCorkle's eyes flashed toward the sound of

his voice, and in that instant, Roth clamped his big hand down around the derringer and pointed it at the floor. Both barrels fired, raising splinters inches from his feet. Kate struggled against him until his free arm lifted her up over his shoulder Then she beat his broad back with her fist until he wrenched the derringer from her hand and tossed her over on a seat. "We're all right back here," Hart called out to the conductor.

"What's going on there?" The conductor took a few cautious steps forward, the man in the striped suit joining him, still holding his fingers to his bloody nose.

"We're federal deputies," Roth said as the conductor ventured closer. "This is a matter of the law. What did we hit?"

The conductor stopped. "Some damn fool left a crummy sitting on the track. Can you imagine that?"

"I'm getting to where I can imagine most anything," Hart replied. "Tell the engineer we'll be out there to help as soon as we check on our horses." He turned back to Kate McCorkle as the conductor and the man in the striped suit left. "Listen real close, Miss McCorkle. The ones we're looking for are JT Priest, Cleveland Phelps, and anybody else connected to *Los Pistoleros*. As far as Quick Charlie Sims is concerned, I'd personally like to twist his neck like a watch stem. But he is not the focus of this manhunt. You're going to have to take our word on it."

"The fact is, lady," Twojack Roth added, shoving her derringer down into his belt, "we believe Charlie Sims is trying in his own way to lead us to *Los Pistoleros*."

"Oh?" Kate McCorkle eyed the derringer in Twojack's belt, thinking about the extra cartridges she had in her dress pocket.

"That's right, Miss McCorkle." Sullivan Hart pushed up his hat brim and let out a breath. "We really need to talk about some things."

Outside, the engineer stood among the brakemen, all of them holding up glowing lanterns, looking at the mangled remnants of the red caboose strewn about them in pieces. A set of steel wheels lay on its side ten yards from the track, one wheel still turning. Another set of wheels lay upside down in the tall grass on the other side of the track.

"Boys, that was a close one," one of the brakemen whispered in the hushed silence. "Damned lucky we didn't derail." He reached out with a toe and kicked a flattened man's hat to one side. "Luckier than whoever was wearing this hat, anyway."

The engineer stepped forward and picked up the busted lantern frame from among the debris. "At least somebody was smart enough to leave a lantern burning." He looked at the high-turned wick, then pitched the broken lantern away. "Let's check the engine, clear the rails . . . and highball the hell out of here."

As the railroad men stood staring at the wreckage, Red Lohman moved forward out of the weeds. He ran in a crouch, his pistol in his hand, until he straightened up, standing with his back flat against the stock car door. Without a sound, he lifted the latch, let it down silently, then slid the door open just enough to crawl up inside. Horses nickered low as he slipped over to the nearest one, picked up a set of reins from a tack peg on the wall, and prepared the horse for the road. He didn't take time to saddle the horse right then, but instead picked up a saddle from a rack and carried it as he eased the horse over to the door.

The sound of the brakemen's voices drifted back to him. Red Lohman reached down and slid the boarding ramp out to the ground. He tensed, listening. When the voices paid no attention to the board hitting the ground, he led the horse down and out into the grass. Then he slipped atop the big horse, the saddle hanging from his hand down the horse's side, and heeled the

animal farther out into the darkness away from the
idling train.

"Did you hear something, Sully?" Twojack Roth
asked as the four of them stepped down to the
ground, Hart leading Briley Barnes while Roth
helped Kate McCorkle. She fell against him as her
foot touched the ground. Her hand slipped the derringer from his belt, but his hand caught her wrist,
took the gun, and put it back in his belt, as if he'd
been expecting her move.

"Yes, I did. From back near the stock car." Sullivan
Hart drew his pistol, pulling Barnes along behind
him. Twojack Roth followed close behind. At the
open door to the stock car, they spread out. Twojack
Roth slipped forward, up into the car. In a moment
he called out, "Whoever was here is gone now."
From the ground, Hart saw the glow of a lantern
appear as Roth lit it and stepped back into the open
doorway. "So's one of those Kentucky racehorses
being shipped north," Roth added. "If you want me
to, I can be saddled up and tracking in about five
minutes."

Sullivan Hart blew out a tired breath. His eyes fol-
lowed the hoofprints in the flickering lantern light to
where the tall grass lay bent in the darkness. "No.
We've got enough to do right now." He looked at
Briley Barnes, then at the woman. "The only tracking
I want to do is on the streets of Chicago."

Chapter 17

The three-car train rolled slower and slower past the small farms and flat grasslands surrounding the city. Soon the passing shadows of grain silos in the evening sunlight fell away, replaced by telegraph poles and endless wood-slat cattle pens where steers bawled and stood pressed together in a sea of glistening horns. The cattle pens soon fell away, and tarred and metal shed roofs drifted by.

Beyond the low shed roofs, the blank faces of ragged children and of old men who leaned on rickety back porch banisters followed the rhythmic clack of rail as the train slowed even more, making its way into the Chicago railway station. "This is crazy, Sims!" JT Priest sweated, sitting with his right wrist cuffed to the arm of his heavy chair. "For God sakes, man, look at what we could do together—just the two of us. To hell with Mabrey and *Los Pistoleros*. We can be rich! Don't do this to me! Please, I'm begging you."

Quick Charlie Sims sat across the green felt-topped table with one knee crossed over the other, and JT Priest's pistol lying in his hand. He stared at Priest without a trace of a smile, no gleam in his eyes, no expression on his face. "Game's over, Tuck. You played me, and you lost." He leaned forward slightly, picked up the bottle of bourbon from the table, and reached over and filled Priest's shot glass, then his own. He then leaned back in his chair and sipped the bourbon.

Earlier in the day Sims had the engineer stop the train in the town of New Hope Siding. With JT Priest's pistol beneath his jacket, Sims had escorted him to the New Hope Sidings Bank, where he'd stood back a couple of feet to the side, making certain Priest used his own name as he cashed a bearer bond in the amount of twenty thousand dollars—a large amount for a small-town bank. There was no way the teller would forget Priest's name or face if ever called upon. Priest knew it, and it had him worried.

On the table lay a short stack of phony bearer bonds—that had him worried too. But what had JT Priest worried the most was the string of dried human ears that Quick Charlie had taken from a lockbox beneath the bed in the sleeping quarters and pitched onto the table only moments ago. Two of those ears had once belonged to Federal Marshal Coleman Hart.

JT Priest tried to give a shaky smile. "If this was a game, where's my chance to get even?"

"I've never understood a man thinking someone owed him a chance to get even when the whole object of the game was to win in the first place." Sims sipped at his bourbon. "But you don't have to wait for my invitation. If you've got something left, pitch it on the table. I came here in handcuffs with the law on my trail and nothing in my pockets. You liked seeing me that way . . . so I threw myself in the jackpot. Now you ask for a chance to get even?"

"What do you want from me, Sims? Just name it." JT Priest looked even more desperate now that the train had stopped—Sims had timed it that way.

"I can't think of a thing. What have you got worth playing for?" Sims shrugged and looked out through the window as the train finally ground to a halt. Sims had told him everything, about stuffing the carpetbag with fake bearer bonds and taking the money. He'd told him about sending Hart and Roth the telegram telling them the train was headed to Chicago. The lawmen should be arriving any time. The one thing he hadn't mentioned was the bank job in Creed. Priest would have to bring that up on his own. And he was about to, Quick Charlie could tell.

A tense silence passed. Then Priest tossed back the shot of bourbon and ran his free hand across his mouth. "Okay, Sims. Let's quit fooling around. I know what you want. I'll give it to you."

"Oh? Really? What is that, Tuck?" Sims cocked his head slightly.

"The bank . . . the one in Creed. I set you up for it. I shot the guard with a Colt Thunderer, then dropped it on the floor . . . it had your name carved into the grips."

Sims shook his head real slow. "That was the best you could come up with? And you call yourself a sporting man?"

"Well, it worked." Priest looked down, embarrassed. "Now, there, I admit it."

"Little good your confession does me, Tuck. What good will it do me to tell the law you admitted it? Who's going to take my word on it?" He shrugged again. "Sorry, bad offer."

"Jesus, Sims! Listen to me! When Mabrey sees the money's missing and hears about the bearer bonds, I'm dead! If Hart shoots me, or if he takes me back to Fort Smith to hang for murder, either way I'm dead. I'll take my chances on a fast horse and a head start. I'll sign a confession for the bank in Creed, saying you had nothing to do with it. Take these cuffs off me. What do you say?"

Sims sipped his bourbon, seeming to consider it for a second. Then he said, "Naw, I don't think so. Those cuffs look good on you, Tuck. I'd rather wait and see who shows up first, the two deputies or some of Mad-dog Mabrey's *Los Pistoleros*. Besides, it's been a long time since you lived on the run. I'd hate for you to get out there and starve to death . . . cheat everybody out of killing you."

Priest ran his hand across his wet brow. "Come on, Sims, give me a break. I sign a confession, you're off the hook. I'll be on the run for murder anyway. A bank robbery charge isn't going to make me much difference."

Sims took a deep breath and let it out, allowing Priest to talk him into it. "Okay, Tuck. Just to show you I'm a sport." He cocked an eye at Priest. "But I can't promise the cuffs will be off in time for you to get out of here."

"Then hurry it up, Sims! Get a pen and some paper."

Sims stood up, walked behind the bar, and brought back a pen, some ink, and a writing tablet. He dropped the items on the table and sat back down. "Start writing." Sims reached into his shirt, took out the folded legal document he'd taken from the safe, and pitched it out on the table. "While you're signing, sign this too."

JT Priest looked at it, then back at Sims. "Sign my shares of stock over to you? You're out of your mind," he hissed, sweat beading on his brow.

"Suit yourself, Tuck," Sims said. "But I won't take one without the other."

Priest thought about it, but only for a second. Whatever he signed now, he'd deny later on if he had to. Getting out of here was the main thing. "Damn you, Sims!" Priest reached out, snatched the folded document and spread it out on the table.

Kate McCorkle looked into Sullivan Hart's eyes and told him the only thing she could tell him when he asked about the money. "It's money I managed to put aside over the past year." Her answer drew a short laugh from Briley Barnes.

"You must have had one hell of a sugar jar," Barnes offered.

Kate gestured at Barnes and said to Hart, "He's going to make me lose my temper. Believe me, he doesn't want that to happen."

Sullivan Hart yanked on Barnes's handcuffs to shut him up. "There's close to a hundred thousand dollars there, ma'am?" Hart nodded at the bundle of money lying on the seat between her and Twojack Roth. "Unless it's marked and proves to be stolen, we have no claim on it. It's not against the law how a person decides to carry their money." He looked at Twojack Roth, then back at her with a questioning gaze.

She shrugged. "Priest has men everywhere. I didn't want to be spotted. I figured it was also a good way to keep my money close at hand. Who'd be watching for a woman carrying a baby?" She wasn't about to mention the other two hundred thousand she'd left in the leather valise and shipped off to New Orleans.

"Well, it had us fooled." Sullivan Hart sank back into his seat, feeling the sway of the train. He took out the keys to the handcuffs, unlocked them from his left wrist and pulled Briley Barnes's arm forward. "Twojack, do you want to take Barnes out back and let him relieve himself?"

"Sure," Twojack Roth replied, standing up and steadying himself. "Come on, Barnes."

"Hey, I'm fine till we reach Chicago," Barnes said, not wanting to miss out on anything.

"Come on, Barnes, let's go." Twojack Roth took the empty cuff from Hart, raised Briley Barnes to his feet, and pulled him forward down the aisle.

Once they were gone, Sullivan Hart leaned forward in his seat. "Ma'am, another couple of hours and we'll be in Chicago. If I find out you and Quick Charlie Sims are pulling some sort of scheme, it's going to go bad for him—you too, if I find out you're carrying stolen money. How far I investigate you and your money depends on how honest you're being right now."

"I'm telling you the truth. I've broken no laws. Like I told you earlier, Deputy. Charlie has no idea I'm coming. He sent me south. He said he was taking *Los Pistoleros* down. If you know Charlie Sims, he usually does what he sets out to do."

"I'm starting to believe that." Hart offered a trace of a tired smile. "Then why didn't you go?"

"I couldn't, not with everything that's hanging over his head. Charlie wouldn't do me that way if it were the other way around. For a long time, I thought he'd run out on me. Now that I know he didn't . . ." She paused, thinking about something. "Simply put, I owe him, Deputy. Do you have to take him back to Fort Smith? Charlie didn't rob that bank in Creed. I'd stake my life on it. If he did, he wouldn't be going to all this trouble. He'd just disappear, and you'd never see him again."

"He's got to go back and stand trial. There's nothing I can do about that. But I agree, ma'am. If he shows me something to prove his innocence, I'll see to it the judge in Creed knows about it." He shook his head slowly. "But there's a matter of a guard being killed. It'll take some strong proof."

"Listen to me." Kate McCorkle leaned forward. "He wouldn't want me telling you this, but Quick Charlie Sims has never killed anybody in his life. He's never even shot anyone that I know of. He might use a gun as a prop, like some kind of stage actor. But it's all a bluff, a part of his game. He'd never use one—that would be beneath him. If you understood Charlie, you'd know what I mean. It's all a matter of how he can make things happen with his wits, not with a weapon."

"I understand, ma'am. And what you're saying may be true. But in my job, somebody points a gun at you, you don't stop to consider whether or not it's a bluff—you can't risk it. I'll be honest with you, ma'am, my partner and I are not used to this kind of situation. We're only a couple of frontier lawmen doing the best we can. We get on a trail and we follow it. Where that trail ends, odds are, somebody dies. We've seen signs along the way that Quick Charlie is working with us, but it's not something we'll stake our lives on."

"But you can give him some room, can't you? You told me yourself that if it wasn't for Charlie waving from the train the other day, you wouldn't have had a guess which way to go."

He nodded. "That's true. He even sent us a telegram to steer us to Chicago. But at the end of every hunt there's that time when the hammer cocks. At that point, it doesn't matter who or what brought you there. I'll give Sims what room I can. But room will be scarce. He better understand that."

Chapter 18

The rat's greasy tail whipped back and forth in the dirt, its rear feet spread to steady the tin can. With its head inside the can, it licked and gnawed at the remnants of dried beans. The tin can scooted a few inches across the ground until it stopped against the bottom edge of a rotting shed wall. "Welcome to the big city," said Clifford Mallory, drawing his rifle from its boot, his horse stepping quarterwise out of the line of riders.

At the sound of the rifle cocking, Cleveland Phelps looked back over his shoulder. "Damn it, Clifford, put the gun away. Use your head." Then Phelps called back to Clifford's older brother, "Harvey, you told me he swore off of dope and regained his senses."

Clifford answered for his brother. "I never said I quit altogether. I just backed off some. Besides, anybody says opium is habit-forming is a damned fool. I've been smoking it for years. Look at me, steady as a rock." Clifford grinned at a couple of faces turning toward him as he extended his cocked rifle.

"Do something with him, Harvey," Phelps called back.

A low ripple of laughter stirred across the other horsemen. Clifford Mallory had already taken aim at the feeding rat's rump sticking out of the can. But, casting a glance at his older brother, Harvey, and seeing the look of disdain on his brother's face, Clifford Mallory cursed under his breath, uncocked his rifle, and shoved it back into its boot. "Sorry, Cleveland . . . I see a rat, I'm bound to shoot it."

"Not in this town, you don't. It's illegal. They don't even allow a man to *carry* a rifle around in public."

"What kind of a sorry-assed law is that?" Raymond Cloud passed a glance all around.

"They don't have law here," Cleveland Phelps answered with a sliver of a smile. "What they have instead is a police department."

"Damn," said Raymond Cloud. "People stand for that?"

Without answering Cloud, Cleveland Phelps nodded, staring straight ahead from beneath his drooping hat brim. "You'll do some rat shooting before this job's over, Clifford." His long silver gray hair spread down on the shoulders of his riding duster. The line of horsemen moved forward at a walk along the narrow alley, bordered on one side by the rail yard. Weaving around broken bottles and debris, the horsemen looked like apparitions from some different world, their long dusters draped down to their bootwells, sunlight glinting off brass rifle butt plates and spur rowels.

Children stared from rear windows and back porch rails, their mouths agape; contrary to their custom of running out to investigate anything out of the ordinary, they shied farther back. Where blowflies spun above the carcass of a dead cat, the horses stepped wide of the stench and shook out their manes and blew long breaths as if to clear the foul air. At the head of the meandering line sat Cleveland Phelps, followed by Raymond Cloud, then Otis Farnsworth. The Mallory brothers rode behind Farnsworth, and behind them, two hardened killers out of Texas, Max Dupre and young Jake Walls.

"I don't know about opium," Otis Farnsworth said, his heavy body turning back in his saddle toward the Mallory brothers, his right hand support-

ing him on his horse's rump. "But I once quit drinking for three weeks and it nearly killed me—hands
shook so bad I couldn't take a pizzle without abus-
ing myself."

At the end of the line, Max Dupre shot Jake Walls
a glance and asked, "First time in a city, Jake?"

"Yep." Jake Walls gestured toward the backs of
soot-smoked brick buildings where a clothesline full
of flapping men's work trousers and longjohns hung
in the breeze. "How do people live like this?"

Max Dupre chuckled. "They're work mules, Jake.
They don't know no better." A ragged yellow goat
with one horn missing stepped out from beside a
wood pile and bleated at them. "*Baa*, yourself, you
sonsabitch," Dupre said, shooting a long stream of
tobacco juice that splattered between the goat's front
hooves, forcing it back a step. "You don't look a
damn bit better."

When a long train swept past them, slowing in its
approach to the station, it blocked their view of the
rest of the rail yard. An idle porter stared from the
crummy deck and offered a halfhearted wave. None
of the men acknowledged him. "I look at a train,"
said Otis Farnsworth, turned forward in his saddle
now and tugging his wide-brimmed Stetson down
on his head, "and all I see is a bank on wheels."

"Speaking of banks," Raymond Cloud cut in, talking to Cleveland Phelps, "what's the word from
Mad-dog Mabrey? We need to get a bank lined up."

"Soon as we get rid of these lawmen," Phelps replied, "we'll get on to something. Mabrey wants us
to help some new flunkies deliver some more rifles
to the Old English Spread—make up for the ones
that burned up. We're going to charge him a damn
good fee for doing this work, you can bet on that. If
JT Priest keeps messing things up, I'm apt to put a
bullet in his eye, whether Mabrey likes it or not."

Otis Farnsworth had started to speak, but just then
his horse swung sideways and let out a painful

nicker. He halted the animal and stepped down as the other riders drew up around him. The horse seemed to be favoring its left foreleg, and raising the hoof to inspect it, Otis cursed.

"What is it, Otis?" Cleveland Phelps swung his horse in closer, looking down as Otis Farnsworth drew a big Bowie knife from the sheath behind his back.

"A blasted roofing nail," Farnsworth said as he picked at the nail with the point of his knife. "He ain't stove up though." He set the horse's hoof back down to the ground and watched the horse test it, then settle its weight into place.

"If you'd shoe that horse now and then, stuff like that wouldn't happen," Phelps said. "I had mine shod coming through Missouri. Got a set of them thick Thorenson store-boughts with the big T stamped on them."

"My horse doesn't deserve any Thorenson store-boughts," said Otis Farnsworth. "He and I ain't been getting along that well." A short laugh stirred among the other men.

While the men watched Otis and his horse, Cleveland Phelps turned his horse away, took out a cigar, rounded it in his mouth, and lit it, his hands cupped around the match flame. After he took a long draw and blew the flame out, his eyes caught sight of the three-car train sitting on a siding track away from the main station rails. He stared, shaking the match out and flipping it away. "I'll be damned," he said to himself. Then he raised his voice to the men behind him. "Boys, speak of the devil and he shall appear."

"Looks like JT's lost his crummy," Otis Farnsworth said, stepping back up on his horse. Phelps chuckled, drawing on his cigar.

"Either that, or Quick Charlie Sims managed to talk him out of it some way," Raymond Cloud said.

"I met that sucker once, shooting dice in New Mexico. I wouldn't trust him no farther than I can spit."

"But you shot dice with him?" Otis Farnsworth turned facing Cloud. "Who won, Raymond?"

"Go to hell, Otis." Raymond Cloud crossed his hands on his saddle horn as they both chuckled under their breath.

Otis said, "Everybody knows better than to fool with Quick Charlie, yet everybody does."

"Not me," Cleveland Phelps growled. "All I've got for him is a bullet in his teeth."

"Then let's get on up there, Cleveland," Clifford Mallory said, ready to kick his horse forward.

"Not so fast, Clifford." Cleveland Phelps raised a gloved hand, holding the others back. His eyes moved fifty yards across the rail yard to where he spotted the two deputies' battered Stetsons as they stepped down from a train. "Let's take a minute here. Looks like JT might have himself a following."

"That's too good to be true, boss," said Jake Walls, seeing the two tall Stetson hats himself. "It'd sure save us some time and trouble to shoot them right here and be done with it."

"A gunfight? Right here? In Chicago City?" Phelps gave Jake Walls a stern look, but it turned into a trace of a smile. "I don't know what they'd think of an idea like that in Texas, Jake. But I like it. I like it a lot."

After stepping off the train, Sullivan Hart and Twojack Roth had spotted JT Priest's short train—minus its caboose—sitting on a siding track, but they had not spotted the riders as the other long incoming train had blocked them from sight. Hart pulled Briley Barnes alongside of him. "All right, here's how we're going to do this." As he spoke, he loosened the cuff from his wrist and reached out, snapping it around Kate McCorkle's. He said to them, "Both of you stay close. If you try to make a run for it, I'll shoot Barnes in the knee."

"Hey! Why me?" Barnes asked with a nervous expression.

"Because I've never shot a woman, Barnes. So make sure you don't let her talk you into doing something stupid."

Hart turned to Kate McCorkle. "Ma'am, if Sims plays straight with me, he's got nothing to worry about. So help us make this thing go right. You understand?"

"I understand." She nodded at the bundled blanket, now lying on the ground. "What about my money?"

"Carry it," Hart said, and turned to Twojack Roth beside him. "Give Sims a little room. We'll try to see where he stands on this. But the slightest move out of JT Priest . . ."

"I know," said Twojack Roth. "It'll save us hauling him back to Judge Parker.

The fireman and the engineer stood looking back and forth between Quick Charlie Sims and JT Priest, noting the pistol on Sims's lap and the cuffs on Priest's wrists. "I knew it," the engineer said, placing his hand on his hips. He nodded toward JT Priest. "First time I laid eyes on this beady-eyed tub of lard, I says to myself, 'that ol' boy is an outlaw.' "

The old fireman nodded along with him. "I never said it before, but something just told me you were a lawman the minute you stepped on the train. Wearing them handcuffs didn't fool me. I figured you was up to something." He winked at Sims. "And I was right."

Quick Charlie Sims smiled, his eyes on JT Priest as he spoke to the fireman. "Strange how some folks can always tell."

"So, what are you? A Pinkerton man? A railroad bull?"

"It's best you don't know," Sims said. "I'm count-

ing on the two of you to go on about your business
and keep quiet. Will you do that for me?"

"Hell, yes!" The engineer answered for them both.
"Just make sure the Hughes & Lindsy Company has
our pay ready come the end of the week."

"That's who put you to work?" Sims asked.

"Yep. Right here in Chicago. That's who hired us,
and that's who we expect to cash us in," he said as
he and the fireman turned to the door. "We'll get on
out of here—and we'll not say a word about this."

"Thanks, gentlemen." Sims touched the barrel of
the pistol upward in salute. "It's men like you who
make my job easier."

Once they stepped out and closed the door, Priest
started right in, his face red with rage. "Sims, you
double-crossing snake! I did my part!" He gestured
toward the signed confession lying folded on the
table. "Now do like you promised and cut me loose!"

Sims only stared. "I told you I couldn't promise
you'd be uncuffed in time to—"

"That was a low-handed trick, Sims!" Priest
shouted. "Damn you!"

"Relax, Tuck. I checked the rail schedule. We
shouldn't have long to wait." He took out a gold
watch, checked the time, then put it away.

"That's my watch, Sims! I kept it in the lockbox!"
JT Priest raged.

"I thought I'd do you a favor, Tuck." Sims took
out five one hundred dollar bills, folded them, and
shoved them down into Priest's vest pocket. "Look,
I'm even paying you for it."

Priest looked down at his vest pocket, then back
at Sims. "What's that for?"

"For the watch. It's spending money, Tuck. Before
you go into Parker's jail, you roll that money up nice
and tight and hide it in the best place you can think
of. You'll be surprised what five hundred dollars will
do for you in a place like that. Believe me, as you're

sitting there waiting to hang, the last thing you'll want is to hear a big watch ticking."

"They won't hang me, not on that confession, not if I'm sitting here denying it, saying you forced it out of me. You fool! The only way it's worth anything is if I'm gone when they get here. I thought you'd have enough sense to know that!"

"Or if you're dead, Tuck." Sims leaned forward once more, the pistol tightening in his hand, his face like stone.

Priest swallowed hard, then fell silent.

Quick Charlie Sims added, "Don't you ever know when it's best to just keep your mouth shut, Tuck?" Sims glared at him for a tense second, then collected himself, leaned back in his chair, and laid the pistol back down in his lap.

At a distance of eighty yards, across five sets of rails converging into the station, Cleveland Phelps watched through a gap in a board fence as the engineer and fireman stepped down and ambled away from the short train. On the other side, he saw the two deputies follow Briley Barnes and Kate McCorkle across the rail yard. "It's Barnes, that lousy little peckerwood," Phelps whispered to himself. "And sweet Kate McCorkle," he added, smiling. "Now what do you suppose she'd be carrying in that bundle?"

Beside Phelps, at the next gap in the board fence, Raymond Cloud turned to him. "You're going to let them all get inside? If JT is in there, it's going to put him in a bad spot once the shooting starts."

"Exactly." Phelps stepped back from the board fence and jacked a round into his rifle chamber. "How often in life does a man get to kill everybody he'd like to kill at one time?" He looked back over his shoulder at Otis Farnsworth, who stood deeper in the littered back yard, holding the reins to the horses. Phelps's eyes shifted over to an old man who stood above them on a back porch with an open Bible in his hand. Then Phelps drew his gaze back to Otis Farnsworth. "Otis, check him out."

Otis Farnsworth turned to the old man and called up to him, his hand resting on the pistol at his hip. "Hey, you old stump! You ever heard of the James Gang? Huh? Well, you're looking at them. Now sit your ragged carcass down and shut up, or I'll bullitize you where you stand."

The old man dropped down on a stool and raised his hands. Otis grinned at Cleveland Phelps. "Never fails, does it?"

Phelps nodded. "Wait until you hear us shoot, then move the horses up there closer."

"You got it, *Frank*," Otis called out to Cleveland Phelps.

Chapter 19

Sullivan Hart stood with his back against the Pullman car, with Kate McCorkle and Briley Barnes beside him. Twojack Roth ran alongside the car in a crouch, climbed up three short steps onto the back deck, eased the rear door open, and slipped inside. His pistol was out and cocked. He flattened himself against the paneled wall and crept toward the sound of Sims's voice beyond the drape partition. Once he reached the long drapes, Twojack parted them slightly with his hand and peeped through. He saw Sims sitting across the table from JT Priest and noted the cuffs on Priest's wrist.

"Freeze, Sims!" Roth threw open the drapes, his pistol aimed and ready. Without turning to face him, Quick Charlie raised his hands, the pistol hanging on his thumb by the trigger guard.

"Is that you, Roth?" Sims asked. "I've been wondering what's been taking you so long."

From the front end of the car, the door flew open and Sullivan Hart filled the doorway, his pistol also drawn and cocked. "I've got it, Sully," Roth said, stepping forward and snatching the pistol off Sims's thumb.

"Now wasn't that easy?" Sims stood slowly and turned facing them, smiling, his hands still raised. "Gentlemen, meet your new prisoner, Mister Tuck Priest." Turning to JT Priest, Sims added, "Tuck this is Sullivan Hart and Twojack Roth. They'll be hosting your trip back to Fort Smith."

"Shut up, Sims." Sullivan Hart's eyes bored past Sims at Priest. JT Priest sat with a sour expression on his face. But his expression turned to terror as Sullivan Hart took one step forward from the doorway, a look of deadly intent about him.

"Easy, Sully," Twojack Roth cautioned him. "Bring in Barnes and the woman."

"Yes, let's all remain civil here," said Sims. "After all, everything's coming together just the way we all want it." *The woman?*

Hart took a breath, uncocked his pistol, and said over his shoulder, "All right, both of you, come in here."

Sims craned his neck, looking past Briley Barnes as Barnes stepped inside. When Kate McCorkle came in with the blanketful of money under her arm, Sims slumped. "Aw naw, Kate. You were supposed to be out of this."

"Charlie, are you all right?" Kate almost took another step, but Sullivan Hart grabbed Barnes by his sleeve, which in turn stopped Kate at arm's length. "I couldn't leave you that way, Charlie. I'm sorry," she said.

Seeing Kate McCorkle, JT Priest growled, "There's that lousy two-timing—"

Twojack Roth shut him up, tapping his barrel on Priest's forehead. "The least you say, the better right now," Roth said in a lowered voice. He patted Priest down for a weapon, finding none. "JT Priest, you're under arrest for murder, by the authority of Judge Charles Isaac Parker, the Western District Federal Court."

"Listen, Sully!" Sims stepped toward Hart with his hands still raised. "You've got to let her go. Please. I didn't count on her showing up. Kate's got nothing to do with any of this. It's too dangerous, her being here."

"We'll get it sorted out." Hart gestured with his pistol barrel, cautioning Sims back. "One thing at a time." Hart moved to the bar, taking Barnes by the sleeve, pulling him and Kate McCorkle with him. "You two stand right here and keep your hands in sight."

"You don't understand, Sully." Sims spoke fast. "I cut the caboose from the train to let a gunman named Red Lohman get away, so he could telegraph Mad-dog Mabrey. You wanted *Los Pistoleros*—I've been bringing them to you. By now Mabrey's sent gunmen here. This is no place for a woman."

"I beg your pardon," Kate McCorkle snapped at him.

"The caboose?" Hart looked at him. "You're the one who left it sitting on the tracks? With a man in it?"

"Yes, I did. I figured he'd wake up . . . I brightened the lanterns, so it wouldn't cause a wreck. Look, you've got to get her out of here—"

"Settle down, Sims." Sullivan Hart moved to the table and looked down at the folded paper. He opened it, read it, then refolded it.

"See, Priest confessed to the bank robbery in Creed. I'm innocent. Get Kate out of here, Sully, for God sakes!"

"That paper doesn't mean a thing," Priest growled. "He held a gun to my head and made me sign it. To hell with this. Take me to Fort Smith. I'll get some lawyers. We'll see who goes to jail."

Roth nudged Priest with his elbow. "I warned you to keep your mouth shut," he whispered near Priest's face.

Sullivan Hart dropped the folded paper back on the table. Then his eyes caught the string of dried ears. Priest's face turned stark white as Hart lifted the string on the tip of his pistol barrel and leveled the pistol on Priest's forehead. Roth saw the dark resolve in Hart's face, and he took a step away from

JT Priest, saying, "Don't do it, Sully. Not here! Not like this! We're deputies—not executioners!"

"Parker said dead or alive. It's my choice." Sullivan Hart's voice seemed to emanate from some distant place. His thumb went over the hammer of his pistol, recocking it.

Kate McCorkle flinched at the sound of the blast. Beside her, Briley Barnes let out a short yelp. Quick Charlie Sims and Twojack Roth jumped back a step. But something wasn't right, Sims thought, feeling something sharp sting his shoulder. At the same time he heard glass shatter and caught a glimpse of splinters explode off the wall behind the bar.

Kate McCorkle had felt something whiz past her cheek, and she stood stunned at the sound of it. Then Sims cried out, "Get down!" He dove into her and Briley Barnes, taking them to the floor as two more shots exploded through the window, sending Roth leaping in one direction and Hart in another. Rifle fire opened up hard and steady. Bullets thumped into the outside walls of the car. Window glass shot across the car in a widening spray. Chunks of polished oak exploded from the bar rail. JT Priest tried crawling toward the door, dragging the big chair with him. Twojack Roth caught him by his hair and slammed his head down on the floor.

"Lie down, Priest! You're not going anywhere," Roth shouted above the rifle fire.

Sims shoved Kate and Briley Barnes along on the floor and around behind the bar. Bottles and glasses shattered on the wall above them, and liquor showered down like rain. "Damn it, Kate!" Sims yelled, holding her down beneath him. "Why didn't you do like I asked?"

She cowered in the downpour of glass and whiskey. "I wanted to help, damn you!" Briley Barnes rolled up in a ball, his cuffed arm pressed somewhere between Kate and Sims. Across the floor, Sullivan Hart scrambled to the back wall, stood up with his

pistol, and managed to fire two shots out through
the broken window.

"How many?" Roth yelled at him as Hart ducked
back, escaping bullets that pounded along the window ledge. Hart had only caught a glimpse. Two
men had taken up cover behind a stack of cooperage
barrels, while two more fired from behind a short
pile of scrap iron. Behind them more scrap iron lay
in a large mound some twenty feet high. More muzzle flashes could be seen from behind an express
freight wagon.

"Half a dozen! Maybe more!" Hart got two more
shots off, then ducked back again to safety. Roth had
moved forward, dragging Priest and the big chair
with him. He took up position at the other end of
the row of broken windows and blasted off three
quick shots. Then the firing shifted toward his position, and he ducked back just in time as bullets
kicked up chunks of metal and splinters from the
window ledge.

"We can't let them rush us in these tight quarters!"
Roth shouted at Hart. "We've got to get some room!
We need rifles!"

The firing lulled as three of Phelps's men reloaded.
From the station platforms forty yards away, a
woman screamed. A police whistle sounded long and
shrill. A man's voice cried out, "In the rail yard!
They're killing one another!"

Crouched behind the express wagon, Cleveland
Phelps reloaded his rifle, casting a glance at Clifford
Mallory. "Why didn't you wait until we got right
up? We could've moved in and been done with it."

"I saw him through the window, pointing a pistol
in this direction." Clifford Mallory levered a round
into his rifle chamber. "I figured he'd seen us."

"Damn it," Phelps hissed. "He was pointing it at
Priest! He was probably arresting him."

As Cleveland Phelps spoke, Raymond Cloud
nudged him from the other side. "Look at what's

coming here. We've got a constable waving a billy bat."

"Then shoot him," Phelps said. "The police have no business butting in here."

Raymond Cloud turned and fired. The running policeman leaped to one side and rolled away on the ground, the rifle shot clipping his right shoulder. Behind a bale of cotton, the uniformed policeman checked his shoulder, seeing it wasn't a serious wound, just a long cut in his wool tunic. He seethed, cursing to himself. Another policeman came running along the walkway and the cop behind the cotton bale waved him back. "Take cover, Yancy! A bunch of cowboys are shooting it out!" He reached inside his tunic and took out his long Smith & Wesson pistol as the other policeman slid in beside him.

"What are we going to do, Sergeant Duffy?" His breath rasped in his chest. "There's only two of us."

"What do you think? We're going to break it up. This is not Dodge City! Nobody pulls this stuff in my town." He looked at the younger patrolman. "Got your revolver, Yancy?"

"Of course." Yancy patted his side.

"Then follow me, lad. You'll see what it was like back in the war."

Behind the express freight wagon, Raymond Cloud levered another round. "See? That's how it is with these damn city policemen. You shoot at one, then you've got a wagonload coming at you." He shot toward the bale of cotton as the two uniformed patrolmen came running forward, returning fire.

Looking diagonally from his position at the window, Sullivan Hart saw the two patrolmen coming. He also saw a rifleman rise up from the pile of scrap iron, aiming his rifle. Hart fired, his shot hitting Max Dupre an inch above his ear. Dupre fell away in a spray of blood. Hart ducked back as whining bullets sought him out. At the other end of the broken windows, Roth swung into view long enough to catch

Jake Walls rise up shouting and cursing at the sight of Dupre falling dead beside him. Roth's shot hit him dead center in the chest and lifted him backward, Walls's rifle flying out of his hands.

Cleveland Phelps glanced to where the two patrolmen had taken new cover, firing now from around a steel support column. A rifle slug banged loud against a steel rivet plate. Fifty yards past the column, Phelps saw two more patrolmen running forward. "Damn nosy constables!" he yelled at the others through the sound of their rifle fire. "Get ready to rush the train."

Behind the bar, Quick Charlie Sims stripped off his coat and threw it over Kate McCorkle's huddled shoulders. He said to Barnes, "Keep her down. Anything happens to her, I'll kill you!"

"Charlie! What are you doing?" She tried grabbing his arm, but Sims pulled away from her.

"I've got to draw them up! Give Roth and Hart something to shoot at! If they hit us all at once, we're dead!"

"No, Charlie! Don't!" She tried grabbing him again, but it was too late. Sims was already crawling through the wet broken glass over to where Sullivan Hart stood pressed against the wall.

"Get back, Sims!" Sullivan Hart yelled at him as bullets whistled in.

"Both of you, reload. Hurry up," Sims told Hart and Roth.

"What are you doing, Sims?" Even as Roth asked, he popped bullets up from his holster belt and shoved them into his big Colt .45, the pistol hot and smoking. "Get yourself back behind the bar!"

"No. Get reloaded. I can draw them up for you."

Hart and Roth looked at each other, rifle fire stabbing through the windows between them. "You'll get yourself killed!" Hart shoved the sixth bullet into his revolver and snapped it shut. "Now stay down, Sims!"

"Wish me luck!" Sims grinned recklessly, getting into a runner's crouch in the middle of the floor.

"No! Don't!" Hart shouted, but Quick Charlie Sims charged across the floor up onto the green felt table-top with bullets slicing past him like angry hornets. His foot only touched the tabletop long enough to hurl himself through the window with a long, wild yell. He hit the ground rolling, then sprang to his feet, running in a zigzag, charging into the blazing rifles.

"The hell is that?" Sergeant Duffy cried out. He and his partner, Yancy, kept firing from behind the column. Farther back, the other two patrolmen had taken cover behind a luggage wagon. One of them blew long and loud on a police whistle. Cleveland Phelps saw Sims make the charge and turned firing as Sims bounded over a short stack of wooden crates. Raymond Cloud fired with him, a shot streaking across Sims's back, causing him to veer for a second, but not dropping him.

Closing in fast on the short pile of scrap iron, Sims saw a rifleman rise up, taking aim from twenty yards. Another rifleman rose, taking aim and firing. The shot hit Sims in the ribs sending him veering once more, but he still managed to continue racing for-ward. Sims saw one rifleman fall backward, a bullet from one of the deputies hitting him in the chest. The other rifleman let out a scream, a bullet spinning him in a circle before he fell down into the scrap iron.

"Keep him covered," Hart shouted. Now Sims felt the bullets streaking past him from the right as he leaped over the short pile of scrap iron and scram-bled up the high mound. Loose pieces of angle iron and rusty metal buggy springs slid from beneath his feet. Cleveland Phelps, Raymond Cloud, and Clifford Mallory had to turn to fire at Quick Charlie Sims as he scrambled higher, hand over hand, a stream of rust and iron falling behind him.

From the Pullman car windows, Hart and Roth

fired at the express freight wagon, trying to pin down
Phelps and his two men. For a moment it looked like
Sims would make it over the top of the scrap iron
and into cover. But as he reached the top, Clifford
Mallory managed to rise up long enough to fire. His
shot hit Sims in the lower back, causing Sims to
stiffen to a halt momentarily before tumbling forward down the other side.

Cleveland Phelps felt splinters from the wagon
strike his shoulder. The four patrolmen had gathered
closer, crouched down, firing and advancing. From
the Pullman car windows, Roth and Hart continued
to fire without letting up. "We've got three men
down," Phelps said to Raymond Cloud and Clifford
Mallory. "Let's get to the horses and get the hell out
of here!"

On the other side of the high mound of scrap
metal, Sims tumbled and rolled downward until he
slid across a patch of dark mud at the bottom and
slammed into a tall board fence. He lay there, dazed
and bleeding. At the end of the fence, Otis Farnsworth still stood holding the horses, and upon seeing
Sims, he jerked his pistol from his holster and pulled
the horses forward. He fired, the shots kicking up
mud at Sims's feet as he tried darting away. "You're
finished, Quick Charlie!" Otis yelled as he fired
again.

Sims pulled himself up the board fence, his legs
growing numb. The shot thumped into the fence beside his head, and the closeness of the slug seemed
to give him the extra motivation he needed to drag
himself higher and fling himself over the fence into
the railroad tool yard.

Sims hit the ground and lay back against the fence.
His legs had all but stopped working now. Blood ran
freely from the wound in his back. He raised a hand
to his heaving chest and felt the warm blood running
from the wound in his ribs. He heard voices shouting
behind him, a whole army of guns firing, it seemed.

"Bring the horses, Otis!" Cleveland Phelps shouted, and Otis ran along the fence with the string until Cleveland Phelps and Raymond Cloud were close enough to snatch their reins from his hand. Behind them, Clifford Mallory hurried along, struggling with his brother's arm across his shoulders. "Get him mounted!" Phelps yelled. Otis ran forward with the rest of the horses and helped Clifford shove Harvey up onto his saddle.

"There they are," Sergeant Duffy growled, and atop the scrap iron mound three patrolmen rose up, firing with their Smith & Wesson long barrel .38 calibers. In a spinning tangle of horses and men, the gunmen fired back, using their big .45 caliber Colts. The two horses they left behind circled wildly in the hail of lead as Phelps and his men nailed their spurs to the horses' sides and sped away through an alley leading out to a muddy street.

"There's another one!" The patrolmen trained their fire on Sullivan Hart as he sailed out from atop the mound and down toward the two spooked horses, his duster spreading out like the wings of a large bird. Bullets flew past him, one of them nipping his hat brim. But without stopping, he caught the saddle of one of the terrified horses streaking past him at the bottom of the scrap iron. He swung himself up and into the saddle as it slid sideways making the turn in the alley, and pounded away, following the other riders.

Against the fence, Quick Charlie Sims felt himself fading. That was a stupid thing to do, he thought. But then he smiled faintly. At least Kate was safe. That was all that mattered now. He batted his eyes and tried to keep them focused, but the loss of blood caused the tool yard before him to tilt back and forth like the deck of a tossing ship. Something moved toward him from across the yard. *What was it?* Not one of the gunmen, he hoped.

Sims struggled with his blurred vision. As if

through a darkening tunnel he watched the two big mongrel watchdogs slowly come closer, their thick hackles raised high, their teeth shining beneath their raised flews. "Oh . . . it's only dogs," he murmured, taking all of his waning strength to raise a bloody palm toward them. They stalked forward like dark beasts called forth from a nightmare. As his weak hand fell to his chest, he felt their breath hot and damp on his throat, the sound of their low snarling voices blocking out all other sound.

On the other side of the fence, the patrolmen had stepped down from the scrap iron and spread out along the fence six feet back from it, their pistols pointed. Sergeant Duffy gestured toward the bullet hole in the splintered wood and at the scrapings Sims had left as he pulled himself up. The sound of the dogs rose into a roar, then a rage. The fence shuddered against their weight.

"Holy mother . . ." Sergeant Duffy whispered. "The two yard dogs have gotten a hold of him." He grimaced and shook his head. "No man deserves to die that way." He backed another step and lowered his pistol. "Come on, officers. Let's get around front. Get the yard keeper to let us in."

Chapter 20

Police had converged on the rail yard from all directions, some running on foot, others arriving in a horse-drawn paddy wagon. Among the officers gathered in a firing line surrounding the train, three railroad bulls stood with shotguns, their neckties flapping in the wind. Farther back from the firing line, a tight crowd of spectators had gathered, and more were gathering yet.

"Cease firing," a voice boomed out above the roaring volley of pistol fire. A man in a long wool police coat uniform stood behind a cooperage barrel with a hand raised in the air toward the riddled Pullman car. "You in there. Are you going to give yourselves up?" He gestured his pistol toward the two dead gunmen on the ground where three officers had dragged them forward. "There's two men dead out here. It doesn't have to happen to the rest of you."

Twojack Roth called out, "I'm a federal deputy with prisoners in here. One of them is Briley Barnes. You have a warrant on him. We brought him back to you. Those two men were gunmen trying to kill us."

"Think it's the truth, Captain Bennington?" an officer asked.

The man in the long wool coat looked at him. "How would I know? Go get the warrant list out of the paddy wagon and check it out." As the officer scurried away, Captain Bennington turned back toward the broken windows of the bullet-riddled

Pullman car. "If you're telling the truth, throw out your weapons and surrender. We'll hash it all out."

Twojack Roth looked over at Kate McCorkle and Briley Barnes, who crouched low and moved across the car toward him. He motioned them down, and they dropped to the floor. Cringing, the big chair clutched to his chest, JT Priest lay with a trickle of blood running down his forehead where a sliver of flying glass had nicked him. "We're coming out," Twojack Roth yelled through the broken window. "But don't let anybody go free until you've talked to Judge Charles Isaac Parker in Fort Smith. Is that a deal?"

"Yes, you have my word, sir," Captain Bennington replied. He looked toward the two railroad bulls, who held their shotguns at port arms and added to them, "One false move, gentlemen . . . you have permission to blast this bird out of his boots."

"Yes, sir. Thanks, Captain," one of them said. "Two of them escaped from the car about the time we showed up." He nodded toward the scrap iron. "They both took off in that direction. Some of your men followed them."

Captain Bennington nodded. "Real good. They won't get very far." Then he turned back to the Pullman car and saw Twojack Roth lay his pistol on the window ledge. Soon after, Kate McCorkle and Briley Barnes stepped down out of the car handcuffed together. Behind them Twojack Roth walked out, carrying the chair, with JT Priest still handcuffed to it.

The police captain waved a cautious hand, motioning his men forward. He looked Twojack Roth up and down as the big deputy stood there in his western trail clothes, an empty holster belt swung low on his right hip, the leather wells of his high-topped moccasins reaching high up his calves, his long black hair hanging down past his broad shoulders. Behind the half-open front of Roth's shirt, the captain spied the bandage from Roth's wounds at

Little Red Springs. "I can't wait to hear what this is all about," Captain Bennington said over his shoulder.

Six blocks away, Sullivan Hart saw a horse pulling a milk wagon across an intersection. The wagon driver jerked back hard on his reins, stopping the horse so fast that it reared high. The four escaping gunmen's horses galloped past it. The milk wagon horse had settled, only to rear again as Sullivan Hart swung his horse wide of it and sped on. An angry curse resounded from the milk wagon driver as bottles rattled and spilled out, breaking on the cobblestone street.

Raymond Cloud looked back as the four horses turned the corner, struggling to stay upright on the stone street. "We got one on our tails!" Cloud shouted to Cleveland Phelps riding beside him.

"Then shoot the sonofabitch!" Phelps yelled back.

Riding on, Raymond Cloud and Clifford Mallory turned in their saddles with their pistols drawn. Pedestrians on the sidewalk who'd turned at the sound of the racing horses' hoofs stood taken aback, stunned at the sight of the outlaws speeding past, two of them with their arms stretched out and big Colt pistols blazing steadily. Faces followed in awe, seeing the brims of weathered Stetsons stand high and long duster tails licking back in the wind.

"I'll break off and get him!" Raymond Cloud shouted to Cleveland Phelps. Before reaching the next corner, Cloud cut away from the others. He gigged his horse toward the sidewalk, then jumped it over a short stone wall. A man and a woman huddled down with a scream as the horse vaulted up over their heads and came down at a hard run across a broad green lawn.

Hart saw Cloud spin his horse to a halt and yank a rifle from its saddle boot. Thinking of what would happen to the people on the sidewalks once rifle fire erupted, Hart cut his horse straight for Cloud and made the same jump, coming up with his pistol as soon as his horse's hoofs touched down. On the street below, Cleveland Phelps and the others sped out of sight.

Sullivan Hart saw Raymond Cloud drop from his saddle and take aim with his rifle. Hart fired first with his pistol, pulling his horse to a halt, the horse rocking down on its haunches as chunks of manicured lawn flew high in the air. Cloud's first shot grazed Hart's thigh, and before he could lever a round and fire again, Hart took careful aim with his pistol.

The first shot caught Raymond Cloud high across his shoulder. The second shot missed his head, but sent his hat sailing in the air. Needing time to lever a round into his rifle chamber, Cloud ducked out of sight, flying up a set of granite steps onto a wide tile porch. "Come and get me, lawdog!" Cloud shouted, swinging his rifle over an ornate porch ledge supported by a row of concrete cherubs holding vine-trimmed vases on their shoulders. His rifle shot went wild as Sullivan Hart fired twice, his bullets raising flecks of concrete into Cloud's face.

"Give yourself up! It's over!" Hart shouted as he lunged his horse forward and up the steps, seeing Cloud go for the door with his rifle butt. Raymond Cloud battered in the leaded glasswork on the front door, ran his hand inside, unlocked the door, and threw it open. As he spilled inside the large house, a maid screamed and ran out of the way. Raymond Cloud hurried across a Persian carpet and climbed a rounding staircase three steps at a time.

Sullivan Hart shouted, "Stop right there!" At the top of the stairs, Cloud froze for a second, then spun around with his rifle up, taking quick aim. Two shots slammed into his chest, the first one knocking him back a step, the second one spinning him around like a top. A man ran out into the hall with an old cap and ball pistol in his hand, just in time for Raymond

Cloud's blood to spray across his face. Raymond Cloud tried to right himself and raise his rifle, but his faltering legs collapsed sideways. He staggered, hit the banister, and flipped over it, landing in a bloody clump at the screaming maid's feet.

"Easy, ma'am. It's all over. I'm a lawman," Hart said, still atop his horse in the middle of the wide living-room floor. He stepped down from his saddle and walked toward her, his right hand still holding the pistol pointed at the body on the floor, his left arm out as if to comfort her. But the woman would have none of it. She backed away slowly until the horse blew out a breath and shook out its mane; she went screaming past it and disappeared through the shattered front door.

A mile deeper into the heart of the city, Cleveland Phelps, Otis Farnsworth, and the Mallory brothers slowed their horses to a walk, looking back over their shoulders. "We've gone the wrong way," Phelps said. On the busy sidewalks, heads turned toward them. A horse-drawn trolley stopped on its tracks, the driver and passengers alike staring wide-eyed at the four men in their long dusters, their horses winded and streaked with white froth.

At a crowded intersection, the horses halted, and the four men looked all around at the gathering crowd. "What are you looking at, you fine-haired sonsabitches?" Otis Farnsworth drew his rifle out of its boot, levered a round into the chamber, and swept it back and forth across the faces of the dumbstruck onlookers. The people moved a cautious step back. Otis poked the barrel toward a woman wearing wire-rim spectacles, carrying a snow white cat in a wicker basket. "That damned cat can't hear a lick, ma'am, in case you don't know it," he sneered. The woman only stared up at him, terrified, with no idea what he was talking about.

"Come on, Otis," said Cleveland Phelps. "You're not making any sense!"

But Otis had singled the woman out and wouldn't let up. "She knows what I mean. Sit that cat up on your head, lady, and I'll do you and it both a favor." He started to raise his rifle to his shoulder. The woman appeared ready to faint. "Don't worry, skinny lady," Otis added, "if I had a sister that looked like you I'd wrap her in barbed wire and nail her chin to a fence post."

"Damn it all, Otis, come on! Max here is bleeding like a stuck hog, and you're babbling like an idiot." Phelps tried grabbing his arm.

But Otis pulled free, his hard icy stare fixed on the helpless woman. She swooned in place and almost sank to the ground. A man in a derby hat stepped forward from the crowd. "Now see here, sir," he said in a British accent, "that's quite enough." He swept the woman back behind him with his forearm, shielding her.

Otis shot him in the leg without batting an eye. The crowd let out a shriek and scrambled back. "There, you John Bull peckerwood . . . walk with that in your knee." The man crumpled to the sidewalk, his derby hat falling and rolling beneath Otis's horse. "Anybody ever asks you, tell them you been shot by Jesse *by-god* James."

"Hell, Otis! Quit shooting people." Cleveland Phelps grabbed him, this time in a stronger grip, and shook him. "Snap out of it! Let's get out of here."

"What about them damned deputies?" Otis blinked his eyes, then turned to Phelps, shoving the rifle back down in its boot.

"Get your wits about you! Forget the deputies for now. I know where they live. We've got a shipment of rifles we've got to meet." Phelps pulled his horse back a step and slapped Otis's horse on the rump, sending it forward. The Mallory brothers followed, Max weaving a bit in his blood-soaked saddle. Then

Phelps looked down at the crowd and batted his heels to his horse's sides. "To hell with all you pumpkin heads!"

The crowd watched them streak across the intersection and ride out of sight. A lady riding sidesaddle on a fancy bay fell back at the sight of them in a flurry of stockings and petticoats as her horse turned skittish. Her gentleman friend on a matching bay jumped down to her aid and shook a tight fist in the horsemen's wake.

While Twojack stood with his hands raised chest high, relating to Police Captain Douglas Bennington a shortened version of what had happened and why, the paddy wagon came in from the front of the rail station and rolled to a halt alongside the bullet-pocked Pullman car. Police uniforms swarmed in and out of the car. Sergeant Duffy stepped in close to the captain, holding out the string of dried ears looped on his finger, "Begging your pardon, Captain, sir. But we found these lying on the floor. What do you make of it?"

Captain Bennington reached out and cupped the ears in his hand, examining them for a second. Then his face turned a pasty white, and he jerked his hand back as if he'd touched a rattlesnake. "My God, man!" He turned slowly to Twojack Roth with a look of stunned disbelief. "Is this . . . ?"

"Yes, Captain," Twojack said. "Those are human ears." He nodded toward JT Priest, still handcuffed to the large chair. "This man collects them." Roth pointed at one of the pair of ears, less dried and blackened than the others. "Those two belong to my partner's father. That's why we're here. This man killed him."

"That's a damn lie!" Priest blurted. "I've never seen them before. You have no right taking me into custody. I want a lawyer."

"A lawyer, eh?" Captain Bennington looked down

at Priest, a sharp gleam coming into his steel gray eyes.

"That's right," Priest sneered. "I'm a born American citizen, and I have rights that must be adhered to."

"Here, adhere to this," Captain Bennington said to Priest, and backhanded him across the mouth. Priest's head bounced from shoulder to shoulder. Captain Bennington caught him by his hair and added, "How dare you ask for a lawyer! You come in here like some Wild West show, shooting up my city—"

"Judge Parker will verify everything I've been telling you, Captain," Roth cut in. "I only ask that you hear from him before turning this man loose."

"Don't worry, Deputy Roth," Bennington said, keeping his temper in check. "Nobody's turning anybody loose—including you—until we get to the bottom of this. Fair enough?"

"Fair enough, Captain." Roth nodded.

"Captain, here comes Yancy, O'Leery, and Tate!" Sergeant Duffy said, getting excited. "They've apprehended one of them!"

Through the parting crowd of onlookers, three patrolmen carried Quick Charlie Sims between them, blood running down Sims's chest, his head hanging limp and bowed. "Give them some room," Duffy barked at the crowd. He moved in and helped the officers lay Sims down on the ground.

"Charlie! Oh, my God!" Kate McCorkle rushed forward before anyone could stop her, dragging Briley Barnes with her like a rag doll. She flung herself down beside Quick Charlie Sims, cradling his head against her bosom with her free arm, Briley Barnes forced into being a part of it. Sims's eyes opened halfway. He managed a weak smile and tried to speak, but he couldn't find the strength to get the words out from his lips. "Oh, Charlie, please," Kate sobbed, "don't die, please don't die."

"Get him on a gurney, then load him on the wagon!" Sergeant Duffy shouted. "Get him to the hospital! Step lively, lads, this man is bleeding to death on us!"

"All right, lady, back you go. Give us room here." Officer Yancy pulled Kate away from Sims, Briley Barnes staggering back with her, as two officers came running in from the paddy wagon, carrying a canvas gurney between them.

"Can somebody please uncuff me from her," Briley Barnes pleaded.

Captain Bennington reached out with his big hand and raised a finger in Barnes's face. "You shut up, boy. We found your name on our warrant list." Bennington turned back to Officer Yancy. "How bad is he? Where did you find him?"

Yancy answered with a grave expression, "He's lost a lot of blood, Captain. We found him over yonder, in the tool yard."

"The tool yard? Good Lord. Then the dogs must have done all that to him?"

"No, sir, Captain," Yancy went on. "He's been shot all over, but he's not dog-bit. He tried running through that lead storm. We saw it all."

"Why did he do a fool thing like that?" Bennington turned his question to Twojack Roth.

"You'd have to know him, Captain. He's a strange one," Roth replied. "He said it would cause them to get up and give us a shot at them." Roth shrugged his broad shoulders. "He was right—it did."

"And the dogs never touched him?" Bennington posed the question to Officer Yancy.

"No, sir, they didn't," Yancy responded.

"I'm surprised those two mongrel devils didn't eat the man alive." Bennington winced. "They've torn up their share of prowlers in the past."

"I know, sir," Yancy said. Behind him, the officers loaded Sims into the paddy wagon. The driver slapped the traces to the horses' backs and sped away. "But the dogs are what took us so long to bring him in. They wouldn't let us near him! He finally came to long enough to call them off of us. They seemed to be guarding him, Captain . . . lunging against the fence at us! I never saw anything like it."

"That's my Charlie, all right." Kate McCorkle stared after the paddy wagon, her eyes growing wet. She brushed a tear from her cheek. "All animals love Charlie Sims . . . dogs, horses, you name it. He just has a way with any dumb animal, I suppose."

Twojack Roth looked at her, then slumped, let out a long breath, and shook his lowered head. "Yep, I suppose," he whispered to himself.

It took over an hour and a half for the uniform police, along with two plainclothes inspectors and the railroad security agents, to go through the train. They impounded the blanket full of money Kate McCorkle had stashed behind the bar, along with the string of ears, Twojack's pistol and his big knife, and the crates of explosives in the car surrounding the big safe. The money and the string of ears now lay in a box at Captain Bennington's feet, along with JT Priest's big Colt pistol. When a freight wagon backed up to the car door and workers from the station began unloading the small crates of dynamite, Captain Bennington turned to JT Priest. "What's in the safe that's so important you'd rather blow up the whole train than have it found?" Bennington reached down as he spoke and picked up Twojack's big knife in its fringed rawhide sheath and hefted it in his hand, looking it over.

"I never saw that safe before in my life," Priest replied, looking down at the floor. His handcuffs had been removed from around the chair arm and replaced with a new set.

"Don't lie to the captain." Sergeant Duffy reached out and slapped Priest roughly on the back of his head.

"It's all right, Sergeant Duffy." Captain Bennington glared at Priest. "We'll see for ourselves what's in

that safe once the dynamite is cleared away."
Bennington looked back at Kate McCorkle, Briley
Barnes, and Twojack Roth. They stood at the far end
of the car, guarded by three patrolmen. Bennington
looked at the big knife in his hand, then down at the
string of ears. "Ever wonder what makes people live
this way, Sergeant?" he asked Duffy.

"Sir, I believe it comes from too much space and
too few people around. It must make them all a wee
bit crazy."

"Perhaps you're right," Captain Bennington pon-
dered, then dropped the big knife back into the box.

Sergeant Duffy gestured toward Twojack Roth at
the far end of the car. "Do you suppose he really is
an Indian, sir? I mean, he doesn't talk the way I
always heard they talk."

"Oh, really, Sergeant? And just how is an Indian
supposed to talk?" Bennington stared at him. "This
is an unusual situation here, Sergeant. Let's try not
to offend anyone." He gestured at Twojack Roth. "If
this man and his partner really are federal deputies,
then they're lawmen, no different from ourselves."

"No different, Captain?" Sergeant Duffy nodded
at the string of ears in the box on the floor.

"That's right, Sergeant Duffy, we're all lawmen."
Captain Bennington offered a thin smile. "Three
armed assailants are lying out there dead on the
platform . . . how many of them did you or your
officers shoot?"

Sergeant Duffy looked embarrassed. "Captain, that
only means they're less civilized."

"Well, perhaps they're not as *civilized*, not as *re-
fined*, and certainly not nearly as *smart*." Captain Bennington winked. "But other than that, they're no
different from us, I'm sure."

A young policeman stuck his head inside the car
door. "Captain, I think you better come quick, sir."
His voice sounded excited. Behind him, the buzz of
the crowd rose higher.

From a block away the crowd had begun to part, making room for Sullivan Hart as he limped forward, leading his horse behind him. The body of Raymond Cloud lay across the horse's saddle, arms swaying with each click of the horse's hoofs on the cobblestone street. Ten feet behind Hart, a group of children had formed, following him over the past four blocks. At first, one of them had ventured forward with a short stick and poked it against Cloud's lifeless back. But when Hart had looked around at them, they'd fallen back and kept their distance.

"My heavens! What's going on here?" a voice called out in the parting crowd.

Sullivan Hart had taken his badge from his shirt and pinned it to the front of his riding duster, the right side of his duster drawn back behind the butt of the big pistol. The spurs on his high-topped riding boots rang low with each step. The tail of the broad bandanna around his neck fluttered on a breeze. A long brown bottle of beer sweated and dripped from his gloved hand.

Ten yards in front of Hart, Captain Bennington and three armed police officers stepped into the narrow cobblestone street. They stared as Hart walked closer, seeing the badge on his chest. The crowd fell silent. At a distance of twelve feet, Bennington raised the pistol in his hand. "Stop right there. Raise your hands."

Sullivan Hart obeyed. As the patrolmen moved in around him, Captain Bennington lifted the pistol from Hart's holster, then snatched the bottle of beer from his hand. "A beer?" He turned his stare from the bottle and into Hart's eyes.

"I stopped at a tavern," Hart offered. "They wouldn't give me any water." He glanced sidelong at the three patrolmen as they lifted his duster tails and patted him down for more weapons. "I'm Federal Deputy Sullivan Hart, here under the authority of Judge Parker's federal court, Western District."

"We've already heard who you are, Deputy." Captain Bennington eyed him, then glanced at the body hanging over the saddle. "What about the rest of them?"

"I had to let them get away," Sullivan Hart replied. "The way they were shooting, I didn't want to risk the lives of your citizenry."

"Good thinking." Captain Bennington nodded. "We'll catch them sooner or later."

"I doubt it." Hart looked disappointed. "It's my bet they're headed out of here. I don't think this is one of their usual haunts."

"So much the better." Captain Bennington shoved Hart's pistol down in his coat pocket. "It's my duty to take your weapon, young man. Don't worry, though, you'll get it back if everything checks out."

"I understand," said Hart. "How's my partner and the others?"

"Everybody's fine, except the man who took a jump through the window. He's shot up pretty bad."

"That's Quick Charlie Sims. He did a crazy thing there."

The captain seemed to run the name through his mind. "Charlie Sims . . ." He cocked his head slightly. "That name sounds familiar. I think I've heard of him."

"I wouldn't be surprised, Captain." Sullivan Hart smiled faintly. "Everybody seems to know Quick Charlie."

Captain Bennington looked around at the crowd and leveled his shoulders. "All right then . . . it might take us a while to verify a few things. Until then, good show. For the time being you and your partner are officially in the custody of the Chicago Police Department. I'll expect your full cooperation, of course."

Sullivan Hart let out a long breath, allowing one of the officers to take the reins from his hand. "You've got it, Captain. You've got it all." The surrounding crowd gave up a vigorous roar of applause.

PART 3

Chapter 21

One full week after the shootout had taken place, Judge Charles Isaac Parker stepped down from a train at the Chicago train station. Deputy Daniel Slater made the trip with him in order to assist in escorting JT Priest back to Fort Smith. They were met by Captain Bennington and two of his men as soon as they stepped down from the train. Captain Bennington swept his hat from his head, stepping forward. "Judge Parker, I'm Captain Lowell Bennington, at your service. I'm in charge while our police commissioner is out of town. This is indeed an honor, sir, even under the circumstances. My men and I admire your reputation for . . . well, you know, sir."

"My reputation for hanging criminals, of course." Parker gave a flat smile. "I also teach Sunday school and coach team sports. I hope they admire that as well."

"Oh, yes!" Captain Bennington blushed. "If they knew about it, I'm certain they would. At any rate, it's a pleasure meeting you."

"Likewise I'm sure." As they shook hands, Judge Parker looked around the platform.

"As you requested, Your Honor," Captain Bennington added, "we've kept your coming here quiet, to avoid the newspaper reporters."

Judge Parker nodded. "Good, Captain. What did the newspapers say about the incident?"

"It wasn't as bad as you might expect, Your Honor.

The main headline read, 'Outlaws Hold Railway Station At Bay.' " Captain Bennington shrugged. "Then it gave the details, most of them true. Your deputies made a favorable impression on everyone—that helped take the sting out of Hart's gunning one of the thugs down in the parlor of one of our leading physicians. An innocent bystander was wounded in the leg a couple of miles from here. Luckily, he was only a touring Englishman."

"Then I'm glad my deputies didn't cause you too much trouble, Captain." Judge Parker gestured toward Daniel Slater who stood with his shotgun in a fringed leather boot, which only covered the weapon up to the hammers and trigger guard, its polished walnut butt clearly visible. "This is Deputy Dan'l Slater."

Captain Bennington and his men introduced themselves to Slater, then Bennington stepped closer to the deputy and extended both hands. "I'm afraid I'll have to ask for your shotgun, Deputy Slater. It's illegal to carry a deadly weapon out in public here."

Slater hesitated and took a step back. "What if I just put it under my coat then?"

"I'm sorry," Captain Bennington said, "but I'm afraid it's also illegal to carry a *concealed* deadly weapon here."

Slater looked confused. "Wait a minute . . . then how the hell *does* a feller carry his deadly weapon here?"

"Don't argue, Dan'l," Parker interceded before Captain Bennington could respond. "Just give them the shotgun. I'm certain you won't be needing it while we're here."

"All right, Your Honor." Slater grumbled under his breath, "Sounds like Hart and Roth could've used one the other day," he said as he handed the shotgun to Captain Bennington, who in turn passed it on to one of his men.

"What's that, Dan'l, speak up, man." The judge gave Slater a reproachful glance.

"Nothing, Your Honor, just thinking out loud." Slater cinched his knee-length blanket coat across his middle, hoping to hide the big Colt .45 strapped to his hip and the smaller double-action Colt Thunderer riding in a shoulder harness up under his arm. One of the men started to make note of the pistols, but Captain Bennington stopped him, saying, "There now, out of sight, out of mind, eh, Deputy?" He gave Slater a half wink.

"We're going to get along, you and me," Slater said, grinning at Bennington. "I can see that already."

On the way to the station house in a covered two-horse carriage, Captain Bennington took a paper bag from underneath his seat and handed it to Judge Parker. "Deputy Roth asked me to give these to you in private. They're . . . *ears*, Your Honor. Two of them belong to Sullivan Hart's father, I believe. Deputy Roth said you'd know what to do with them. Apparently, he didn't want Hart to see them again."

"Yes, thank you, Captain. We'll bury them." Judge Parker passed the paper bag to Slater with no further comment on the subject. Parker settled back in his seat, and as the carriage wound its way through busy streets, he and Captain Bennington discussed what had happened and talked at length about *Los Pistoleros*. At the end of the ride as the carriage pulled off the cobblestone street into a dirt alley beside the brick station house, Captain Bennington shook his head, saying, "It all sounds rather incredible. But I suppose it was bound to happen any time—East meets West crime-wise, so to speak." He let out an exasperated breath. "I wish there was more our department could do to help, but given our limited jurisdiction, and as elusive as these men are, I'm afraid your men are on their own."

"My men are used to that, unfortunately." Parker adjusted his tall silk top hat, then rose and stepped down from the carriage. "What about this Briley Barnes my deputies have mentioned? Have you learned anything from him?"

Captain Bennington winced. "Your Honor, Briley Barnes was only wanted on a simple petty theft charge. Yesterday his employer posted a bailment bond on his behalf. He's gone, sir. It's doubtful he'll even show up for court next week."

Judge Parker stopped abruptly on the sidewalk. He started to say something, but then he caught himself. "Yes, bailment . . . I'd almost forgotten there is such a terrible practice. But perhaps it doesn't mater. We have one of the leaders in custody—the one who killed my deputy. That's not a bad day's work. We'll manage to get the others, somehow."

Bennington looked at Slater and asked the judge, "Will only the two of you be transporting the prisoner back to Fort Smith?"

"No," said Judge Parker. "We've made arrangement with the Pinkertons. They're sending a couple of guards along."

"Not that it's necessary," Slater huffed.

They ascended the concrete station house steps, where on either side stood a large round lamp globe atop an ornate metal stand. A pigeon cooed atop one of the globes, and Slater slapped his hip, then pointed a weathered finger at it and said, *"Bang."* The police officers only gave one another a curious glance and stayed close to him, taking note of the pistol bulge beneath his dusty blanket coat as they walked through the wide oaken doors.

Heads turned and officers rose from their seats as the Hanging Judge, Charles Isaac Parker, walked past them, his top hat cradled on his forearm. He offered a curt nod back and forth, Slater staying close to his right side, one step back like a trained guard dog. When the judge, Slater, and Captain Bennington were settled in Bennington's office, a young officer brought in coffee and an assortment of warm muffins. A few moments later, Sullivan Hart and Two-jack came down from a police dormitory upstairs and joined them.

Judge Parker and Deputy Slater greeted the other deputies, and before stepping back, the judge asked them both, "Well, how are they treating you boys here?"

"We're fine," Hart replied, nodding.

Twojack Roth added, "You know us, Your Honor . . . we always make do. Sorry you had to make this trip, sir."

"Nonsense, Deputy." Parker spread his hands. "I wouldn't have had to come here. This could all have been handled by wire. But I wanted to come here . . . air out the ol' robe so to speak." He beamed, smiling all around. Then, getting down to business, he asked Captain Bennington, "You have the confession JT Priest made on Charlie Sims's behalf?"

"Yes, Your Honor, right here." Captain Bennington picked up the battered paper from his desk and passed it over to Judge Parker. The judge only glanced at it before he folded it and put it inside the lapel pocket of his swallowtail coat.

Hart and Roth looked at each other, then at the judge. "Aren't you going to read it, Your Honor?"

"Later, perhaps." Judge Parker turned his gaze to Captain Bennington. "Would you please excuse us, Captain?"

"Yes, of course. I need to speak to some of my officers anyway." Captain Bennington stood up from behind his desk, brushed muffin crumbs from his wool tunic, and left the office. When the door shut, Judge Parker stepped closer, Slater at his side.

"The fact is, this confession means little in and of itself." Parker smiled and patted his lapel. "But this, along with your reports, prompted me to speak to the authorities in Creed on Mister Sims's behalf. Suf-fice it to say, Sims has been exonerated of all charges." He narrowed a gaze on Sullivan Hart. "Unless you choose to arrest him for horse theft, that is."

Hart and Roth both looked relieved. "No, Your Honor. I have my morgan back, no worse for the wear. For all Sims's aggravation and trickery, he did help us out a lot. He'll be glad to hear this. Will you be going with us to visit him at the hospital, Your Honor?"

"No." Parker gave Hart a flat stare. "And don't be too hasty in telling Sims he's off the hook just yet. I only want you two to know he's a free man. I don't want him knowing it yet."

"Oh . . . ?" Hart looked puzzled.

"Deputies," Parker said in quiet tone, drawing them closer. He cast a quick glance around the office to confirm their privacy. "I have been passing along all the information you've sent me about this gang of plunderers to the *highest* source in Washington." He paused and let the meaning of his words sink in. "The name William Mabrey has come up in several Senate investigations—I'm talking about bank fraud, bank robbery, large-scale gunrunning to a foreign government, misallocation of government funds for purchase of beef. You name it, William Mabrey and his friends have been in on it."

Again Hart and Roth looked at each other. Slater nodded as if to confirm the judge's words. The judge went on. "The government wants these men stopped, and since you two are already nipping at their heels, Washington has agreed that you're the men to do it."

Sullivan Hart's expression went blank for a second, then he replied, "But Your Honor, we have no experience in investigating something this large. We track and grab. This was just something we hooked in to . . . most of this happened because Sims led us to it."

"Exactly." Parker nodded. "And if it takes Sims to get this done, hire him, threaten him, do whatever it takes. My last wire from Washington tells me that something has already made a chink in Mabrey's armor. Two officials in the Bureau of Indian Affairs have come forward willing to testify against his so-called Midwest Investment Corporation. So apparently, something you or Sims has done is starting to dry up Mabrey's cash flow. Without money to buy people, this man will fall. I want you two to be the ones who make it happen."

"We'll do our best, Your Honor," Twojack Roth cut in. "But this is going to take some time and money. We had to pawn our rifles to get here."

"Does one hundred thousand dollars sound adequate?" Judge Parker looked back and forth between them. "Because it's within my power to confiscate that amount—the money found on this Miss McCorkle you told me about in your report." He spread a knowing smile. "I believe it to be stolen, don't you?"

"But we have no proof." Twojack Roth stared at Parker.

"Proof is a word we might as well forget for now. I want to see results. We'll sort through the proof when the time comes. Whatever money is left in your expense account, she can claim when it's over. If the money turns out to not be stolen, I'll reimburse what we've spent catching these scoundrels."

Sullivan Hart shook his head slowly. "This is going to be a hard blow to Sims and the woman."

"Make it work, Deputies." Judge Parker stepped over to the small table beside his chair and picked up his cup of coffee. He sipped it and touched a white napkin to his mustache. "If Sims balks on it, tell him it's coming straight from the Hanging Judge." Parker smiled with wide satisfaction. "Tell him I said there's more than one way to hang a man."

An hour later, after Judge Parker and Deputy Slater left to meet the Pinkerton guards and pick up JT Priest, Twojack and Sullivan Hart walked along the cobblestone street toward the hospital. "This case must have some awfully big eyes on it if his source in Washington is pushing it," Twojack said.

"Well, there's no question that his source in Washington is the president himself. I reckon the president wouldn't be asking for help if he didn't need it. My question is, where do we start?"

They walked on, ignoring the faces staring at them, Hart still in his trail clothes, boots, and spurs. Twojack Roth wore his trail clothes and moccasins, but he was also wearing a heavy Navy watch coat one of the officers had lent him until his riding duster came back mended and patched where bullets had nicked and creased it.

"I say one of us needs to pay a visit to that labor contractor, Hughes & Lindsy," Roth offered. "Since we don't have Briley Barnes to show us around the way we wanted him to, I might as well look them up and do some snooping around on my own." Roth smiled. "I can do that while you're breaking the bad news to Sims and Kate McCorkle."

"Thanks," Hart said in a wry tone. "I hate facing Sims with this. Why couldn't we just ask him for his help?"

"Parker didn't want to chance Sims turning us down," Twojack offered.

"Yeah, but still . . ." Sullivan Hart dismissed the subject. "Maybe we ought to search for this Hughes & Lindsy Company together. How will you even know where to start?"

Twojack Roth turned the collar of his big Navy coat up against a gust of wind, then stuffed his hands down into the pockets. The brim of his belled-out Stetson flattened up against the crown. "If I can track men in the mountains and the badlands, I think I'll be all right tracking skunks in the streets of Chicago."

They stopped and stood on a street corner a block from the hospital. Sullivan Hart leaned against another sharp blast of wind sweeping in off Lake Michigan. "I feel wrong lying to Quick Charlie. I wish the judge hadn't ask me to do it."

"Follow your conscience, Sully. I'll back your play whichever way you go with it."

Hart bit his lip, thinking about his options. "I'll see how it goes when I get there." They parted a step. "Good luck, Roth. Watch your back out there."

"You too, Sully." Roth nodded, and Sullivan Hart watched him turn and walk away along a meandering cobblestone side street that looked more to Hart like a long narrow tunnel leading nowhere.

Chapter 22

For the past four days Quick Charlie Sims had been lying flat on his stomach, the surgery healing on his lower back where the bullet had been removed. Kate McCorkle had been at his side throughout it all, the policeman on guard outside his room allowing her to help feed Sims, bring him water, and call for a nurse when he needed one. Sims had been up and around earlier that morning, taking short halting steps—getting his legs back, he called it.

Had things gone the way Sims planned, he would be waiting for William Mabrey when Mabrey got here. But Kate had spoiled his plans, heading this way when she should have gone south and stayed out of things. Okay, he thought, there were a few minor setbacks, but nothing he couldn't straighten out. He didn't like working from a hospital bed, but for now it was the best he could do.

Sims had every intention of taking care of William Mabrey right here in Chicago, then being back in Fort Smith when JT Priest made his escape from Parker's jail. And there was no doubt in Sims's mind that Priest would try to escape. That's what the five hundred dollars was for—the money he'd shoved down into Priest's pocket before the shooting had started. Quick Charlie Sims wasn't through with *Los Pistoleros* yet . . . not by a long shot. With a pillow beneath his head, Sims lay adrift in the bed, reworking his plans in his mind.

"Charlie, are you asleep?" Kate McCorkle had left the room for a moment to get a fresh pitcher of water. She now set the pitcher down on the wooden stand beside the bed and brushed a hand across Sims's forehead.

"No, Kate," he answered in a drowsy voice without opening his eyes. "Just thinking."

"Those people are still out in the hall, Charlie." She leaned down closer to his face. "They're really getting on the guard's nerves."

"Have they caused any problem?" Sims smiled, keeping his eyes closed.

"No . . . but he seems nervous anyway."

"Did you tell them I'm doing fine?" Sims asked.

"Yes." She paused. "But do they understand English, Charlie? I mean . . . they all huddled real close to me, then just stared as if I weren't there."

"How close?" Sims asked.

"I don't know, just close," she said and shrugged. But then her eyes took on a knowing expression as she caught on.

Quick Charlie reached out with his left hand. "Come here, Kate." She stepped closer and watched his hand reach down into her dress pocket.

"Jesus. Charlie!" She managed to keep her voice down, seeing Sims take out a deck of playing cards and a small ball of silk string with a long hat pin stuck in it. "They're good," she whispered.

He reached into her other dress pocket and took out a pocket knife and a folded one dollar bill. "I mean real good, Charlie!" she added. "I know, because I'm good myself, and I didn't feel a thing." She looked herself up and down. "But why? What's this all for?"

"Just their way of showing they care." Sims took the hat pin from the ball of string. He put the pocket knife and hat pin under his pillow, and handed the dollar bill to Kate McCorkle and played out a few inches of string. "The idea is, I should be able to get

anywhere in the world with a dollar in my pocket.
If I can't, I don't deserve to." He smiled up at her,
tying a quick series of complicated knots in the
length of string. "They'll go away when you give this
to them." He handed her the string. "It tells them my
fingers and mind are working—lets them know I'm
all right."

"What are they, Charlie, Gypsies? Are they all
pickpockets?"

"They're Roma, Kate, and no, they're not all pickpockets. That's just Uncle Breldi and some of his family. They're silversmiths, but they're real good at
moving things around unseen. It comes from years
of persecution, I suppose."

"Uncle Breldi . . . ." A silence passed as Kate studied the knots in the silk string. Then she put the
string in her pocket and asked, "Are they your family, Charlie? All the time I've known you, you've
never talked about your relations." She brushed a
lock of dark hair from his forehead, then sat down
in the chair beside his bed.

"They're not my family. They're old friends of my
family," he said in a soft voice. "My family has been
dead for years."

"But . . . I always thought your family was from
New York or New Jersey, or somewhere back East."

"My folks lived all over. They could never sit still
for long. They were wanderers, Kate. That's where I
get it from." Again he spread a relaxed smile, his
eyes closed, his left arm hanging down the side of
the bed.

Kate sighed. "Sometimes I look at you, Charlie,
and read you like a book. Other times I wonder if
I've ever known you at all."

"You know me better than anyone else does, Kate.
Maybe there's not that much to know." He changed
the subject. "Did you manage to put the rest of the
money in a safe place? The other two hundred
thousand?"

"Yes, it's—"

"Shhh, don't tell me where. It's your money. I just wanted to know you've still got it."

"Yes. I'm in good shape, Charlie. There, does that help you make your plans?"

Sims only smiled without answering.

Kate waited a few minutes, and when she was sure Sims had dozed off, she walked back out in the hall and a few yards past the guard to where the small group of people sat on the floor. An elderly man with a long gray beard, three elderly women in long dresses, and a younger woman with a child on her hip stood up and gathered around her again. "Whoa, now." Kate raised a hand toward them, keeping them at arm's length. "Uncle Breldi? Charlie asked me to show you this."

Kate held the small ball of string out to the old man, who stood short and powerful in his high-collar fur coat, his face nearly hidden beneath the brim of a battered derby hat. But instead of taking the string from her, he examined the knots, the others leaning in, doing the same. Then the old man looked up at Kate with a smile of satisfaction, ran his thumb and finger along the string, and watched Kate's eyes widen in astonishment as the knots disappeared.

Uncle Breldi nodded to the others as Kate stood staring at the length of string. "Charlie, he is doing well," the old man announced. Without another word, each Roma filed past her in turn, smiling and nodding, the bottom edge of Uncle Breldi's fur coat almost brushing the floor as he passed her. Kate stood with the length of string hanging from her hand as they moved away along the hall.

Coming from the opposite direction Sullivan Hart turned to look the Roma up and down as they passed him. With his battered Stetson in his hand, Sims walked up to Kate McCorkle, gesturing his hat back down the hall. "Who are they?" Hart asked, noting the length of string in Kate's hand.

"Just some old acquaintances of Charlie's." She rolled the string back onto the small ball and dropped it into her pocket.

"How's he doing?" Hart asked as they turned and walked to Sims's room.

"He's coming along. He's asleep right now. Did the judge get here this morning?"

"Yep, he's here." Hart walked on without facing her.

"Well? What did he say?" She tried placing a hand on his arm to stop him, but he kept walking. Kate followed him past the police guard at the door and into the room. "Is everything all right, Hart?" she asked.

"No, Miss McCorkle, I'm afraid not," Hart said in a hushed tone, looking down at Quick Charlie Sims.

The sound of their lowered voices caused Sims to stir and open his eyes. "What's not all right, Sully?" Sims, flat on his stomach, raised his face and looked up at Sullivan Hart.

"Judge Parker is reviewing your case, Sims. So far you're still not off the hook for the bank robbery or shooting the guard."

"Even with the confession? Even with me bringing Priest to you?"

"Sorry, Sims." Hart shook his head slowly. "He says it looks better for you, but he wants your help bringing down the rest of this gang. He won't clear things up for you in Colorado until it's done. And that's that."

"I see . . ." Sims turned onto his side, studying the deputy's eyes, seeing something more there than Hart was revealing. "Well, I've done all I can to clear myself. Looks like I'm headed back to jail." He closed his eyes as if dismissing the whole matter.

"What?" Sullivan Hart looked at Kate McCorkle, then back at Sims. "You'd rather go face a hanging than help us?"

"Yep." A trace of a smile moved across Sims's lips.

"You're not a good liar, Sully, so don't try me."
Without opening his eyes, Sims fluffed up his pillow
with one hand and settled back into it. "Come back
when you've practiced some."

Sullivan Hart stood squeezing his hat brim for a
second, considering something. Then he reached out
with his hat and nudged the brim against Sims's forehead. "Open your eyes when you talk to me, Sims."
Quick Charlie looked back up at him. Hart gestured
a nod in the direction of the hall. "I saw those Gypsies out there, Sims. This thing between you and JT
Priest—it goes back further than the bank in Creed,
doesn't it?" When Sims only stared at him, Hart went
on. "I heard a story about a band of Gypsies JT Priest
killed years ago. He took their ears, the same way
he took my father's."

Sims held up a hand. "Stop right there, Sully.
There are things I don't talk about. If you're asking
me if I'm one of the Roma Gypsies, it's none of your
business. If you're asking me if I'm looking for re-
venge on Priest and Mabrey for something more than
the robbery in Creed . . . Let's put it this way. A
Gypsy never admits vengeance, even to himself."

Hart nodded and let out a breath. "Okay, Sims, if
we have to talk in circles about it, here's the truth.
Listen close. If you got out of that bed and left, legally
there's not a thing I can do about it. In fact, there might
even be a letter in my pocket right now, signed by
Judge Parker, saying you're a free man. Twojack Roth
and I are going to stay on *Los Pistoleros'* trail until we
put them out of business. Care to help us?"

"Of course." Sims smiled and lowered his head
back onto his pillow and closed his eyes. "There
now, Sully, was that so hard to do?" Kate McCorkle
and Sullivan Hart stared at one another until Kate
shrugged and turned away.

It was evening, rain slanting in on a blowing wind,
when Twojack Roth looked up at the sign that read:

HUGHES & LINDSY. The sign was located in the second-floor window of the large crumbling brick building. The building stood amid the smaller faded buildings and loading docks on the south side of town. For the past three hours, Roth had been asking directions to the place, but none of the shopkeepers he approached had ever heard of Hughes & Lindsy.

Finally, he'd asked an old Italian pushing a peddler's cart. The old man repeated the names Hughes & Lindsy to himself and came up with nothing. But then he tapped his forehead and searched through his ragged coat. He took out a thin, worn business index, leafed through it, and held it out for Twojack Roth to read. Roth had thanked him and walked away in the direction of the old man's pointing finger. Three blocks later he'd spotted Briley Barnes walking in the same direction across the street, and Roth had stayed back and began following him—about time he did some tracking, he'd thought.

That had been an hour ago; and now, having seen Briley Barnes just go through the doorway of the building, Roth read the sign above the door. It read: SOUTHSIDE MEN'S ATHLETIC CLUB. Beneath the peeling letters, the caricature of a muscular arm flexed itself to the street. Inside the main entrance, Twojack tried the knob on a dirty glass door with HUGHES & LINDSY stenciled on it. The door was locked, so Twojack turned and walked along a littered hallway toward the sound of men's voices beyond a set of wooden double doors.

"Hold it there," a short, wiry man in a plaid English wool cap said, stopping Roth inside the double doors. "Are you a fighter or a spectator?" When Roth only stared at him, the man looked him up and down, taking in Roth's thick neck, broad chest, and shoulders. Then he waved Roth on inside, saying, "Dumb question. Sign in with the man at ringside."

But instead of walking over to where a rope lay spread out in a wide circle on the floor, Roth moved up into a gathering of men and stood for a moment looking all around for Briley Barnes. He finally spotted Barnes sanding at the front of the crowd, shaking rain from his waist-length wool jacket. Roth smiled to himself and edged forward through the spectators, stopping right behind Barnes. Looking down for a second at Barnes's bowler hat, like a large bear finding its next meal, Roth clamped a hand around Barnes's neck, raised him a few inches from the floor, and whispered in his ear, "Briley Barnes, you little weasel."

"Oh, no! Please, Deputy!" Barnes whined, writhing back and forth trying to free himself. "Let me down! I'm out on a bailment! You're not supposed to bother me!"

"You said you would show us around, Barnes. You don't want to hear about the vision I just had of you sailing against a brick wall, do you?"

"I wanted to show you fellows around, Deputy, honest! But I didn't know how to find you!"

"Then aren't you glad I found you? Now we can start all over."

Inside the circle of rope on the floor, a big white man, his head shaved clean and wearing a broad handlebar mustache, held the roaring crowd's attention as his bare fists pounded another man backward and out of the rope circle. The big man turned facing the crowd with his fists raised in victory.

"Sure, Deputy! I'll still do it," Barnes pleaded. "Just put me down!"

As the roar died down and the crowd settled, some of the spectators moved away from Barnes and Roth, seeing Barnes's feet peddling the air beneath him. From within the rope the big man's voice called out, "Hey, Cochise! You can't take scalps in here."

A ripple of nervous laughter rose from the crowd, then stopped under the big Cherokee's gaze. "This is a private matter," Roth called back to him, ignoring the man's barbs. "I apologize for the distur-

bance." Roth lowered Briley Barnes's dangling feet
to the floor, but clamped his hand down, crushing
Barnes's bowler hat and pinning him in place.

"Who let this Injun in here?" The boxer glared
across the large room at the double doors where the
small man in the English cap shied back a step.

"I did, Mister Lindsy," the man called out. "He
said he's a fighter."

Lindsy? Of Hughes & Lindsy? Twojack Roth looked
the big man up and down.

"Is that true, Cochise?" Lindsy banged his big fists
together. "You're a pugilist, boy? If you are, you
need to pick on somebody your own size. Don't go
crippling Briley Barnes. He's my employee, in case
you don't know it."

An employee . . . Good enough, Roth thought. He
let go of Barnes's collar, brushed by one of Barnes's
shoulders, and said close to his ear, "Try to run, and
I'll shoot you a whole bunch of times." Then Roth
looked back at the big man. "You're the man I came
looking for, Mister Lindsy," Roth called out. "Maybe
we can talk after the event?"

"You didn't answer me yet, boy. Are you a pugilist
or not? If you're not, go sell your beads elsewhere.
We're real busy here." Even as Lindsy spoke, Roth
could feel himself being sized up, the big fighter's
eyes moving across Twojack's broad shoulders, com-
paring them to his own.

*Injun, Cochise, boy. Now the remark about selling
beads . . .* Roth felt himself start to smolder, but he
tried to let it pass. "I'm a federal deputy, Mister
Lindsy." He spread the front of his Navy coat open
wide enough to show him the badge on his chest.
"I'd really like to talk to you when you get a chance."

"Man, that's Porter Lindsy—he'll kill you!" a
hushed voice said beside Twojack Roth. Roth stared
straight ahead at Porter Lindsy as the big man
walked toward him and stopped less than a foot
away.

They stared eye to eye, their broad chests jutted forward like brewer's barrels, neither backing an inch. Before Lindsy said another word, Twojack Roth began shucking off his Navy coat. As he pitched it to the side, Porter Lindsy allowed himself a bemused half smile. "Injun, you must be reading my mind."

"Yes, and I'm getting a real bad vision, Lindsy," Roth said, reaching down, unbuttoning his shirt-sleeves, and rolling them up over his thick forearms. "After I bat your head around, think we can talk some?"

"I'll talk . . . but you won't hear a word I'm saying, boy." Porter Lindsy chuckled and took a step back, banging his big bare fists together. "What do you say? You ready to fight, Injun?"

Twojack Roth stepped forward, his shirt stretching tight across his shoulders. "I'd love to, paleface," he said.

Chapter 23

"Gentlemen, toe the line," a referee said, shoving Twojack Roth into position. Roth looked awkward and out of place in the center of the rope circle.

"Don't worry," Porter Lindsy said to him, his guard up high, his left toe out against the line on the floor, "when the bell rings you're free to move around—even *run*, if you've a mind to." His grin at Roth was cruel. "Sure you don't want to take your shirt off before we start? Might be cooler."

"I don't plan on working up a sweat." Twojack Roth just stared at him as the referee stepped back. The crowd fell to a hushed buzz around the ring.

"All bets are down," a voice called out. As soon as the hammer struck the bell, Porter Lindsy was ready. Roth wasn't. Two sharp left jabs shot through Roth's guard as easily as if he'd had his hands in his pockets. His head snapped back with each punch. No harm done. Porter Lindsy looked surprised that his jab hadn't staggered the big Indian. His left hand stung from the impact.

"Pay attention now, Injun." Lindsy still displayed the same cruel grin. "I seldom find a fighter my own size. Let's give the crowd their—"

A straight blow from Roth's big right hand seemed to come out of nowhere, causing Lindsy to rock back and replant his feet farther back from the line on the floor. "My name's Roth. Don't call me Injun."

A surprised look came over Porter Lindsy's face,

shocked that this big Indian could get a punch on him like that. He still grinned, but it turned waxen. "Well. So we will see some sport out of you after all." He jumped forward a step on the balls of his feet, his first in a rapid succession of jabs glancing off Roth's guard, a second flurry catching Roth's shoulder as Roth ducked to one side. As Roth straightened, Lindsy came up under his guard, and launched a hard right to Roth's ribs, only inches from the wound in his chest. Roth almost doubled over, but caught himself in time, backing up a step as Lindsy advanced across the line. The crowd roared.

Porter Lindsy had found a weak spot, and wanted to work on it. He hooked upward with his right again. But Twojack Roth hunched enough to catch the blow on his elbows and come back with a left-right combination that sent Lindsy back across the line, a trickle of blood running from an open gash above his eyebrow. The crowd sliced its breath and groaned.

Roth stalked forward, not standing as straight now with the crushing pain in his wounded chest, but still coming. A roundhouse right snuck its way through Porter Lindsy's guard and sent him tottering side-ways. But Lindsy collected himself quickly when Roth moved in, and once more landed a powerful right up into Roth's ribs. The crowd went wild seeing Roth fold like an accordion and stagger backward. Had Porter Lindsy moved fast, he would have fin-ished Roth. But right then Lindsy needed a second to shake off the rest of the big roundhouse that had made him see stars. When he did start forward, the bell resounded.

"You need the bell, Roth?" Lindsy called out, his words sounding a little slurred coming from his throbbing jaw.

Roth now. No more Injun . . . Much better, Twojack thought, shaking his head. "Uh-uh," he called out to Lindsy. Roth forced himself to straighten up, the pain

in his chest deep and cutting. He felt warm blood
soaking through his shirt as the wound opened up.

"All right then," Porter Lindsy said, the grin gone
now, his breathing labored. He glanced outside the
rope circle at the referee. "Ring that blasted bell
again, and I'll bend it over your head." He shook
out his hands, his knuckles raw and aching. "Come
on, Mister Roth, let's see what else you've got." He
stepped to the center of the ring, redoubled his big
fists, and gestured Roth toward him.

The cheering of the crowd soon leveled down to a
steady murmur of apprehension. The big men fought
from one side of the rope circle to the other, one
forcing the other back, but neither one able to knock
his opponent out of the ring. Then the fight pushed
back in the other direction until after a while the
fighters were in the center of the circle, both of their
guards all but down, swapping punches with arms
that appeared to be made of lead. "You've got to
stop this," a spectator said to the referee.

"You heard what Mister Lindsy said. You stop it
if you want it stopped." The referee tried to hand
him the hammer and the bell, but the man stepped
away.

Twojack Roth almost went down to his knees, taking a hard shot in his chest that swept the breath out
of him. "Go . . . down," Porter Lindsy gasped, his
right hand broken and swollen, one of his large
knuckles jammed back halfway to his wrist. But Roth
straightened up with a powerful uppercut that raised
Lindsy onto his toes. Porter Lindsy's left eye was
swollen shut and bleeding freely; his right jaw had
puffed out to twice its size. Twojack Roth looked
no better.

Both fighters staggered forward until they leaned
against each other like trees in the aftermath of a
terrible storm. They sank together to their knees in
the center of the ring, still swinging, but their blows
falling limp against each other's back. Porter Lindsy

managed to shove himself off Twojack Roth and summon enough strength to make a swing, but before his big swollen fist came around, Roth fell over on his side, blood running from the newly opened gunshot wound in his chest.

The crowd roared and cheered once again as Porter Lindsy rocked back and forth on his knees. With the room swirling around him, Lindsy focused on Twojack Roth as the Cherokee struggled to raise himself up, not making it. Roth's shirttail had worked its way halfway up his chest. Lindsy saw the bandaged gunshot wound just as the referee and three other men came in to drag Roth away and carry him to the alley out back.

"Wait . . . a minute," Porter Lindsy rasped, his breath heaving in his chest. "He's with me . . . leave him alone." Lindsy peered at Roth through his right eye, his left eye nothing but a bloody slit in the purple swollen flesh. "Why didn't . . . you say something, Roth? I wouldn't . . . fight a man in that shape."

"What shape?" the referee asked, leaning in between them.

"Never mind!" Porter Lindsy shoved him away, glad that no one but him had seen the bloodstained bandage before Roth jerked his shirttail down and covered it. Lindsy reached down and helped Twojack up onto his knees

"I told you . . . I came to talk." Roth held a hand pressed to his bleeding chest wound. "You're a hard man to talk to."

Porter Lindsy looked all around. "Get us up from here. What the hell's wrong with you people? Get Mister Roth some ice, some water!" Porter Lindsy looked back at Twojack Roth and shook his bloody head. "Jesus," Lindsy muttered under his breath.

It was close to midnight when the carriage pulled up out front of the station house. Sullivan Hart had been

pacing back and forth on the limestone porch, out of
the rain beneath the shelter of an overhang above the
doors. Hart hadn't seen or heard from Twojack Roth
since early afternoon, and it had him worried. He
stopped pacing and watched with curiosity as a big
man with a battered swollen face stepped out of the
carriage into the rain, then turned and helped Roth
out onto the sidewalk. Hart bounded down the limestone stairs through the gusts of rain.

"My God, Roth!" Sullivan Hart looked back and
forth between the big men, both of their faces in-
flamed and dabbed with spots of iodine. "Who did
this to you?" he asked them both.

"We did it to each other. It's a long story," Roth
said as Porter Lindsy looped Roth's arm across his
shoulder and helped him across the sidewalk and up
the stairs. Hart hurried ahead and opened the door
for them. Once inside out of the rain, Lindsy eased
Roth down onto a wooden chair. "This is Mister Porter Lindsy," Roth said to Hart. Then to Lindsy he
said, "This is my partner I was telling you about,
Sullivan Hart."

"My pleasure, Hart." Porter Lindsy raised his
bandaged right hand to show why he couldn't shake
hands. "Roth told me what happened to your father
and why you're here."

"So you're Lindsy, of Hughes & Lindsy?" Hart
saw the glistening black leech stuck to Porter Lindsy's swollen eye.

"Yes, but I want you to know I have no part in
this gang you're after. I told Roth everything I can
about the laborers we've been sending out. That little
rat, Briley Barnes, has been recruiting men for Midwest Investment. My partner, Hughes, probably
knows what's going on, but not me. I'm more of a
silent partner—it's been a place to stick some of my
fight winnings."

"It's the truth, Sully," Roth said, raising his bruised
face to Hart. "He's given me a list of six new men

they sent west just this morning, to pick up a shipment of cargo in Missouri and head out with it, destination unknown at present." Roth smiled across split and swollen lips. "Care to guess what that cargo's going to be?"

"Guns," Hart said in a flat tone, "to make up for the load we cost them."

"That's what I figure," said Roth. "When you make a deal with the *federales*, you better be able to keep your end of it."

Porter Lindsy looked uncomfortable, touching his fingertips gingerly to his purple cheek. "Gentlemen, I hope I've helped, giving you those names and information. I'll be on my way now." He raised his bandaged right hand, backing toward the door. "You take care of yourself, Roth," he added reaching back for the knob. "Thanks for our gentleman's agreement." He turned and left.

Sullivan Hart gave Twojack Roth a questioning look.

"He didn't want any of his cronies to know I was fighting him with a bullet wound in my chest." Roth shrugged. "Must've thought it would make him look bad. How did it go with Quick Charlie Sims?"

"From the looks of you and Lindsy," Hart replied, "I'd say Sims and I got along *real* well. Him and Kate McCorkle are both upset about the judge using the money. But he's agreed to help us."

"How did you handle it?" Roth asked, raising a hand to his aching chest.

"I told him the truth. He's a hard man to bluff. Besides, it turns out there's more behind all this than just the bank robbery in Creed being pinned on him. He's got something working with JT Priest from a long ways back. I think it was Sims's folks Priest killed—the Gypsies Barnes told us about. A band of Gypsies were at the hospital today. Sims called them Roma. Said a Gypsy never admits his vengeance, even to himself, if you can figure that out."

"He means his vengeance is so deep it's become second nature to him. He doesn't dare think about it, for fear it will cloud his vision of anything else." Roth considered the notion, then added, "So why didn't he do something to Priest back when he had the chance? Back when they were in Colorado together?"

"Who knows?" Hart replied. "But if we're going to catch up to the men and that cargo, we need to get a move on. Sims will have to wait here. That's okay with him, though. He feels like William Mabrey is headed this way after him and the money."

"Think one of us needs to stay here and wait for Mabrey?" Roth looked at him through his swollen eyes. "Sims is in no shape to take care of himself."

"No. We'll both have our hands full out there. I'll talk to Captain Bennington and make sure the police keep guarding him until he's on his feet. Besides, he has Kate McCorkle with him. Between the two of them, I'm sure they can hold their own."

The carriage pulled up in front of the Southside Men's Athletic Club in the wind-driven rain. As Porter Lindsy started to step down, the carriage driver said, "Are you sure, Mister Lindsy? I don't mind taking you to your home."

"No thank you, Miller, not in this blow. It's a two-hour ride. I have a cot in my office, I'll be fine. Get yourself and the horses out of this deluge."

"Yes, sir." The driver tipped his silk top hat and pulled the carriage back into the empty street.

Once inside the brick building, Lindsy saw that the door leading up the stairs to the offices of Hughes & Lindsy was not locked. He saw the glow of a lantern at the top of the stairs and as he walked upward, he saw that the door to the offices stood partly open. He called out before walking inside, "Hughes? Is that you, sport?"

"Yes, Porter," his partner's voice replied from beyond another open door, this one on the right of the reception area. "Come in. I thought perhaps you'd stay the night here rather than press home in the rain."

"It's a terrible night, no question about it." Porter Lindsy slipped out of his raincoat, shook it out, and hung it on an oaken coatrack. He stepped into James Hughes's office and saw the grave look on the man's face in the dim light of a desk lantern. Hughes looked at him across his desk.

"Yes, Porter, terrible indeed." Only then did Porter Lindsy turn slightly and see the faces of the three men step out of the shadows. "Now, what have you told that lawman about our business here?" Lindsy recognized two of the men, William Mabrey and Briley Barnes. The third man had a red beard, and held a cocked shotgun pointed at Porter Lindsy's stomach. Lindsy's first instinct was to make a lunge for the shotgun, but the man must've seen the thought cross his mind. He steadied the shotgun in his hands, his finger on the trigger.

Porter Lindsy tried a bluff. "Nothing, Hughes. I gave the poor fellow a ride, dropped him off, and came right back here." He looked around again at the three faces, Mabrey's somber and silent. "What's the meaning of this? I won't be treated like some—"

"Shut up, big man," Mabrey hissed, cutting Lindsy short. "Barnes here was watching, said the two of you were in this office. Then he followed your carriage to a tavern and saw the two of you have dinner together."

Porter Lindsy looked at Briley Barnes, knowing there was no point in denying anything. "Barnes, you rat. What did you hope to gain by this? When these men are through with you, they'll serve you for breakfast."

"Don't worry about Barnes," Mabrey said. "Barnes is doing all right for himself. What did you tell the lawman?"

Lindsy played it hard, without so much as a flinch. "I told him everything I could think of, about you, about your gang, about the six men we dispatched out this morning. I put the lawmen right on your trail, Mabrey. Now do what you will." Lindsy jutted his chin as Mabrey and Barnes stepped back a couple of feet. Mabrey gave James Hughes a malevolent look.

"He's lying, Mister Mabrey," Hughes said, his voice sounding worried all of a sudden. "I never told this dupe anything more than I had to. He knows nothing about your business. He's a barroom brawler. All he knows is that we provide laborers for Midwest Investment—nothing more."

Mabrey stood silent, as if weighing Hughes's words. "Very well," he said at length, seeing Hughes take a breath of relief. The tension seemed to lift from the room. Then Mabrey took another step back as if to leave, and nodded at Red Lohman. The shotgun blast lit up the office with an orange-white flash, like a bolt of lightning. Briley Barnes ducked away, but not in time to keep Porter Lindsy's blood from splattering up his side and in his face.

Porter Lindsy lifted backward off his feet, slammed into the wall, and sank down, his chest a smoking mass of mangled flesh. "For God sakes, Mabrey!" Hughes was shaken. "Not here! Look at this mess! We'll never get it cleaned up!" His eyes darted about the office. Blood had even showered upward onto the ceiling.

"Briley Barnes will see to it you have nothing to worry about, Hughes." Mabrey nodded at Barnes. "Do it, Briley boy." Barnes lifted the pistol out from beneath his coat and aimed it at Hughes.

"Mabrey, please, no!" James Hughes pleaded, starting to rise up from his seat. "I'm on your side!"

"Sorry, you know too much, Hughes." Mabrey turned his gaze to Barnes. "What are you waiting for, Briley boy? First time is always the hardest."

Briley Barnes swallowed back the knot in his throat. "Yes, sir." The pistol bucked twice in his hand, the first shot hitting Hughes low in the stomach, causing him to jackknife forward with a tortured groan. The second shot hit him in the top of his lowered head and set him down hard in his chair. Barnes stood staring at the strange expression on Hughes's lifeless face.

"There now, well done," William Mabrey said. He reached out, patting Barnes's shoulder as he took the pistol from his hand. "The two of you put a torch to this place . . . leave not a trace. I'll meet you back at my Pullman car."

Red Lohman broke the shotgun into two pieces and placed them both inside his coat. "What about the shipment of guns? Think we better head that way, now that the law is onto it?"

"No." William Mabrey stared at him. "Phelps is paid to take care of that business. Let him handle it. I need the money that that two-bit grifter Sims stole from JT Priest. Without it, I've got the government breathing down my neck." He looked at Briley Barnes. "You're moving up fast, Briley boy. First thing in the morning, you're going to show us to the hospital where Sims is staying. We'll get the money and kill that grifter . . . his lady friend too. You can bet they're both in on it. Kill them both real slow for all the trouble they've caused me."

Chapter 24

Twojack Roth and Sullivan Hart met Captain Bennington in the hospital hallway the next morning on their way to Sims's room. "Good heavens, man," Bennington remarked, looking at Roth's swollen face, "you look like you should be a patient instead of a visitor. Who did that to you? I'll arrest them for attempted murder."

"It was only one person, Captain. I got involved in a sporting event with Porter Lindsy."

Captain Bennington nodded, his expression of surprise melting. "Yes, I heard. I only wanted to hear you say it." He looked at both of them now as they stood with their big Stetsons in their hands. "There was a fire before daylight this morning. Luckily, the rain was still falling hard, or we'd be rebuilding this city. The men's club where you fought Lindsy has been gutted, and so were the offices of Hughes & Lindsy. We found two charred corpses. No way of being certain, but I have a feeling it's the two of them." He watched Hart's and Roth's expressions.

"I hope not," Roth said. "Porter Lindsy turned out to be a great help to us."

"We have an arson investigation going on now," Bennington said. "We'll have to see what we dig up."

Hart winced. "Captain, I hope you're not going to tell us we can't leave town. We're headed out on the morning train—we put our horses on board on our

way over here. Lindsy gave us a tip on some cargo
being moved west. It sounds to us like a load of
rifles."

"No, I'm not saying you can't leave town,"
Bennington replied. "In fact, the sooner you get after
these scoundrels the better. Just wanted to see your
reaction when you heard about the fire. It's my job."

"We understand, Captain," Roth said.

"What about Sims and the woman?" Bennington
asked. "I hope Sims isn't traveling with you, is he?"

"Not right now," Hart said. "Can you keep some
men watching over him and the woman? He thinks
there's some trouble coming his way."

"Don't worry about Sims." Captain Bennington
smiled. "Whatever it takes, I'll make sure he's safe.
I have a personal reason."

"Oh?" Hart looked at Roth, then back to the big
captain.

"Yes. I finally recalled where I'd heard the name
Quick Charlie Sims before. Do you realize that man
is a devil with a golf club in his hands?"

"I'm not real familiar with the game," Hart said.

"Nor am I," Roth offered.

"Well, at any rate, Sims is highly respected among
the golf set. In fact, last evening I spoke to the
mayor—our mayor is quite a golf enthusiast—he
can't wait to meet Sims. Said he saw Sims play a few
years ago, in Yonkers, New York." Captain Bennington smoothed down the chest of his wool tunic. "So
don't worry about Sims and Miss McCorkle. Unless
they refuse it, they're under my protection."

"Well, there you are," Hart said with a beaten sigh,
"Sims and the mayor." He gave Roth a bemused
look. Roth chuckled under his breath.

"Maybe we need to take up that game, golf. It
seems to open a lot of doors," the Cherokee said.

Sullivan Hart gave him a flat glance as they walked
on. "I've always thought about it. Just can't find
the time."

Inside his room, Quick Charlie Sims lay on his side, dealing a hand of blackjack to Kate McCorkle. They'd been talking about JT Priest, Mabrey, and their situation, and Kate was very interested in when and how she might get her money back from Judge Parker and his deputies. "There's more to life than money, Kate." Sims flipped a card down onto her hand. "I need to get in shape to be in Fort Smith when JT Priest makes his escape."

Hart and Roth stepped past the door, and hearing Sims's words, Hart looked straight at Sims and said, "What makes you so sure JT Priest is going to make a break, Quick Charlie?"

Sims looked up from flipping another card onto Kate's hand. "Good morning to you too, Deputies." Sims smiled, then added, "Call it intuition, Sully." He looked at Kate McCorkle, saying, "Twenty-two, Kate—you're busted."

"How do you know that?" She frowned and threw her hole card down.

Sims didn't answer her. Instead, he riffled the deck, fanned it, then closed it and dropped it on the bed, looking up at Hart. "If you were in Priest's shoes, wouldn't you be trying to break out?" As he spoke, a card appeared out of nowhere into Sims's hand. It danced across the backs of his right knuckles, then disappeared. "Besides, as large as this gang is, who knows . . . there might be a couple of other *Los Pistoleros* in that jail on other charges. If so, they'll either cut his throat or help him escape. What do you think?"

Hart let it pass. "We came to tell you we got a tip on some of the gang moving some cargo. We're heading west to catch up to them. You can join us as soon as you're able to travel."

"A tip, huh?" Sims relaxed on his side. "Is it a shipment of rifles, to make up for the ones they lost in the fire?"

"You already knew about it?" Hart took a step closer. "Then why didn't you tell us?"

"Easy, Hart." Sims held a hand up toward him. "I didn't already know about it. But it just makes sense. They don't want to lose their *federales* business, not with Mabrey needing cash the way he's bound to."

Sullivan Hart looked from Sims to Kate McCorkle, and in doing so saw the hickory shaft of a golf club leaning against the oak stand beside the bed. Shaking his head, he reached over and picked it up. "Let me guess, Sims, a golf club . . . Captain Lowell Bennington's, right?"

Sims shrugged one shoulder. "He asked me to take a look at it. Says it doesn't feel just right to him. What could I say?"

Twojack Roth gave Sims a wary stare. "Bennington told us the mayor wants to meet you, Sims. You seem to be making your share of new friends here."

"Yeah, that's what Bennington told me." Sims smiled. "I thought that was interesting—the mayor, of all people."

Sullivan Hart pointed the handle of the club down at Sims's face, sighting down it with one eye as if aiming a rifle. "I'm sure you've already heard about the fire at Hughes & Lindsy, being so close to the captain and all."

"Yeah, Bennington mentioned something about it." Sims leaned forward to peer at Roth's swollen face. "Whooie! Looks like this Porter Lindsy made quite an impression on you, Twojack."

"Are you paying attention here, Sims?" Hart asked, poking the golf club toward him.

Sims looked back at Hart. "Oh yes. My chips are in the pot. I want you to do me one favor, though— take Kate with you. Get her out of here."

"No you don't!" Kate snapped at Sims. "I'm not leaving you here alone. You can't even walk yet without falling."

"Kate," Sims said in a firm tone, "it could get real dangerous here. I want you out of it."

Hart and Roth looked at her. "He's right, ma'am. Why don't you go with us? The police will watch after him. Come on with us." It was more like an order than an invitation.

"I'm free, right? No charges against me?" Kate looked back and forth between them, then said before anyone could respond, "So I'm the one who decides where I'll be and who I'll be with. I'm not going anywhere, so there!" She folded her arms and stiffened in her chair.

"She's got a point, Sims." Hart reached over and put the golf club back where he'd found it. "You can't get around yet. You're not armed—even if you were, you won't shoot anybody."

Sims gazed at him curiously. "Where did you get that notion, Sully?"

"She told us all about it, Sims." Hart gestured toward Kate McCorkle. "Maybe it's best that she stays with you."

Sims closed his eyes for a second and let out a long sigh. "All right, Sully. I'm too weak to argue with her. You two get going. I'll join you as soon as I can make the trip."

"Good enough then," Hart said, he and Roth both nodding. "We'll see you in Fort Smith." In a moment they were gone.

Sims rose back up on his elbow and cocked an eye at Kate McCorkle. "I won't *shoot* anybody? Where on earth did you come up with that?"

"What was I supposed to do, Charlie? For all I knew they might have shot you down like a dog when they caught up to you. I made it up . . . evidently they believed it."

Sims chuckled. "Who else have you told that to?"

"Just Deputy Hart, on the train coming here." She thought about it. "He mentioned it later to Roth . . . and that Briley Barnes character might have heard it,

I think. Why? What's the big deal? You've said so yourself that you never want to be looked at as a big hardcase."

"That's true . . ." Sims thought about it. He smiled, laying his head back down on the pillow. "Dear Kate, you never cease to amaze me."

On the cobblestone street across from the hospital, William Mabrey and Red Lohman sat waiting in a covered buggy for Briley Barnes to return. "After what Sims did to me, boss, I'd appreciate you letting me do the killing," Lohman said.

Mabrey looked at him. "Red, after what you *allowed* him to do to you, I'm not sure you can."

"I came right to you though, boss. I didn't run and hide and leave you wondering, did I? No, sir, I came to you and admitted it. And don't forget, I killed that pugilist for you."

"Yeah, Red, you did." Mabrey looked across the street to where Briley Barnes came walking out of the shrubbery surrounding the hospital with his hands shoved down in his coat pockets, his new bowler hat cocked at a jaunty angle. "But Barnes there did just as well, killing Hughes. So what's your point? You're lucky I didn't have you shot. Mess up again, and I might." Mabrey chomped down on his cigar.

"So what's the story, Barnes?" Mabrey asked as Barnes stepped up into the covered buggy.

"Nothing doing, Mister Mabrey. He's in the police prisoner's room. There's bars on the window." Briley Barnes slumped down in his seat next to Red Lohman, who grudgingly made room for him.

"How the hell do you know he's in that room?" Lohman asked in a harsh voice.

Barnes's voice was equally harsh in reply. "Because I went in through the back delivery door and asked one of the workers if they knew where the man was who got all shot up at the rail yards. It's called using your head, Lohman!"

"You punk," Red Lohman hissed, his red-gray beard appearing to bristle, his face turning stark white in rage.

"Look here, both of you!" Mabrey nudged Red Lohman, and all three of them watched as Sullivan Hart and Twojack Roth stepped out through the main entrance of the hospital and started walking along the street. "So they haven't left town yet," Mabrey contemplated. "Too bad there's no time to get some gunmen on them. What do you want to bet they're headed for the train station right now?"

"Probably so. Let's take them ourselves, boss," said Red Lohman. "There's three of us. They're not expecting anything."

"Did you read the Chicago newspaper, Red?" Mabrey worked on the cigar in his mouth, watching Hart and Roth walk away. "Those two men held off Phelps and some of his best gunmen. You want to go jump down their shirts, be my guest. I don't look for fights I can't win. What about you, Barnes?"

"No sir, Mister Mabrey. Only an *idiot* would want to jump them right here on the city street in broad daylight." Barnes cocked his bowler hat forward, a smirk of satisfaction on his face.

"Why, you little turd!" Red Lohman started to backhand him, but Mabrey caught his wrist.

"Listen to the lad, Red. You might learn something. After all, nobody jackpotted him and left him knocked out in a caboose with a train boring down on him." Mabrey's grin was cruel. "I won't have the two of you fighting each other. I want you to stick close to Briley boy for a while, Red—sort of show him how we do things. It's time he takes a step up with us."

Red Lohman looked at Mabrey. "What does that mean for me—a step up or a step down?"

"That all depends on you, Red. I need men around me who can get the job done." Mabrey just stared at him. "You've got some making up to do."

"Just tell me what you want done, boss." Red Lohman sounded submissive. "I'll do whatever it takes."

"All right, Red, you go follow those two lawdogs,
but stay back aways from them. Either make sure
they get on the train, or else find out where they're
staying. Briley boy and I will be right here somewhere, keeping an eye on things . . . if we can figure
a way to get to that grifter and his woman."

Briley Barnes stepped down to let Red Lohman out
of the buggy. When Lohman started to turn and
leave, Barnes leaned close and said in a snickering
whisper, "Watch out for any stray cabooses."

"Laugh it up, you Irish punk," Red fumed. "See
if I don't bend a gun barrel across your jaw."

When Briley Barnes stepped back into the carriage,
Mabrey grinned around the end of his thick cigar.
"You think on your toes, Briley boy . . . I like that.
With JT Priest out of the picture, and Phelps losing
some men, you stand a chance of doing yourself
some serious good working with me—especially now
that you've proved you can drop a hammer on a
man when he's looking you in the eyes."

"I want whatever I can squeeze out of this life,
Mister Mabrey," Barnes replied.

They sat silent for a few minutes until William
Mabrey spotted Kate McCorkle come out the hospital
doors, a tall policeman at her side. "Pay attention
here, Briley boy . . . maybe you can squeeze something out of sweet Kate McCorkle." They watched as
Kate seemed to be arguing with the policeman. Finally he threw up his hands and Kate shooed him
away. As the cop walked back inside the hospital,
Kate McCorkle shook her head and stalked off along
the sidewalk, mumbling under her breath.

"Stupid little fool," Mabrey whispered to her as if
she were standing beside him. "You just chased
away the one person who might have saved your
worthless life today." He turned to Barnes. "Get behind her, Briley boy." Mabrey gave Barnes's pistol

back to him. "First chance you get, grab her and bring her back here. Sims will give up the money if we're holding her. Once he does, we'll take her somewhere nice and quiet, and you can cut her pretty little throat for me."

Chapter 25

Kate McCorkle felt she was being followed, but what confirmed it for her was the sight of Briley Barnes walking behind her when she stopped abruptly and looked into a dress shop window. He'd been caught off guard, and instead of stopping, he breezed by her with his face turned away toward the street. She let out a breath, pretending to stare at a long velvet dress in the store window. Okay, she thought, if Barnes wanted to play, she'd play.

She walked into the store, browsed for a few minutes, then picked herself out a nice sturdy parasol with a good strong blunt tip on it. She paid for it and came out with it raised over her shoulder, twirling it leisurely on her way along the busy street, headed toward the firearms store, where she'd been headed to begin with. Only now she would take her time— give Barnes a little lesson in following helpless women. She gazed around, taking note of a darkened alley across the street as she drifted along the sidewalk.

Barnes hung back, watching. If there was one thing he was good at, it was following people without them knowing it. Barnes thought about it for a second. How was he supposed to bring her back? He looked around the busy street. *Jesus!* He couldn't just heave her up under his arm and carry her kicking and screaming. He needed to get her somewhere alone, smack her face back and forth a few times, get her attention, then show her the small pistol in his waist. That ought to do it.

Listen to me, Kate. One false move and you're dead, understand . . . ? Maybe whip that pistol out, shove the barrel up under her nose, lift her head up a little, her arm already twisted up behind her back. Barnes smiled to himself. *Oh yeah, that would work.* At the corner he hung farther back as she crossed the street and doubled back in the same direction. She'd make a slip before long, get off this main street, give him a chance at her. He'd spent time handcuffed to her. She hadn't seemed either that strong or, to tell the truth, that smart. *All right, lady . . .* Forget the Kate part—too friendly, he thought. *You know me, and you know I'll kill you. Now move it, or die.*

He followed, stopping when she stopped, looking into windows at things he otherwise would have no interest in. Forget the you know me, you know I'll kill you part—too dramatic, he thought. Keep it simple. Smack her once in the mouth, pull out the pistol, jam it in her ribs. *Come with me, somebody wants to see you.* He watched her stop at the corner of the alley fifteen feet ahead. She wasn't about to go in that alley though, he thought. That would be too good to be true. But surely she would have more sense than to— *There she goes!*

Barnes's heart raced in his chest. He waited for five seconds, then ten. Then he hurried to the corner of the alley and peeped around it. The sunlight was blocked by the tall buildings on either side, bathing the alley in darkness. He saw her grow smaller in the shadows as she moved away. He hurried, trying to run on his tiptoes without making any noise. *Where was she? In the shadows? Up there?* He looked at where some empty crates stood stacked up the side of the brick building.

Barnes quickened his pace, looking all around for her. But then, as suddenly as she'd disappeared, she sprang back in front of him from behind a wooden crate, facing him in a flurry of petticoats, startling him to a skidding halt less than three feet away. Barnes's left hand went for the pistol in his belt; his right hand drew back to slap her. "Lady, I—Kate, you're coming to talk to—" But neither of his hands completed its move.

The hard, blunt tip of the parasol came straight up under his chin, his teeth slamming shut on his tongue. Blood spouted. Barnes's hands went instinctively to his mouth, not even seeing the parasol tip draw back and shoot forward like a warrior's spear, the blunt tip striking deep where his ribs met in the center of his chest.

Barnes bowed forward and struggled for breath, hobbling in a short painful circle around the narrow alley and coming right smack back to Kate McCorkle. He saw her shoes and the hem of her dress through a watery veil. Her hands took him by his ears. For just a second he felt she was leading him somewhere, maybe feeling sorry for what she'd just done to him. But then his head struck the brick wall.

Barnes was on the ground now, smelling something terrible where his cheek met the hard damp cobblestone. Kate McCorkle's foot was on his neck, and she reached down and pulled his pistol from his belt, then cocked it and jammed it down in the exposed corner of his mouth, good and tight against his eye tooth.

"Barnes, you son of a bitch," she whispered a few inches from his ear, squatting, her feet spread wide with one foot on his neck. "You're with Mabrey, aren't you?" Barnes nodded as best he could. She jammed the barrel against his tooth. "He's here in town right now? To kill Charlie?" Again Barnes nodded, whimpering under his breath, his eyes turned wildly up to her. "How many more men are with him?" She poked the pistol harder, his chin crooking sideways against the grimy cobblestone. He groaned and held up one trembling finger.

"One more, huh? Red Lohman . . . that figures, that murdering bastard!" She eased the pistol up enough for him to talk. "Why'd he send you after me? The money? He wants the money back and me and Charlie dead, right?"

"Uh-huh." Barnes nodded. "He . . . he told me to bring you back. Said get rough . . . if I had to." His breath rasped in his chest.

Kate McCorkle spoke through clenched teeth, taking her foot off his neck and stepping back. She leaned the parasol against an empty crate and smoothed a hand down her bodice, straightening. "I'd kill you for two cents, Barnes. But since you didn't get rough . . ." She looked him up and down. "You go back and tell William *Mad-dog* Mabrey I was too busy shopping to come see him right now. Tell him when I do see him it'll be to put a bullet in his eye. If he or you or anybody else makes a move on my Charlie, I will kill that person graveyard dead. Can you remember all that, Barnes?"

"I'll remember." Barnes nodded. His voice sounded thick and odd, not at all as he wanted it to sound. Rising up onto his knees with a hand pressed to his ribs, he spat out a gout of dark blood. "My tongue is cut bad . . ."

"That's not my fault." Kate helped him the rest of the way to his feet, then gestured with his pistol. "Now get your trousers off. Hurry up."

"Hunh?" Barnes gave her a strange, frightened look, a hand moving down instinctively to shield his crotch.

"You heard me! Get them off. You're giving me a head start out of here. It's either that, or I knock you cock-eyed cold with your pistol butt."

Barnes loosened his belt and let his trousers fall, his wrinkled knee-length underwear looking ridiculous and large around his knobby knees. "Mabrey will kill me," he slurred, his injured tongue now swelling up nearly twice its normal size.

"Somebody was bound to kill you, Barnes. Just be glad it wasn't me." She took his trousers, stood on one leg of them and jerked up, ripping them apart at the upper seams. Barnes moaned, watching her. Then she ripped each leg seam up to the pockets and pitched them at his feet. "There, that'll slow you down." She picked up the parasol, shoved the pistol somewhere up under the waist of her dress, and walked away.

When Kate McCorkle came to the firearms store, she walked inside, leaned the parasol against the counter, and pointed to a pair of big Colt pistols hanging on display. "Yes. Give me two of those," she said when a clerk stepped forward and asked if he could help her.

"Ma'am, if you don't mind my saying so, I hope these are for your husband, or perhaps some gentleman friend? Because quite frankly, these are far too powerful for a lady."

She gave him a steady, determined stare. "Will they knock the 'nads off a bull buffalo at fifty yards?" The clerk looked as if she'd slapped him. His face reddened. He could only nod. "Then that's what I want, sir," Kate said in a resolved tone. "And two boxes of cartridges. I'm through carrying little pistols that won't shoot a man in half."

Red Lohman was the first to return, and when he didn't see Mabrey's buggy, he dropped back out of sight into the cover of some low-hanging willow branches that drooped down over the edge of a stone wall across the street from the hospital. Five minutes later, Mabrey's buggy came around the corner of the block. Lohman sidled up close and waved his hand up and down. "You weren't here, boss," Lohman said, stepping up and taking a seat beside Mabrey. "I started getting concerned."

"See that blasted policeman?" Mabrey nodded at the blue uniform across the street near the hospital door. "He keeps coming out to the street and waving me on. I've circled the block four times since you left. He shouted out, 'You can only stop here to let someone in or out'—and we call this a free country." Mabrey spat the bad taste of it from his mouth. "Where'd the deputies go, Red?"

"You were right, boss. They got on the train. They're headed west."

Mabrey thought about it. "They're onto Phelps and the rifle deal. They'll be tracking Phelps down in two days, if they haven't already wired ahead and sicced the law on him and his men. Damned telegrams! Damned trains! I'm really getting sick of all this so-called progress."

"Uh, boss?" Red Lohman looked worried. "I better tell you this. I happened past your Pullman car on the way here. There were two men there, so I asked them who the hell they were. They said they're with the railroad, and they needed some money. Claimed they haven't been paid for the use of the engine for the past three months. Said they're cutting it loose from your car and putting your car on a siding over in the coal yard till you pay them something."

"The coal yard! Damn it to hell!" Mabrey ran a hand across his brow, starting to sweat now. "I've paid those buzzards. I know I have! For last month anyway, I'm certain . . . or at least the month before last. I'd swear to it!"

"I'm only telling you what they said, boss." Lohman leaned back from him.

Mabrey settled himself down. "I didn't bring a lot of cash with me this trip. But I'll get this straightened out before we leave here. I'm not traveling by horseback, I promise you that!" Mabrey leaned out of the buggy and looked back, seeing the police officer walking toward them. "This is like some crazy nightmare!" He lashed the reins to the horse's back and sent the buggy forward to circle the block again.

On the next trip around, Red Lohman spotted Briley Barnes moving along close to the stone wall across from the hospital. "There he is, boss." Lohman squinted. "But what the hell happened to him?" Barnes hugged even closer to the stone wall, looking scared and embarrassed, his new bowler hat gone, his trouser legs flaring open all the way up the sides of his pale legs.

"I don't know." Mabrey already began to boil. "I know he didn't get that woman. Looks like somebody beat the living hell out of him!"

Red Lohman smiled to himself. "Get in, Barnes," he said as the buggy drew near. Barnes leaped up into the seat beside Lohman and pulled his trouser legs closed. "Well, how did *you* do, you lousy little punk?" Red Lohman looked him up and down, loving it. Briley Barnes kept quiet, and just stared straight ahead.

On the third floor of the hospital, Quick Charlie Sims stood at the barred window and looked down, unable to see the buggy or even the main street from where he stood. He used Captain Bennington's golf club as a walking cane. "I hope you haven't scared them away." He smiled to himself. "You really need to work on that temper of yours, Kate," he added, over his shoulder.

Behind him, Kate McCorkle sat on the side of his bed, the two new Colts laid out on the sheet beside a box of cartridges. "I know, Charlie. But when I saw him sneaking around following me, I just saw red. I couldn't help it." Kate shoved bullets into each pistol in turn, spun them, then laid them back down.

Sims turned from the barred window and limped back to the bed. He reached down and cupped her cheek. "You did fine." He smiled, looking into her eyes. "It feels like old times."

Kate, still wound tight, turned her face from him, looking back down at the pistols. "I probably should

have gone on and shot him." She'd come into the
hospital moments earlier through the rear doors, to
avoid being seen. The big Colts had been hidden in
a brown paper bag with a loaf of Italian bread sticking up from it. The guard at the door hadn't questioned her. "At least we know they're here. There's
no more guesswork." She shrugged. "If they want a
fight, I'll give them one."

Sims turned around and eased himself down on
the side of the bed, propping both hands atop the
golf club and resting his chin on them. "We need to
get things rolling, get finished up here. I still want
to be in Fort Smith when Priest makes his break."

Kate looked at him. "Should you be sitting up like
that? Doesn't it hurt?"

"No, this is all right. It's a little sore. But I've got
to push myself a little more each day." He paused,
thinking about something.

"Charlie, are you okay?" Kate leaned toward him.

"Hmm?" He blinked, looking back at her. "Oh,
yeah. Just working on something. We need to get rid
of some of this police protection so Mabrey will make
his move." He paused for another second, then
added, "Captain Bennington said he and the mayor
play golf on a private meadowland outside of town.
I wonder where that is?"

"Oh," Kate said flatly, "you want to play golf?
Good luck, Charlie. You shouldn't even be walking
yet."

"I'm not going to play—but it's always fun to
watch." He closed his eyes, his forearm across his
brow. "When did Bennington say the mayor wanted
to meet me?"

"One day next week, why?"

"It'll have to be sooner than that. I won't be here
next week." Sims paused, then asked, "Think you
can slip in and out of here without Mabrey seeing
you?"

"If he does, I'll blast a hole in him." She hefted one of the big pistols from the bed.

"No, Kate. I don't want you or the police or anybody but me to take down Mad-dog Mabrey. All right?"

"All right. Sure, I can slip in and out." She straightened up, letting the pistol down onto her lap. "What do you want, Charlie?"

"I need you to go to Uncle Breldi. Tell him I want to play golf with the mayor . . . but not next week. Tell him to set it up as soon as possible—tomorrow if he can."

Kate looked astonished. "Uncle Breldi can do that?" She snapped her fingers. "Just like that? He has that kind of pull with the mayor?"

Sims smiled. "You'd be surprised what Uncle Breldi can get done if he wants to."

"But where do I find Uncle Breldi?" she asked.

"Go find a horse auction barn and just mention his name. Believe me, Kate, he'll find you."

Kate stood up, the big pistol hanging in one hand, her other hand resting on her hip. "Is this one of those deals where you're only going to tell me a little bit at a time?"

"Kate, right now, a little bit at a time is all I've got. You're not going to get out of here with that pistol and lose your temper, are you?"

She raised the Colt with both hands, sighted it on something across the room and out through the window, closing one eye. "I'll try not, Charlie." She smiled and lowered it. "But you know how I am."

Chapter 26

Sullivan Hart and Twojack Roth stepped down from the train at Little Red Springs and walked forward toward the engine. The engineer and the fireman had just stepped down as well, the engineer holding a leather grip bag. Seeing the deputies, the engineer held up two fingers, saying to them, "Don't forget, gentlemen, in two hours this train leaves come hell or hailstorm. Can't spare you no more than that."

"Thanks," Roth said, "that's plenty of time." He and Hart then headed on to the sheriff's office with their saddlebags over their shoulders. They'd had the conductor talk to the engineer the day before, and let him know the urgency of their trip. He'd agreed to let them off at an unscheduled stop of their choosing should the need arise. For the past two days and nights, the conductor had pushed a little harder than usual for their sake. The train had made excellent time.

At the sheriff's office, Sheriff Bud Kay stood up from behind his battered desk with a mug of coffee in his hand. "I figured I hadn't seen the last of you two." He offered a thin smile, then let it drop, taking note of Roth's swollen face. He winced. "Twojack walked into a lamppost, I see. Lots of people do that their first trip to the city. Can't help looking up all the time." He chuckled. "How's the manhunt going?"

"Sheriff, you wouldn't believe it," Sullivan Hart replied.

"I bet I would. It came out over the wires, you know. Told about a big shootout in the Chicago rail yards. I'm glad to see you boys are all right. They said one man get et up by guard dogs."

Hart and Roth looked at each other. "That was Quick Charlie Sims, Sheriff. He fell in among two rail yard dogs. But they didn't even try to bite him."

"Sims, huh? That figures." Sheriff Kay shook his head. "Did you ever get your black morgan horse back from that rascal?"

"Yep, I got him back. He's on the train." Sullivan Hart looked embarrassed. "We're still on Cleveland Phelps's trail, Sheriff." Roth spoke. "We would have wired you, had you keep an eye out for him, but we both knew you would anyway."

"You're right, I have been. Him and three of his men were through here day before yesterday. One of them looked to be wounded. They met some men at the train, unloaded three wagonloads of cargo, then headed out." Sheriff Kay lowered his eyes for a second. "I know I should have done something to stop them, but I'm not as young as I once was. Plus, I didn't want to interfere with anything you two had going on. Didn't want to put them on guard. I stayed back and observed, you might say."

"Thanks, Sheriff, you did good," Roth said.

"Which way did they head out of here?" Hart asked.

Bud Kay pointed southwest. "In my opinion, they're going straight back to the Old English Spread—no house left there, but plenty of room to hole up and wait for the *federales*, if they're hauling what I think they are." He tapped a bony finger to his forehead. "I ain't forgot how to think, fellows." He grinned. "I did some snooping around in their tracks after they left. Phelps's horse is wearing a pair of new Thorensen store-boughts. You can see the big

T in the dirt plain as day, should you have to track him down."

"That's good to know." Roth smiled. "How's the coffee?"

"Help yourself." Sheriff Kay gestured with his cup toward the small stove.

"Thanks." Roth walked over, picked himself up a cup, and filled it halfway. As he sipped, Roth noticed the empty jail cells with their doors standing open. "What became of the prisoners?"

"The circuit judge turned them loose, just like I said he would. He came through earlier than I expected. It was plumb wild around here for a day or two, until they all drifted off. One tried stealing old Gus Brambley's mule, Hazel. Of course if you know Hazel, she ain't the kind of mule you want to steal. She bucked him right through the barbershop window, cut him to pieces."

"And the rest of them?" Twojack Roth asked.

"Aw . . ." Sheriff Kay waved it off. "One got into it with Big Nancy—she nearly drowned him in the water trough. Another got snakebit." He shook his head. "I almost felt sorry for them."

Hart smiled at Roth. "It's good to be home."

"Yep." Roth tipped his cup toward him in salute.

Sullivan Hart turned to the sheriff. "We've got a couple of hours to get some supplies and have a sit-down meal, Sheriff Kay. Care to join us? It's on Judge Parker's court."

"I'd never pass up a chance to eat a meal out of the Hanging Judge's pocket. He's so tight his shadow collects dust."

"Speaking of the judge," Hart said, "I need to wire him. You two go on. I'll get our rifles out of hock and join up with you later."

By the time the train let out a blast from its steam whistle, Hart and Roth had checked on their horses in the stock car, watered and grained them, and were back on board, their rifles back in hand, their saddlebags supplied with a week's worth of provisions. They'd made arrangements with the conductor to wake them before they reached the water stop a hundred miles ahead. Then they both wiped their rifles down with their bandannas, loaded them, and leaned them against their knees.

They slept like dead men for the next three and half hours, until the conductor said, "Time to wake up, deputies." The few other passengers watched as Hart and Roth stood staggering slightly with the sway of the train. Carrying their rifles, they shouldered up their saddlebags and headed back toward the stock car.

"Feels like forever since I've been in a saddle," Hart said as they prepared their horses for the trail. Soft evening light flickered through the slats on the stock car.

"Me too," Roth said, "but I've got a feeling we're about to get caught up." They strapped their saddlebags down, feeling the train decrease its speed with a long shriek of its whistle.

"We've saved ourselves a full day or more, railing it out this far. Maybe we'll have some element of surprise," Hart said as he took his leather gloves out of his duster pocket and put them on. "It should be a straight shot from here to the Old English Spread. This is where they shipped their cattle from."

"I'm rested." Roth looked at Hart. "We can ride all night if you want to." He reached for the reins to his horse.

"Sounds good to me." Hart adjusted his battered Stetson down on his forehead. The sway of the train lessened as the big wheels turned slower and slower beneath the straw-covered floor. When the train bumped to a halt, they threw the doors open, slid the loading ramp out, and in moments stood with their horses while the conductor checked the stock car doors and stepped back up between two cars.

"Good luck to you, Deputies," the conductor called

out as the train chugged slowly forward. He focused on Roth. "Hope you find whoever did that to your face." Hart and Roth tipped their hats to him, then waved a gloved hand to a young boy whose small hand wagged up and down at them until the woman beside him reached out and turned him forward in his seat.

"It's going to be a long night," Roth said.

"I know it," Hart replied.

Darkness loomed, the long shadows of wild grass on the plains giving way to coming moonlight. In the distance, the rise of the hill country stood in a black streak across the horizon. They turned in silence and stepped up into their saddles, Sullivan Hart liking the familiar feel of the black morgan cross standing beneath him. They turned their horses and looked out across plains. "Back into the breech," Hart whispered, patting the big morgan's withers. They heeled their horses forward and rode away.

Cleveland Phelps sat beneath the canvas lean-to on a folding stool the *federales* had left behind. He counted the large stack of money on the small empty ammunition crate in front of him, with his pistol lying near his hand. Light from the campfire out front of the lean-to glowed in his eyes. Next to the stack of money lay a worn folded document he'd taken out of his saddlebags earlier and read to himself three or four times throughout the day.

When Otis Farnsworth stepped forward from the other side of the campfire and over to the lean-to, Cleveland Phelps gave him a menacing stare. Phelps reached over and cocked the pistol, making sure Otis saw him do it. "What do you want, Otis?" Phelps kept his hand covering the pistol butt. "You better get some sleep like everybody else. We're breaking up and getting out of here before dawn."

"Yeah, I know." Otis spoke in a hushed voice, glancing back over his shoulder at the sleeping camp.

"That's why I want to talk to you." He came closer, but stopped at the edge of the lean-to. "Can I come in?"

"Hold on a minute." Cleveland Phelps kept his eyes on Otis as he picked up the stack of money and shoved it into the open saddlebags at his feet. Then he straightened up and laid his hand back on the pistol butt. "Come on in."

Otis Farnsworth grinned, his big round face seeming to take up lots of space beneath the lean-to. "You don't trust nobody, Cleveland Phelps . . . that's what I always admired about you."

"You know the rules, Otis. Everybody watches out for his own share. You got your cut along with the rest." Phelps took out a short thin cigar and stuck it in his mouth. With his eyes still on Farnsworth, he took a long match from his shirt pocket, lit the cigar and let out a stream of gray smoke. "What's on your mind?"

"You and me go way back, boss." Otis kept his voice low. "And all the way from Chicago I've been asking myself, when is Cleveland going quit fooling around and take over this whole show? Without you and us"—he gestured toward the others, sleeping around the campfire—"Mabrey and Priest ain't nothing. *Los Pistoleros* might go all the way back to them two years ago. But it's changed. You know it has. With JT Priest out of the picture, what's to stop us from—?"

"Power," Cleveland Phelps cut in. "Mabrey has the right people in his pockets right now. These *federales*? They're people he knows. How did he get to know them?" Phelps grinned and rubbed his thumb and finger together in the universal sign of greed. "I'll tell you how. His contacts in Washington."

"But they know you, Phelps. You're the one who just put the deal together, not Mabrey and Priest."

"Funny you should mention that, Otis." Cleveland Phelps puffed his cigar. "Before they left awhile ago,

I told them that from now on they deal directly with me and you. Told them Priest is in jail, and Mabrey might not be far behind him."

"Yeah? You mentioned me too?" Otis beamed.

"That's right, buddy. You and me." Cleveland Phelps was only half lying. He had said that to the *federales*, but he'd only said Otis Farnsworth would be his middleman, the same as Priest was with Mabrey. "These others are good gunmen," he added, lowering his voice. "But like you said, you and me go way back. They've got no head for the business end of it. Clifford's a plum idiot and Harvey . . . well, the shape he's in, I'm not sure he's going to make it anyway."

"So, it's me and you. When do we take the rest of this thing over?" Otis Farnsworth leaned forward, eager for direction.

"Well, first things first, Otis." Phelps picked up the folded document off the crate and put it inside his shirt. "I want to see if Mabrey lands on his feet or not. Quick Charlie Sims has hit him hard." He patted his shirt where he'd placed the document. "This paper right here, Otis? This is twenty percent ownership in the Midwest Investment Corporation. Mabrey has fifty-one percent, Priest has twenty percent, and the rest is spread out among some of their contacts. I've been carrying this around for three years now. Mabrey and Priest probably think I forgot all about it. But no sir. I've been waiting, watching. This is what I call my keys to the *Los Pistoleros* kingdom."

"I don't get it." Otis Farnsworth scratched his head.

"Otis, Midwest Investment owns holdings not only in America, but in countries around the world. Africa, England, Australia. Lord Tillford, the Englishman, set me straight about it. He offered to buy my share. I wouldn't sell. See, it's not just about robbing banks and pulling cattle schemes. That's what Mabrey would have Priest and us think. But according to Tillford, Midwest Investment is into everything—a lot of it strictly legal."

"Damn . . ." Otis Farnsworth blinked his eyes, trying to take it all in.

"When I take over, I want more than a fast horse and a handful of banks to rob. I want it *all*." He paused. "And that's where you come in, Otis."

"How, Cleveland? I'll back your play," Otis offered.

"I'll need operating cash for a while, just like Mabrey. But I'll take better care of you and the boys than Mabrey did of Priest and the rest of us. You can count on that."

"But if Priest and Mabrey both go to jail, or even hang, won't that be all of Midwest Investment? What happens to it then?"

"It just keeps on going. That's the sweetest part, Otis. They sell their legitimate shares to somebody— and guess who that somebody will be?" He grinned. "See why I'm sticking with Mabrey and Priest for now? I figure once it's a sure bet that Priest is going to hang, I'll ease in there and get his share from him. He'll be needing money to make one of those *appeals* that's going over so favorably lately."

"I'm with you, boss. Let me know what to do."

Cleveland Phelps studied his eyes for a moment. "Okay," he said at length. "I'm taking you into my confidence . . . don't let me down. I'm heading out of here in a little while. Come daylight, before the rest of you split up, you make sure these new laborers are dead. I don't want a trace of them blowing on the wind. Then you get to El Paso and wait for me there. Will you do that?"

"I damned sure will." Otis stood up with him. "What about those two deputies? If you run into them, you'll have your hands full."

"I'm not worried. Besides, if they're on our trail right now, they'll be coming down out of the north.

I'm headed south. So, if you get a chance at those two . . ." Phelps grinned and chewed on his cigar. "Be sure and kill them for me."

"You've got it, boss." Otis Farnsworth grinned.

Chapter 27

Sullivan Hart and Twojack Roth had ridden hard and steadily throughout the night, and before dawn they lay covered by a low rise of rock eighty yards back from the smoldering campfire. They'd left their horses a few yards farther back, tied to a deadfall of cottonwood. Hart raised his pistol, checked it, and reholstered it. He squinted in the pale moonlight, faintly hearing the sound of men's voices, their wake-up coughs mingling among the low nicker of horses. "I wish we could get a little closer first, or else wait for daylight." A wagon tailgate squeaked open, then shut.

"No time," Roth whispered. "They're getting ready to move out. I'd hate to get caught on open ground, as many men as there are."

Hart considered it, then said, "You're right . . . here goes."

"Do it when you're ready. I'll flank them to the right first chance I get." Roth braced himself, his rifle cocked, aimed, and ready.

Sullivan Hart moved ten feet away in a low crouch, then lay flat and aimed his rifle, searching for a target of any kind close to the low glow of firelight. Something white moved in the darkness. *A shirt?* He hoped so. The sound of his rifle shot split the silence. A startled yell rose up near the campfire. Twojack Roth's rifle exploded a streak of fire as Hart levered another round, then another.

Otis Farnsworth dove to the ground and crawled farther away from the fire, one of the new men stumbling over his back as the whole camp scattered back and forth, yelling. Otis made it beneath an empty wagon where Clifford Mallory had already taken position and lay firing his rifle at the muzzle flashes in the darkness. Otis turned, firing his pistol between the spokes of a wagon wheel.

"Where's Cleveland?" Clifford Mallory shouted to Otis.

"He's gone!" Otis fired six rounds, dropped his pistol, and grabbed another one out of his belt.

"Gone? Gone where?" Clifford shoved more rounds into his repeating rifle.

"Never mind! He had business to tend!" A rifle shot from the deputies careened against a wooden spoke, sending off a spray of splinters. Otis Farnsworth ducked away, then emptied his other pistol toward the deputies. "It's those lawdogs! I know it is," he shouted. One of the new men rolled under the wagon beside him and fired a small pocket pistol toward the roaring rifles. Otis Farnsworth shoved him away. "Get the hell out of here! All that little thing's doing is making them mad!"

Harvey Mallory had crawled in among the horses at the sound of the first rifle shot. With his wound broken open and bleeding, he gathered the reins to their horses, only two of them saddled, and steadied them amid the gunshots. A bullet whistled past his head; another one kicked up dirt at his feet. The horses tried to rear and bolt away, but he held them tight.

The rifle fire continued to pound the campsite. "Harvey? Can you hear me?" Clifford called out to his brother. "Need some transportation here!"

"It's coming," Harvey yelled. But before he could gather the horse around himself for cover, a bullet tore through his shoulder and spun him around in a tangle of reins.

Another of the new men scrambled in, hearing Harvey let out a groan. "Here, I'll help you!" He took the reins and looped Harvey's arm across his shoulder as rifle shots sliced the air around them.

The man with the small pistol rolled in around two more of the new men, lying flat in the dirt with their hands covering their heads. Immediately rifle fire whistled past them. "Jesus! Get out of here with that!" one man shouted at him. "Don't shoot over here! We're unarmed! We surrender!" the men shouted from the ground. The rifle fire turned away from them and thumped back into the wagon where the flames from Otis Farnsworth's and Clifford Mallory's guns flared in the darkness.

Twojack Roth rose up, ran ten yards to his right, then dropped down and fired three rounds to show Hart his position. Then he darted farther right, flanking the campsite. He caught the flash of a white shirt rise up and run in a thin streak of pistol fire. Twojack fired and saw the white shirt fly backward. *Got him.*

With the new man helping him, Harvey Mallory tried to get the horse around behind the wagon a few yards back. But the rifles held the wagon under relentless fire. "Hold up here," Harvey said, his arm across the man's shoulder. They stopped.

"Don't worry, I've got you," the new man said as Harvey staggered in place, blood from his fresh shoulder wound running down his chest.

"Thanks, I'll remember this," Harvey replied beneath the deafening gunfire.

Under the wagon, Otis Farnsworth had taken a graze along his cheek. He fired with one hand raised to his face to stem the flow of blood. "Where the hell's your brother?" he shouted at Clifford Mallory.

"He's bringing the horses!" Clifford yelled back.

"When, damn it!"

"He can't get to us!" Clifford stopped to reload.

"Then let's get to him!" Otis dropped down on his

belly and crawled away. Clifford stopped reloading and followed him.

As soon as the firing stopped beneath the wagon, Sullivan Hart scanned the gray darkness, knowing they were making their move. At the sound of Clifford Mallory calling out to his brother, Hart swung the rifle and fired. Roth did the same from thirty yards to the right. But their shots found no substance, and the firing from the camp had now stopped completely. Roth continued to fire as Sullivan Hart rose up and ran back to their horses.

"Let's go! Let's go!" Clifford Mallory snatched a set of reins, helped Harvey up into the saddle, then grabbed a horse for himself. Otis Farnsworth had already mounted and kicked his horse out across the flatland toward the hills. Hearing the sound of his horse's hoofs, Roth fired in his direction, the shot veering wide of Otis's back by mere inches.

"What about me?" The new man grabbed Harvey's leg before Harvey could spur his horse away. Clifford had just spun his horse and kicked it forward.

"Oh, you . . ." Harvey reached down with his good arm. "Come on. Get behind me." He helped the new man scramble up onto the saddle as he spurred his horse. The new man felt a bullet sing past them. He grabbed Harvey around his waist and hung on tight, the horse bolting forward so fast it nearly pitched him backward.

"Glad you didn't forget me!" the new man said close to Harvey's ear above the sound of the horse's pounding hoofs. Another bullet zinged through the air.

"Yeah, you should be—stupid son of a bitch!" Harvey shouted in reply.

"What?"

Harvey didn't answer. But when he heard the man let out a grunt and slam forward against him, he grinned to himself and reached around with his good arm, keeping the man's limp body from falling out of the saddle until the sound of fire grew distant behind him. Then he turned the man's body loose. *"Adios, amigo,"* he said. "Thanks for being my shield." He felt the horse's pace quicken as the dead weight flew from its back.

Hart and Roth converged on the campsite from both sides, their pistols drawn and cocked. "Everybody up! Hands high!" Hart demanded. They kept their horses sidestepping and moved in a circle around the camp. Four of the six new men stood up, and a fifth lay stretched out flat on his stomach, dead, his small pocket pistol an inch from his hand.

Roth spoke down to the nearest man. "There's supposed to be six of you boys. Where's the other one?"

They all looked around, their hands high. The one Roth had asked shook his head. "I don't know. But we never fired a shot at you, honest. We just took cover is all."

Hart's eyes swept the campsite, seeing one empty wagon riddled with bullets, a canvas lean-to that had been shot to the ground, and a shattered ammunition crate. "You've already delivered the rifles?" Off to the left in the gray darkness, a mule brayed long and loud.

"They were waiting when we got here," the man replied. "Took the other two wagons with them and left us this one to get home on."

"How many men just took off?" Roth asked.

"Three of them. Mister Phelps was already gone when I woke up. At least, I never saw him."

Hart and Roth looked at each other. "Can you men find your way back to Little Red Springs from here?"

The men only milled in place, looking stunned at the prospect. "You better hope you can," Roth said, wanting to get a move on. He looked at Sullivan Hart and nodded in the direction the gunmen had fled. "They're not getting any closer."

Hart backed his horse, stopping it beside Roth. "All right, you men scatter. Get your mules and clear out!'' He turned to Roth as the men ran in all directions. ''Think Quick Charlie Sims is up having breakfast about now?''

''Nah. It's too early for Sims.'' Roth spread a wry smile. They turned their horses and heeled them forward as the first traces of sunlight glowed on the eastern sky.

Kate McCorkle pushed the big wooden wheelchair into Quick Charlie Sims's room, then turned and closed the door behind her. Rolling the wheelchair across the floor to the bed, she looked at Sims and shook her head. ''I hope you know what you're doing, Charlie. If Mabrey and his men see you, they're going to kill you.'' She picked up the new black bowler hat from the wheelchair and held it out for him.

''With the mayor and his bodyguards? I doubt it.'' Sims looked up at her from the side of the bed. He was dressed in his trousers and a clean white shirt a nurse had brought him. He had a wool shawl thrown over his shoulders. ''You did tell Uncle Breldi to have the mayor bring some bodyguards, I hope?''

''Yes I did. Uncle Breldi said, don't worry . . . the mayor *will* have bodyguards. But, Charlie, I've got a bad feeling about this. What if Mabrey—?''

''Don't start worrying, Kate,'' Sims stopped her, standing up from his bed and sitting down in the wheelchair. He reached over, picked up Captain Bennington's golf club, and laid it across his lap. Kate set the new bowler hat on his head. Sims cocked it back, high up on his forehead. ''Mabrey is not going to kill me without trying to get his money back first.'' He glanced up at her over his shoulder. ''As soon as I leave here, I want you to come back to this room and stay put, okay?'' She didn't answer. ''Okay?'' he asked again in a stronger tone.

''Okay,'' she relented. ''But at least take one of the pistols with you.''

"I've already got one."

"Where? I didn't see it." Kate leaned out over his shoulder and peered down into his lap.

"That's the whole idea." He pulled his wool shawl tighter around his shoulders and made sure the new bowler hat sat high on his forehead.

"Charlie, you never wear a hat that high." Kate started to adjust it on his head, but he stopped her, and pushed it back up.

"Do you mind, Kate? I want to keep the sun off my neck. Now are you going to take me downstairs, or do I have to walk? The mayor will be here any minute."

William Mabrey sat in the covered buggy a half a block away, looking back at the hospital. When he saw Kate McCorkle walk out to the street and look both ways, he ducked out of sight, then carefully peeped back again, this time barely showing part of his face. "There she is! What's she looking for?"

Lohman and Barnes both started to lean out the other side of the buggy, but Mabrey stopped them. "Sit still! I can see her. She's up to something."

When Kate walked back to the doors of the hospital and out of sight, Mabrey cursed under his breath. "Damn it, now I can't see her." He reined the buggy forward. "We've got to get turned around and get closer." At the corner a block away, Mabrey swung the rig around in a complete circle and headed back, keeping the buggy close to the edge of the cobblestone street. "Can you see her yet?" Mabrey asked Red Lohman and Briley Barnes, trying to keep the buggy close to the stone curbing.

"No . . . yeah! There she is!" Red Lohman raised a hand to shield his face as Kate looked in their direction from fifty yards away. Mabrey kept his head tilted forward, his tall top hat hiding his visage. Barnes bowed forward as if in prayer. "What's this about, boss?"

Lohman nudged Mabrey, nodding toward the big

glass-enclosed four-horse carriage that had just rolled around the corner and pulled over toward Kate McCorkle. Kate stepped back and smiled up at the driver.

"I don't know," Mabrey said under his breath, "but I don't like it." He pulled back on the reins, stopping the buggy. "Red, work your way up there—see what's going on!"

"What about me?" Barnes asked. "I can slip around from the other side."

"Shut up, Barnes! You're lucky I haven't strangled you to death!"

Barnes slumped back in his seat, his head still bowed. They watched through hooded eyes as Red Lohman slinked from tree to shrub until he got within fifteen feet of the big carriage. Two big men in long black coats had already stepped out of the carriage and walked into the hospital. Now they came back, carrying Quick Charlie Sims, wheelchair and all, between them. Kate McCorkle stood back, her hands folded in front of her.

"Good morning, Mayor, Your Honor," Lohman heard Sims say as the door opened and the two men lifted him inside. "Glad you could make it on such short notice." Lohman was taken aback. He blinked his eyes as if to clear them, then squinted at the engraved brass plate on the side of the carriage.

"I'm sure the fresh air will do him good," Kate said through the half-opened carriage window. Lohman saw a tall top hat tip toward her, then he watched Kate McCorkle step back and wave as the carriage made a wide full circle on the cobblestone street and move away beneath the crack of a long black whip. Kate McCorkle turned around and walked through the hospital doors.

What the hell? Red Lohman stood transfixed for a second. Then he heard Mabrey call out in a harsh whisper as the buggy rolled up in front of him. "Get in, Red. Hurry up!" Red Lohman snapped out of it, bounded out and up into the covered buggy. "Well? Who was it? Where are they going?" Mabrey spoke fast.

"Boss, I don't believe this. Sims just left with the mayor!" Red pointed as he spoke, the big carriage already swinging around the corner and heading back the way it had come.

William Mabrey stared for a second, then a sly smile came across his big face. "You're right, Red . . . I don't believe it either. This is some kind of Charlie the Wizard scheme. If that's the mayor, I'll eat my shoe. Sims no more knows the mayor of Chicago than I know the king of England! The mayor wouldn't dirty his carriage wheels for Quick Charlie Sims!"

"But that's the damn mayor's rig!" Red pointed out. "I saw the brass plate on it!"

"You saw what Sims wanted you to see, Lohman. Sims is slippery as an eel. You ought to know that by now!" Mabrey stood up from his seat. "Get over here, Barnes. Take the reins."

They swapped seats, Barnes getting nervous, holding the reins up with both hands. "Where are we going?" He looked at Mabrey.

"Follow them, you damn imbecile," Mabrey hissed. "Don't let them out of your sight." He let out a nasty chuckle under his breath and settled himself into the seat. "Watch me close, boys. You might both learn something."

Chapter 28

Kate McCorkle raced through the hall of the hospital, holding her hemline up to her knees with both hands, almost knocking over a cart full of linen. She burst through the back doors and down off of loading dock to the horse she'd rented earlier and had left tied beneath the shade of a wide maple tree. Charlie was going to be mad, she knew. But that was too bad . . . she wasn't about to take a chance on him facing William Mabrey and his men alone.

She climbed up into the saddle, felt up under her waist-length vest, and adjusted the big Colt at her waist.

"I hope you ride better than I do," she said to the horse. Then she batted her heels to the big bay's side, sending him up into the wide stretch of commons behind the hospital grounds. In a moment she'd cut diagonally through the sparse wooded commons and back onto the cobblestone street. Ahead of her a hundred yards, she saw the black covered buggy that had followed the carriage. *Mabrey . . . !* Beyond it she saw the tail end of the mayor's big carriage as it topped a hill and descended out of sight. The big bay jostled and high-stepped quarterwise, its hoofs clacking on the stone street until she righted its head and put it forward again.

When she'd shortened the distance between her and the buggy by fifty yards, she let the horse wind down to a slower pace, not wanting to get too close.

For the next half hour, the big glassed carriage led the discreet parade through the city streets, businessmen and workmen alike tipping their respective caps, top hats, and bowlers toward the mayor's impressive four-horse rig.

Briley Barnes remarked as he drove the covered buggy, "I don't know, Mister Mabrey, that sure looks like the mayor, the way people are acting."

"People are fools! Don't ever forget that, Barnes." Mabrey sat tense, his long wool coat open down the front, his hand inside it on the pistol he wore in a shoulder harness. "Quick Charlie Sims will not out-slick me. I've seen him do it too many times to others. But this time he's met his match." In another few minutes the cobblestone beneath them turned into hard rutted dirt as the skyline of the city formed itself behind them in a gray pall of swirling industrial smoke.

In another twenty minutes the hard dirt streets had turned into a wide country lane. On either side of the winding lane stood tall maples and oaks, whose branches reached out across the road like a translucent canopy shimmering in the morning sunlight. "Where in the hell are they going?" Mabrey cursed, his pistol out of his coat now and lying on his lap. "What's out here, Barnes?"

"Nothing, Mister Mabrey." Barnes stared straight ahead.

"Nothing?" Mabrey gave him a flat, sarcastic look. "You mean the earth just comes to a stop? There's only a void? What?"

Barnes swallowed hard. "I mean, only some country estates. A private hunt club, maybe some—"

"Ah, a private hunt club! Where golfers congregate to knock their little ball around. Now I get it." Mabrey smiled to himself.

"Get what?" Barnes looked bewildered.

"Nothing, Barnes, just drive on." Mabrey turned to Red Lohman. "I hope you're prepared to torture my money out of him. We take a piece or two of Sims to Kate McCorkle, and my money will be in hand."

Red Lohman stared ahead, a killing shine in his eyes. "Either your money, or your money's worth." He paused, then added, "Unless you'd rather Barnes get a taste of how it's done." A faint trace of a smile played beneath his red-gray mustache.

"Good idea. We'll let Barnes do the slicing." Mabrey held out a hand. Red Lohman lay a closed straight razor in it. Barnes saw it in his peripheral vision and swallowed hard.

Kate McCorkle reined the big bay off into the grass when she saw the buggy pull over and stop. Ahead of the buggy, she watched the big carriage turn right and move along a wooded entranceway toward a large brick-and-stone mansion set back over a hundred yards atop a sculptured knoll. "Goodness, Charlie," she whispered to herself. A buffer of thin woodlands lay beside her, but beyond the woodlands, a sloping hillside rose up plush and green and finely cultivated.

In the buggy, Mabrey poked Barnes in his ribs. "Leave the buggy here. Let's get going." They stepped down, Mabrey's pistol hanging in his hand. "Stay inside the trees," he said, gesturing with his pistol. "This is one game that grifter will wish to God he never played."

They stepped into the cover of the woods and moved like stalking wolves along the entranceway. Where the woods stopped some thirty yards from the sprawling mansion, they stayed back in their cover, and in moments saw the two big men lower Sims and his wheelchair from the carriage. One of the men took out a wide leather golf bag and stood it on the ground. The other looked all around, then pulled Sims's wheelchair back and gave the heavyset man room to step down from the carriage. "Golf! That son of a bitch!" Mabrey raged under his breath.

"He knows I'm waiting to kill him, and he plays golf!"

"Shhh, hold it, boss. What's this?" Red Lohman ducked down a little, his pistol out. Behind a tree ten yards to their left, a young man stood hiding, watching the two big bodyguards prepare for the outing.

"Here it is, boys," Mabrey whispered. "This is the scheme I was talking about. Sims lures me out here . . . and he's got a gunman waiting." Red Lohman raised his pistol toward the unwary man's back. But Mabrey shoved it down. "No," he whispered. "Let's take him without a sound!" He glanced back out at Sims and the others beside the big carriage. Sims's black bowler hat was still cocked high, back above his hairline.

"Mayor, my arse," Mabrey said, as if speaking to the heavyset man who stood at the carriage in his dark wool suit and golf knickers. Mabrey spread a sly grin, watching him take a practice swing with a long hickory driver. The two big bodyguards stayed close behind him as he walked toward a flat driving area, stretching his arms and loosening his wide shoulders. One bodyguard carried the big bag of golf clubs; the other pushed Sims in his wheelchair.

Hidden behind the large maple tree, the young man had no time to think or yell. Red Lohman's rough hand spun him around, clamped around his throat, and pinned him to the tree. The young man stared wide-eyed, his mouth agape, at the open bore of Red's cocked pistol only inches from his nose. "Okay, punk, spill it, and spill it fast," Mabrey hissed in his face. "What's his scam here? What's your role in it?"

"Oh, God!" the man whimpered, his hands trembling. "Please don't shoot. I'm sorry!" A short pencil stub fell from one hand. In his other hand the pages of a small writing tablet fluttered open like pigeon wings.

Briley Barnes stepped forward and jerked the tab-

let from his hand. He glanced at the scribbled lines
as Mabrey threatened the young man. "Boss, look at
this. He's a newspaper reporter!"

"Like hell. Let me see that." Mabrey snatched the
tablet from Barnes and read it, murmuring the
words. "While crime grips the city, the mayor finds
time to, so-forth and so-on . . ." Then he turned back
to the terrified young man. "Who are you? What are
you doing here?"

"I'm . . . I'm Markland Beale . . . I'm investigating
the mayor." He shook so hard his teeth chattered.
"But I'll kill the story, I swear I will! Just don't shoot
me! My editor knows I'm out here."

Mabrey reached up and scratched the side of his
head with his pistol barrel, looking out through the
cover of low hanging branches at the foursome stepping back from the driving area and walking along
the side of the long green fairway. "You're telling
me you're tracking the mayor?" He gestured toward
the distant fairway. "And that *is* the mayor?"

Red Lohman eased off and lowered his pistol, un-
cocking it. Young Markland Beale collected himself,
rubbing his throat. "Not after the next election, he
won't be. Not if I can help it." He caught himself,
then said with caution, "I mean . . . you gentlemen
don't work for him, do you?"

"I'll ask the questions, Beale," William Mabrey
grumbled, pitching the tablet against Beale's chest.
Beale caught it, clinging to it with shaking fingers.
"Now what are you doing out here?"

"I got a tip from City Hall. The mayor broke four
important appointments this morning just to play
golf with some hotshot sportsman who's in town."

Mabrey let out a long breath. He looked at Lohman, then at Barnes, then back at Beale. Markland
Beale stammered, asking, "Who . . . who are you?"
As he asked, he managed to bend down and pick up
his pencil. When he stood up, he'd stepped wide,

gotten the tree out from behind his back, and now stood with a few feet between them, ready to write.

Mabrey looked him up and down, Beale staring at the guns in their hands. The guns were only meant to scare the truth out of him. Mabrey wouldn't have blown their cover with a gunshot. Now that he saw Barnes wouldn't get close enough with the straight razor, Mabrey shrugged. "We're Pinkertons, Beale. There's been threats on the mayor's life. If you're a reporter, you should already know about it." He watched Beale's eyes to see if he would buy the lie.

"No. I haven't heard of any threats—I mean, any more than usual. Sorry. Now can I go ahead and do my job? Please, gentlemen?"

Mabrey still wasn't convinced. He took a step forward. "Come here, Beale, I want to tell you something."

"No, sir. I can hear you just fine from here." Beale took another step back, as if realizing they didn't want to go blazing away at him. "Let me ask you this, Detective," he said. "When he first started receiving these death threats, how did it affect his state of mind? I mean, did he become—"

"Get out of here, Beale," Mabrey interrupted, raising his pistol and kicking dirt and twigs at him. "We see you in here again we're going to assume you're some kind of anarchist. You understand me?" Mabrey stepped toward him, aiming the pistol. Beale raised his hands chest high in a show of peace and backed away.

Kate McCorkle ducked back behind a white oak and watched the young man run past her through the woods. She breathed a little easier, seeing him make his getaway. When the sound of his running footsteps faded away, she stayed down and looked around at Mabrey, Lohman, and Briley Barnes, the big Colt pistol gripped tight in her hands. She was tempted to raise the pistol and start shooting, but she didn't trust her shooting from this far away, some twenty yards or more.

"Come on, they're getting too far ahead," Mabrey said. Kate watched them spread out, keeping a few feet between them as they moved along just inside the edge of the woods. She waited until they stalked a little farther away, then slipped out from behind the tree and followed from cover to cover until she stopped and saw them stare out at the golfers. "Look at this," Mabrey whispered to Lohman, who crouched near him. "That grifter is actually showing the mayor how to hit a golf ball!"

"Then it *is* the mayor?" Red Lohman asked.

"I don't know. Maybe it's one of Sims's scams, maybe it's not. But it doesn't matter. First chance we get, when they bring the game a little closer to these woods, Sims is mine."

"Whooa, boss." Lohman moved closer to him. "That's risky, getting into something when you don't know whether it's a scam or not. That's how Sims works. He gets you focused on one thing, then hits you with something else. I know that better than anybody." Red's hand went up to touch his still tender forehead.

Mabrey glared at him, recalling how he had recently given JT Priest similar advice about Quick Charlie Sims. Recalling it only fueled his rage. "Red Lohman, don't you ever presume to question me! And don't you tell me a *damn* thing about Sims. I see through him like glass. If this is one of his scams, he's lost his touch."

"Boss, alls I'm trying to say is we need to know what to look for here," Red Lohman reasoned.

Mabrey intensified his glare. "You stay here, Red. Cover our backs. Barnes and I will keep alongside them. If this breaks into a shooting, you be ready back here. Can you handle that much?"

Red Lohman only nodded, biting his lip. Barnes gave him a skeptical look as he eased past him and followed Mabrey along the edge of the woods. *Arrogant bastard* . . . Lohman slumped back against a big maple tree and slid down to the ground, shoving his pistol back into his holster.

"What's going on, Mister Mabrey?" Barnes asked as the two of them stopped behind a tree, Mabrey peeping around it and seeing Sims in his wheelchair, sitting all alone while the other three men walked out on the fairway forty yards ahead, searching for a ball along the edge of a pine thicket.

From his wheelchair Sims called out, "See, Your Honor? Let that club face open just a little and it'll slice to the right every time."

In the woods, Mabrey whispered under his breath, "That son of a bitch . . . I'll open his club face!" Mabrey watched Sims roll his wheelchair forward over a rise on the path, only his shoulders showing now, along with his bowler hat. A gray stream of smoke swirled upward from his cigar and curled away on a breeze. Out in the fairway, the other three men moved farther away.

"Get ready, Barnes. They go a little bit farther, we might have to snatch him out from under their noses. Take him back in these woods . . . no, wait, we'll take him somewhere else, more private. Once she brings me the money, we'll kill them both—make one watch while we kill the other. Hee! I love it!" Mabrey chuckled, rubbing his hands together, babbling aloud.

Barnes stared at him, getting a little worried at how Mabrey's plans kept changing from one minute to the next. Was that something that Quick Charlie Sims wanted Mabrey to do? If it was, Barnes wasn't about to mention it, not after the way Mabrey had jumped down Red Lohman's shirt.

Mabrey looked out along the fairway, seeing the other three men disappear into the pine thicket, then looked around the tree and saw Sims roll his wheelchair backward a few inches, up from over the rise,

giving them a view of his back, the cigar smoke still
curling upward and away. "Come on, Barnes! Here's
our chance, while they're not looking!"

They hurried over twenty yards, low to the ground
like rats, the plush green fairway grass muffling the
sound of their running footsteps. Sims didn't hear
them, and wouldn't expect a thing, Mabrey thought.
He saw Sims's shawl through the back of the wooden
wheelchair, Sims was sitting tall, his bowler hat
cocked back, the thick cigar smoke rising in plumes.
Mabrey stopped. "Cover him, Barnes!" He grabbed
the wheelchair and spun around with it toward
Barnes. *What the . . . ?*

Facing the wheelchair, Barnes stood stunned, his
pistol pointed at two crossed golf clubs leaning back
beneath the shawl, the bowler hat atop them, a cigar
burning on its brim. He only caught a glimpse of the
contraption before it all fell to one side and toppled
to the ground. "Oh, hell," Barnes said, staring past
Mabrey. He saw Quick Charlie Sims rise up as if
from out of the ground as he stepped over the edge
of a deep bunker and jammed a big Colt pistol in
Mabrey's back.

"Game's over. Time to settle up, Mad-dog," Sims
said close to Mabrey's ear. He reached around Mabrey, took his pistol out, and pitched it on the
ground. "Now then, which one of you is carrying
the razor?"

"What razor?" Mabrey asked. "Don't talk crazy,
Sims. Those days are over! We can deal! I came to
talk, to get the money back and see what I can do
to make things right between us."

"Save your breath, Mad-dog." Sims spoke over
Mabrey's shoulder to Briley Barnes. "You're Barnes,
right?" Briley Barnes only nodded, and Sims said,
"Drop the pistol, Barnes."

But Barnes didn't drop it. He only stared, Sims
seeing the question working hard in his mind. "Lis-

ten, Barnes. I know she told you I wouldn't shoot anybody. But believe me, she didn't mean it."

"You're not going to shoot with all these witnesses around, Sims," Mabrey said. "Now let's talk, straighten this out some way. I'm rich, Sims, for God sakes!"

"Look around us, Mad-dog. The mayor and his bodyguards are gone, swallowed up by the woods."

Mabrey let out a breath, casting a nervous sidelong glance down the empty fairway. "Damn you, Sims."

Sims looked at Barnes again. "He gave you the razor, didn't he? Did he tell you what he wanted you to do with it?"

"Uh-huh." Barnes nodded, looking black and lost and not sure what to do next. "Said to torture you till you gave up the money, that's all." Barnes kept his pistol pointed at Sims as he lifted the razor from his pocket and pitched it on the ground. "There, I don't need that. But I believe her, Sims. She said a pistol is only a prop to you."

"Then you can die where you stand, Barnes. Think about it, what's the best you can do here? Mabrey knows he's finished. What have you got to gain by making a stand here?"

Barnes bit his lip, thinking about having to face Red Lohman in the woods. "I can't go back the way I came," he said.

Sims managed a thin smile. "Nobody can. Now pitch the pistol down, then cut out that way." Sims nodded toward the long fairway. "I'm giving you a chance. If you're smart, you'll take it."

Briley Barnes pitched the pistol to one side on the lush fairway grass. "Sorry, Mister Mabrey. I'm not cut out for this kind of stuff. It's got me a nervous wreck." He stepped sideways a few feet, then turned and ran, shooting sidelong glances toward the woods.

"Have a seat, Mad-dog." Sims kicked the bowler

hat, the shawl, and golf clubs out of the way, and pressed Mabrey down into the wheelchair.

"Damn it, Sims. Show some decency. At least take me over in the woods!"

"This is good enough. The place is closed. There's just you and me here. Now tell me, where is it?"

Mabrey stiffened in the wheelchair. "Where's what?"

"The wagon, Mad-dog, my family's wagon." Sims stepped back and let out an exasperated breath. "We're going to do it one way or the other. You know the only choice you get."

"If you kill me, you'll never find it, Sims," Mabrey said with finality. "So let's deal, shall we?"

"No. If you don't tell me, JT Priest will."

"Priest doesn't know where it's at," Mabrey blurted out, then realized what he'd just done.

Sims spread a thin, tired smile. "That's what I always thought. He wasn't even there, was he? You wanted me to think it was him, but it was you all along. You put Tuck Javin out front and made him think you'd turn him into a gentleman, a sportsman. He even claimed he did it! He even changed his name to shed that old outlaw image. All that time, you knew he'd have to face me. Did you ever even tell him that?"

"No. He still doesn't know the connection." Mabrey stared at him. "Take me to the woods, Sims. You're getting everything else you came for. Give me that much. Be a sport about it."

A loud pistol resounded from the bordering strip of woodlands. Mabrey started in the wheelchair at the sound. Quick Charlie Sims said in a quiet voice, "If I had to guess, I'd say that's Kate putting a bullet through Red Lohman. I told her to stay out of it. But I knew she wouldn't. So I figured her to take care of whoever you left to cover your back." Sims looked at him with a serious expression now, the smile gone, his dark eyes seeming to bore into Mabrey's. "Still want to go to the woods?"

"Damn it. You always win, don't you, Sims? How does that feel? Knowing you're too slick, too smart, too damn quick to ever take the short end? I want to know, just between you and me, before I die."

"Just between us?" As he spoke, Sims took out the small ball of silk string and let it fall, unwinding from his hand. "I haven't won anything of value since the day I left the wagon. Now where is it?"

Mabrey let out a breath. "It's in a cave on my old spread near the border. It's been there all this time. If I'd ever thought burning it would have changed anything, I would have done it years ago."

"It's not your place to burn it, it's mine." A length of string lay across Sims's wrist, and now the long stiff hat pin was in his hand.

Mabrey watched the hat pin turn back and forth across Sims's knuckles, the way a poker chip or a golf ball might do. In one last attempt Mabrey said in soft whisper, "The past is gone, Sims. Killing me won't change a thing. Let me make you rich. *Los Pistoleros* is so big, so powerful . . . you can't even begin to imagine. Come in with me, Quick Charlie Sims. Nothing could stop the two of us, *nothing*."

"Nothing but the ghosts of my family, Mad-dog Mabrey." Sims uncocked the pistol and shoved it into his belt. He knew Mabrey would make a move once the pistol was out of play. What man wouldn't? Even as Sims reminded himself of this, Mabrey lunged forward out of the chair toward him. Quick Charlie was glad in a way, because this was not something he'd ever looked forward to . . . not this part. But he was sworn to it, not in words or by some laying on of hands. But he was bound to it nonetheless, like some tortured soul bound to eternal chains.

He sidestepped as Mabrey went by, his big head down, leaving his thick neck exposed; and as if guiding Mabrey, Sims caught the back of his hair with one hand, the other hand moving in quick with the stiff hat pin. Sims pivoted, walking Mabrey in a complete circle, Mabrey seeming to melt slowly, barely making it around to the wheelchair before collapsing back into it.

Sims wiped the hat pin on Mabrey's trouser leg. He looked over at the edge of the woods and saw Kate McCorkle step out with the Colt in her hand. He waved her back. She looked across the fairway at him for a second, then turned and stepped into the woods, holding up the hem of her dress with the same hand that held the pistol. When she'd moved out of sight, Sims turned back to Mabrey's body, took out the pocketknife Uncle Breldi had given him, and stepped forward, flipping the blade open in his hand.

Chapter 29

Otis Farnsworth and the Mallory brothers sat atop their horses on the empty street of Whittenville and looked all around at the empty storefronts and abandoned shacks and houses. A skinny cat stepped out across the boardwalk from the open door of the old Blue Pearl saloon and hopped down into the street, rubbing itself against the sun-bleached hitch rail. Otis Farnsworth raised his pistol and cocked it toward the purring animal. "Getting to where if you want to visit a town, you better get there before the paint dries or you'll miss it."

Otis took aim at the cat, but before he could fire, Clifford Mallory stopped him, saying, "Whatever bullets we've got, we best save, Otis. We might have to make a stand."

"No. We got to keep pushing," Otis said as he lowered his pistol.

"I don't know how much farther Harvey can push. He's not looking any better." They both turned in their saddles and looked back at Harvey Mallory, his horse lagging a few yards behind them. Harvey rode slumped in his saddle, dark blood covering his chest and side.

"There comes a time when every dog can't finish the hunt, Clifford." Otis glared at him from beneath his hat brim. "Then it's up to somebody to put it out of its misery."

"That would make sense, Otis, except Harvey ain't

no dog. He's my brother." He looked back at the rise
of dust, then added, "That damn Indian. I hate being
tracked. We've drug him over rocks, through water.
We'll never shake him loose—he's too damn good."

Flies circled and buzzed when Harvey Mallory's
horse came to a stop beside them. "If you're worrying about me, boys, don't dig my hole just yet."
He straightened in his saddle, his face ashen, sweat
flowing down his brow.

"I was telling Otis, we might ought to make a
stand right here, Harvey. There's two of them, three
of us. What do you think?"

"I think it's up to each one of us now, whether we
stand or fold." Harvey searched both of their eyes in
turn. "Far as I'm concerned, I can hold them boys
off a couple of hours, give you both time to get out
of here, rest your horses, and make a run to Indian
Nations."

"You're talking out of your head, Harvey," Clifford Mallory said, dismissing it. He looked back at
the thin rise of dust on the far horizon.

Harvey reached out a weak gloved hand and
slapped Clifford on his shoulder. "Listen to me, little
brother. Anything we owe each other has been paid
many times over." He offered a tired wounded smile.
"Hell, we've had more fun than any devil oughta."

"I ain't listening to this, Harvey." Clifford shook
his head. "You stay . . . so do I." He turned his gaze
to Otis Farnsworth for his reply.

"Damn it, boys . . ." Otis lifted his hat brim and
adjusted it higher up on his head. "I know how this
sounds. But I've business waiting for me in El Paso.
It's the best offer I've had in my whole damned life."

"Then get to doing it, Otis," Clifford said, stopping
him. "Harvey and I will just make ourselves home
here, maybe catch up to you later."

"You two won't think ill of me?" Otis looked at
them.

"No." Clifford spoke for both of them.

"Won't shoot me in the back when I ride out?"

Clifford grinned. "We might, but not over this. I've always wanted to anyway." He looked at his brother. "What about you, Harvey?"

"More times than I can count." Harvey coughed, then looked back at the rise of dust moving closer. "You better kick out of here if you're going."

"Good luck, boys." Otis heeled his horse forward.

They watched him ride away, and at twenty yards, Clifford Mallory slid a glance to his brother and slowly drew his pistol from his holster. "I told him we might," Clifford said in a low tone. But before he could raise the pistol, he saw Otis's horse stop in its tracks. Clifford lowered the pistol to his side, watching Otis turn the horse and heel it back to them.

"Hell, I ain't going nowhere," Otis said, reining back up to them. "I just remembered. Last time I was in El Paso, I got in the most godawful mess you can imagine."

Clifford and Harvey Mallory only nodded. A silence passed, as each of them looked back now at the rise of dust, as if within it lay answers to questions that all men ask themselves. Finally, Otis said, "How you boys want to play it?"

"Hell, why not hard and fast?" Clifford looked back and forth between them, a tight smile on his face. "Just like in the dime novels. Right out here in the middle of the street. Winners take all."

"Suits me. I've always wanted to do that." Otis rose slightly to step down from his saddle and chuckled. "If I'd known this, I could've gone ahead and shot that cat."

Sullivan Hart and Twojack Roth stopped their horses a long way back from the abandoned town and stepped down from their saddles in a stretch of short sourgrass. "They've stopped there," Roth said, seeing no fresh rise of dust ahead of them. "Must be holing up to make a stand." He looked down at the three sets of hoofprints on the ground, one set not as straight or as deep as the others. "This one's in bad shape."

Hart stepped forward and raised his telescope to his eye. He scanned the weathered buildings rising above the earth's curve, unable to see the street. Then he lowered the lens, let out a breath, and handed it to Roth. "Yep. I'm glad of it. Maybe we can get this thing over with and go on to something else."

"Yep." Twojack Roth didn't bother to look out through the lens. He clapped the telescope shut between his hands and tapped it on his gloved palm. "We've still got Cleveland Phelps, William Mabrey . . . and no telling how many others to hunt down."

"We'll get to Phelps, sooner or later." They'd seen the big Thorenson T in a set of hoofprints at morning light. But the prints had only headed south for a short distance, then cut west for the distant border. "As far as Mabrey goes, I've got a feeling Quick Charlie is taking care of him. Miss McCorkle said Sims wouldn't shoot a man, but I never bought that for a minute."

Roth nodded. "Yeah, that was a good one." They passed a canteen back and forth in silence, then stepped up into their saddles and rode on, abreast now, keeping a distance of twenty feet between them.

There was still no sign of dust in the air when they stopped again, this time less than half a mile out of town. "Good place for an ambush," Roth murmured. They checked their pistols and their rifles, then moved their horses forward at a slow walk until they reached the edge of town. They looked forward into the dirt street, where small clumps of wildgrass stood amid old wagon ruts, and where the fresh prints of three horses ended at the horses' hoofs at a weathered hitch rail outside the abandoned saloon.

The skinny cat lay on the boardwalk as if it were dead. But at the sound of Sullivan Hart's voice, it flipped up to its feet and shot through an open door. "This is deputies Twojack Roth and Sullivan Hart! You're under arrest!" Hart called out, his voice resounding through the dried wooden shells of the gutted buildings. "Throw out your weapons and come out with your hands up!"

After a moment, when no response came, Hart started to call out again. "This is deputies Twojack Roth and Sulli—"

"Yeah, we heard you, lawdog," the voice of Otis Farnsworth replied, cutting him off. Otis stepped out slowly from one side of the street, a half a block past the hitching rail. Across the street from him, the Mallory brothers stepped into view at the same time, Clifford with his brother's arm looped over his shoulder.

"Are they serious?" Twojack Roth said in a sidelong whisper to Hart. "With all this cover, they want to shoot it out."

"They look serious to me." Hart and Roth swung down slowly from their saddles and, keeping an eye on the three men, walked their horses over to another weathered hitch rail and spun their reins.

"Are you sure you want to do it this way?" Hart called out, taking his right glove off, he and Roth stepping back into the center of the overgrown dirt street.

"Aw, yeah," Otis Farnsworth yelled back to him. "I'm sick of you dogging us, Injun," he said to Roth. "There's such a thing as privacy, you know."

"Yeah, I know," said Roth, shoving his shirtsleeve halfway up his big forearm. "Do you realize what a good lawyer could do for you? The way the courts are working, you could get out in a couple of years."

"A couple of years? Not in Parker's jail, no way." Otis opened and closed his gun hand. "Besides, I'm wanted everywhere you can name. We're tired, hungry . . . and not going no farther till we settle up." He stood in the middle of the street now, his hand poised near the pistol on his hip. Clifford stood six feet to Otis's right. He dropped his brother's arm from around his shoulder, helped him straighten up, then put four feet between them. Harvey swayed, then righted himself.

"What about you two?" Hart spoke to the Mallory brothers. "We can get you to Little Red Springs, get you fixed up."

"Do you know who we are?" Clifford Mallory had a dark laugh in his voice. "We're the Mallorys, from Tennessee. Does that tell you anything?"

"Yes, it does," said Hart. "Just thought I'd offer."

The gunmen stalked forward, Harvey already lagging back, his legs shaky.

Twojack Roth counted in silence, giving himself a starting point. At the count of ten, when the gunmen where within twenty feet, Roth's hand streaked up, his first shot hitting Clifford Mallory on the upswing as Clifford drew and fired. Clifford staggered sideways with the impact of Roth's shot. But he kept coming, blood spilling down his chest.

Hart's first shot caught Otis Farnsworth dead center and sent him flipping backward landing facedown in the dirt street. Otis struggled to reach his pistol in the dirt. "Don't do it!" Hart yelled, but Otis clawed toward it anyway. Hart's next shot knocked him dead.

Twojack Roth fired again at Clifford Mallory, the man now badly hit but still managing to squeeze off a wild shot at Roth. Farther back in the street, Harvey Mallory struggled to raise his pistol and fire. His hand couldn't get it level, and his shot only thumped into the ground a few feet in front of him. He sank to his knees, his pistol hanging limp in his hand. He winced at the sight of Roth's shot picking his brother up off the ground and spinning him a full circle in a spray of blood. "Go down, Clifford, damn it!" Harvey pleaded.

But Clifford caught himself with one hand and one

knee on the ground, his pistol still returning fire, blood flowing from the two holes punched in his chest. Roth shot him again. Clifford dropped onto his chest, got both hands around the pistol butt, and managed one more wild shot before both deputies came forward, pouring shot after shot into his body until the pistol fell from his bloody hands and his face fell to the dirt.

"That's the end of it, Harvey." Sullivan Hart stepped in as Harvey Mallory rocked back on his knees in the dirt sobbing, trying with all his effort to raise his pistol. Hart reached down, wrenched the bloody pistol from his hand, and tossed it aside. "Take it easy now," Hart whispered. "You did the best you could."

Hart and Roth stepped back in the drift of smoke and the ringing silence. They looked themselves over for wounds, finding none. In a moment Harvey Mallory looked at them and rubbed a hand across his dirt-smeared face. "You said . . . something about a good lawyer?"

Hart just looked at him. Then he turned and got the horses, brought them forward, and took down a canteen. Opening the cap, he handed it down to Harvey, supporting it with one hand while Harvey took a drink. "We'll take a look at you, see if we can't patch you up some. There's a good doctor in Little Red Springs. Where all are you hit?"

"I haven't stopped to count . . . since last night." Harvey struggled with his words. Hart poured water into Harvey Mallory's cupped hands, and after Harvey had splashed it on his face and wiped it around, Roth and Hart both lifted him to his feet and walked him into the slanted shade of a building. "Will you bury Clifford for me?" Harvey asked. "I'd do it myself, but I'm not able."

"Sorry, we don't have a shovel." Roth wet his bandanna, pressed it to Harvey's head, and held it there.

"I can't stand thinking that damn cat will be chewing on him before we're out of sight." Harvey hung his head.

Sullivan Hart looked all around. His eyes settled on the crumbling stone walls of a town well. "We might take up some rock and stone and pile it over him. Will that do?"

"I'd appreciate it." Harvey looked up at them, then singled out Twojack's face, for the first time, taking note of his black eyes and still swollen jaws. "If you don't mind my asking, Deputy, what the hell hit you in the face?"

Roth didn't answer. Instead, he slumped against the weathered building between Sullivan Hart and their new prisoner; and the three of them sat there in silence for a while, listening to the low purr of the skinny cat when it came across the dirt and dropped down on its side in the shade.

By afternoon Harvey Mallory sat atop his horse, his wounds bound in strips of cloth torn from a shirt Sullivan Hart had found in Clifford Mallory's saddle-bags. The deputies had covered the bodies of Otis Farnsworth and Clifford Mallory with rocks and stones taken from the wall of the abandoned well and the stone chimney of a fallen trading post that had been there long before the town of Whittenville had come and gone. "That ought to do it," Twojack Roth said, taking one last look back at the empty street.

That night the deputies made camp, cleaned their rifles and pistols, and each took his turn guarding the prisoner while the other slept. The next morning they struck out for Little Red Springs and by nightfall rode into the town, hearing the sound of a twangy piano through the bat-wing doors of the saloon.

A dim light glowed in the window of Sheriff Bud Kay's office. But before going there, the deputies sat atop their horses for a moment in the middle of the dark street. At length, Sullivan Hart said to Twojack

Roth in a weary voice, "Well, nothing to do now but get back to Fort Smith and get on back to work."

"It's about time . . ." Twojack Roth gave a smile and nudged his horse forward. Sullivan Hart followed, leading the prisoner's horse behind him, the sound of the horses' hoofs falling softly in the quiet of night.

Epilogue

Captain Bennington and two of his officers escorted Kate McCorkle and Quick Charlie Sims to the station the morning they left Chicago. The big captain thanked Sims for making adjustments to his golf club, although Sims hadn't really done anything except wipe the club down with a soft cloth. But when Sims had given it back to him, he'd asked Captain Bennington to make a couple of practice swings. He'd corrected the captain's stance, advised him to keep his left heel on the ground and follow all the way through before trying to see where the ball was headed. "The club worked fine yesterday evening." Captain Bennington beamed, taking a short swing with his empty hands as he spoke. He went on to say how he regretted not getting a chance to see Sims play, and how sorry the mayor was, not getting an opportunity to meet him. But with the newspaper lambasting the mayor's office with a series of ridiculous accusations, the mayor had his hands full right now. Kate McCorkle listened and kept quiet. She held a folded newspaper in her hand, tapping it on her palm. Quick Charlie only smiled.

"At any rate, Mister Sims," Captain Bennington added, shaking Sims's hand, "it's been a pleasure meeting you. I'm glad those thugs Deputies Hart and Roth were concerned about didn't try anything after all. They must've decided my officers were more than they could handle, eh?"

"I'm sure that was it, Captain. As they say, 'All's well that ends well.' " Sims drew on his cigar and let out a stream of smoke, knowing Kate McCorkle would start right in on him as soon as they boarded the train.

And so she did. Once the train had left the Chicago station and gathered speed across the flat grasslands, Kate McCorkle turned to Quick Charlie Sims. She unfolded the newspaper with a great show of patience and spread it out before them. "Mayor denies allegations of abandoning post in midst of crime wave," she read. Then she stopped and looked at Sims. "It goes on to say his entire staff claims he was in his office all day the morning he supposedly played golf at the Meadowland Club. Who was that, Charlie? Uncle Breldi? Some of his friends? Why didn't you tell me it was all a setup."

Sims shrugged and smoked his cigar. "People play a better role when they don't know they're acting. We both know that. Since you weren't supposed to be out there in the first place, let's call it even."

She paused, thinking, then said, "So, it was all about making Mabrey think you really were with the mayor?"

"No, of course not. I knew Mabrey would see through it right away. If he knew for sure that was the mayor and his two bodyguards, there's no way he would have tried anything. It's what you might call a double blind. Once a person like Mabrey thinks they know your game, they can't resist playing it."

"But he must have a least thought it *might* be the mayor?" Kate considered it.

"Yep, a little uncertainty always sweetens the pot—makes a person start rethinking their plans. Once they start rethinking, they're too busy to see what's happening before their eyes. He took his eye off the ball, Kate, long enough for me to make the switch in the wheelchair. It's like any other game. Once you look away, everything changes. Mabrey

looked back at the wheelchair—all he saw was hat
and smoke. By then he was too excited to stop himself." Sims shrugged. "Why am I telling you all this?
You already know it."

"Yes, but . . ." As she thought about it some more,
she worked it out in her mind. "The brass plate on
the carriage?"

"Breldi's whole family are metalworkers, Kate.
That was the easy part for them."

"And the reporter . . . you brought him in just at
a point when Mabrey knew it was a scam? Just a
little kick of doubt to keep Mabrey off balance?"

Sims grinned. "Yep, something like that, as it
turned out."

"I have to admit, that kid was *real* good, Charlie.
He even convinced me." She shook her head, recalling it.

"That's because he was no actor, Kate. He really
is a reporter, evidently." Sims tapped a finger on the
newspaper in her hands.

"So Uncle Breldi tipped off the newspaper? Had
them send out a reporter?" She looked confused.

Sims relaxed into his seat. "I have no idea. Sometimes things seem to happen just right when I'm involved. But it worked. That's all I care about. You're
still alive, I'm still alive. Mabrey's dead . . . and the
money's all yours. You won't have to look over
your shoulder."

"Correction, Charlie. The money's *ours*. I won't
have it any other way." She folded the newspaper
and laid it on her lap. "You have to come out of this
with something."

"I will, once I get to that cave out in the badlands.
I'll set fire to a wagon and walk away a free man.
For years it's haunted me. Soon it will all be over."

"Why do they do that, Charlie? Why do they always burn the wagon?"

"It's their way, Kate. Always has been, always will
be. What's the difference why they do it?"

Kate looked at Quick Charlie Sims, studying his face as if for the first time. "You don't look like a Gypsy, Charlie."

"Oh? And how does a Gypsy look?" He drew on his cigar. "They took me in as a child, and raised me like I was their own."

"Then what about your real parents? What happened to them?"

Quick Charlie Sims didn't answer. Instead, he changed the subject, saying, "Once I burn the wagon, I'm heading to Fort Smith. I still want to be there when JT Priest makes his escape. I might even see if the judge would like my help rounding up the rest of *Los Pistoleros*. I sort of enjoyed working with Twojack and Sully. An interesting game, law enforcement."

Kate smiled. "What makes you think they enjoy working with you?"

"I could tell they did." Sims chuckled. "Besides, they need to work with me if they expect to completely do away with everybody connected to this gang."

"Oh? Why is that?"

"Because *Los Pistoleros* is part of the Midwest Investment Corporation, the same as Hughes & Lindsy was . . . the same as a dozen banks, mines, and business operations still are. Midwest Investment is big, rich, and powerful." He paused, then patted the inside pocket of his new wool suit coat. "And guess what? I own twenty percent of it. JT Priest signed his shares over to me the day he signed the confession." Sims smiled, watching her bemused expression.

"Charlie! You own twenty percent?"

"Yep, for now. I plan on acquiring some more."

Kate stared at him for a second, then she shook her head as if to clear it. "No, wait a minute. What will happen now that Mabrey's dead?"

"It doesn't matter. Ordinarily his shares would go to his estate. But right now, nobody even knows he's dead, Kate. His body will never be found, and neither will Red Lohman's, unless Lake Michigan goes dry." He winked. "But Uncle Breldi promised me it won't."

"But still, Charlie. JT Priest will get a lawyer. Even if he hangs, he'll never allow this. He'll deny signing it. You have no witness."

"That's not so. If he denies it's his signature, I have a bank teller who watched Priest sign and cash a phony bank draft on the way to Chicago. I'm sure he'll identify Priest, and his signature too, if Priest wants to push it." Sims relaxed even further into his seat. "But so much for that. Judge Parker and I still have a chess game to look forward to. So I'm sure he'll be glad to see me."

Kate gazed straight ahead. "Geez, Charlie, I don't know . . ."

"There you go, doubting me again." As he spoke and smoked his cigar, Quick Charlie Sims took a chess piece out of his coat pocket. He looked down at the white pawn as it began turning back and forth across the knuckles of his right hand, the way a poker chip, or a playing card, or a golf ball, or even a long stiff hat pin might do. "Imagine. Of all people, the Hanging Judge *chose me* to play." The white pawn stopped and stood up on Sims's knuckle, suspended there, as if looking out on the world around it. "And you know me, Kate . . ." The pawn began turning once more from knuckle to knuckle instinctively, as if with a mind all its own. "I only play to win."

❑ Cheyenne Justice 0-451-19492-6/$5.99

Jason Coles knows the way of the West—and of the tribes who have inhabited it for countless centuries. So when a stubbornly independent young woman reporter named Abigail Langsforth sets out for Sitting Bull's camp, panicking her wealthy father, Coles is the last best hope to catch up with her and save her pretty hide.

But it will take every bit of skill and grit that Coles possesses, not so much to find the missing girl, but to keep her. Because aside from facing down angry Cheyenne, a Sioux hunting party, and a pair of nasty white traders, he's up against one fierce fighting spirit in Abigail Langsforth herself....

Follow the adventures of Jason Coles:
❑ Stone Hand 0-451-19489-6/$5.99
❑ Black Eagle 0-451-19491-8/$5.99

CHARLES G. WEST